SPYGLASS

Hélène Deschamps

SPYGLASS

AN AUTOBIOGRAPHY

Edited by Karyn Monget

Henry Holt and Company
NEW YORK

Acknowledgments

A very special acknowledgment and all my gratitude to Henry Hyde for his unfailing friendship, from the battlefields in 1944 to the present. Also my thanks to John E. Taylor, the "master" of the OSS files at the National Archives in Washington, D.C., whose endearing friendship helped me regain the confidence needed to finish this book. My grateful thanks to Dr. Henry J. Gwiazda and Dr. George C. Chalou, also at the National Archives, for their support and encouragement.

Henry Holt and Company, Inc., *Publishers since 1866*
115 West 18th Street, New York, New York 10011
Henry Holt is a registered trademark of Henry Holt and Company, Inc.
Copyright © 1995 by Hélène Deschamps and Karyn Monget
Map by Robert Romagnoli
All rights reserved.
Published in Canada by Fitzhenry & Whiteside Ltd.,
195 Allstate Parkway, Markham, Ontario L3R 4T8.

Library of Congress Cataloging-in-Publication Data
Deschamps, Hélène. Spyglass: an autobiography / by Hélène Deschamps.
p.   cm.
1. Deschamps, Hélène—Juvenile literature.   2. World War, 1939–1945—
Underground movements—France—Juvenile literature.
3. World War, 1939–1945—Personal narratives, French—Juvenile literature.
4. Spies—France—Biography—Juvenile literature.
5. United States. Office of Strategic Services—Juvenile literature.
[1. Deschamps, Hélène.   2. World War, 1939–1945—Underground movements—
France.   3. Spies.]   I. Title.   D802.F8D437   1995
940.54'8644—dc20   [940.54'8644]   94-39233

Designed by Victoria Hartman / First edition—1995 / ISBN 0-8050-3536-2
Printed in the United States of America on acid-free paper. ∞
1   3   5   7   9   10   8   6   4   2

Whenever possible the author has used people's real names. However, in a few instances names have been changed to protect those who still require it. Any connection between those fictional names and actual persons is purely coincidental.

To you, Jackie, Hellops,
Didier, Petit-Jean—
I remember our hungry years,
the once upon a time,
a long, long time ago. . . .

Contents

Publisher's Note

One of the first questions we faced when we read Hélène Deschamps's gripping account of her wartime fight against the Nazis was how to verify it. Her story was fascinating, but was it true? We were pleased, then, to receive many confirming documents, including letters from two key people with whom she worked in the Office of Strategic Services (OSS) and a signed affidavit with an official seal from a French officer who verified her role in the Resistance.

Henry Hyde, the chief of the French desk for the OSS, recalled that

> Hélène Deschamps worked from November 1943 to August 1944 for one of our networks. She rendered valuable services in observing and reporting on enemy troops and German order of battle and ran missions through the lines after the Americans landed in the South of France. She was highly commended by our chief agent in Apt. He advised me that she had shown a remarkable sense of responsibility, as well as great courage and loyalty to the Allied cause. Thereafter, between September 1944 and March 1945, she served our unit

in Annemasse, where she was likewise highly regarded. Hélène Deschamps was a genuine, good agent.

Jacques Locquin, who worked for the French DGER (Direction Générale des Etudes et Recherches) to establish who had actually participated in the struggle against the Nazis, wrote that "before starting with network Jacques, OSS Mademoiselle Hélène Deschamps was with network Franc-Croix and also worked with network COMBAT. She accomplished her missions in an extremely satisfactory fashion, never retreating in the face of danger, and she brought back to her network vital information."

Lieutenant General David E. Grange Jr., of the U.S. Army, added that he was "honored to get a chance to know Hélène Deschamps. She is truly a person worthy of deep respect from all Americans."

Spyglass is the undoctored and unsparing record of how she earned that respect.

Author's Note

My name is Hélène Deschamps. During World War II, when I was a teenager and a young woman, I was a spy. Working with the French Resistance and later with the American OSS, I helped to free France from the Nazis.

Secret warfare did not produce glamorous spies hiding behind sunglasses and sporting trenchcoats. We survived by our wits, and a good dose of bravado. In my case, deception and guile toward the enemy came easy.

I began writing about my experiences as a spy shortly after the war ended. It was virtually impossible to keep records during the war, as anything the Germans discovered linking me to the Underground would have meant certain death. Since that time, I have done my best to reconstruct the events I witnessed. Of course, after years of thinking and rethinking through a four-year period in my life, some of the events and missions described in this book are recalled in more detail than others. Nevertheless, nothing has been dramatized or embellished. This is a true story, written as I remember it. My life as a spy was more action-filled than any fictionalized account could ever be.

I risked everything for my convictions, choosing to fight for my country and losing much that I valued, even loved. It started out like a game, and seemed fun at first. But the choice I made was nothing like those you see in novels or movies. If you had to renounce family, friends, any kind of a normal lifestyle to fight a fierce enemy, would you? And yet, had I not made that choice, I could not have lived with myself. This is my story, just as I lived it. It is about the true price of war, and the choices we make every day; the choices that define who we really are.

Faced with the stark choices of courage or cowardice, honor or betrayal, camaraderie or selfishness, I and others who fought for a liberated France rose to the challenge. Though I survived, many who I cared about and loved did not. Their faces, and their memory, will remain with me forever.

PART I

1939–1943

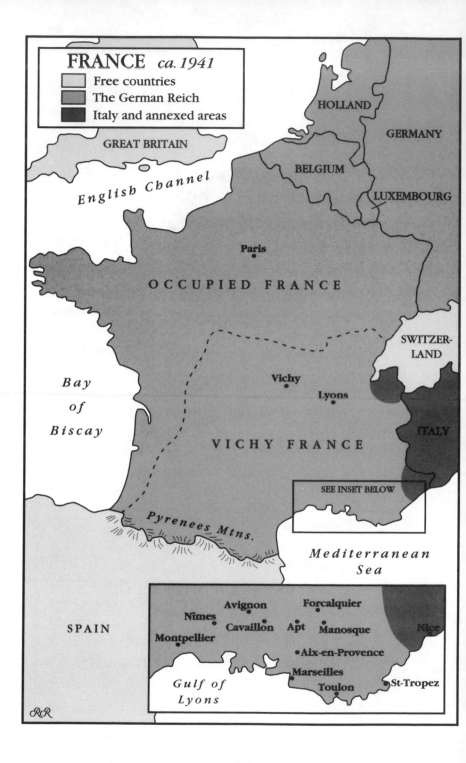

CHAPTER ONE

Invasion

I grew up hearing tales of wartime bravery, fearlessness, and endurance. My father, Gaston Deschamps, was a disciplinarian who raised his children in a stern, formal way. Like the proud line of men before him, he was a distinguished soldier. Father was wounded in World War I and received a Military Legion of Honor citation. It read, "An officer of remarkable bravery and high moral value, Gaston Deschamps demonstrated the most brilliant military qualities of sangfroid and courage under a shelling of rare violence. Gravely wounded, he continued to give his orders and endured his pains with the greatest show of fortitude." Father retired as a high-ranking colonel before the outbreak of World War II.

On my mother's side, patriotism ran just as high. My great-great-grandfather, Jean Hardy, was *général de division* at the age of thirty-eight, during the reign of Napoleon Bonaparte. My grandfather, Raphael Napoleon Hardy, was the police commissioner of Paris. Mother married a successful military man and gave birth to my two brothers, Maurice and Philippe, who, my family hoped, would one day follow in the footsteps of the long military tradition set before them.

I was born in 1923, in the French Concession of Tientsin in Northern China. Being a part of a military family meant spending a good deal of time abroad. As a child, we traveled continuously. After three years in China, we moved to Dakar, the capital of Senegal in Africa. A few years in Madagascar, then three more on the island of Réunion in the Indian Ocean was the pattern of my childhood.

After having such a varied and exotic childhood, my ideas were quite different from those of other girls my age. Mother came to the conclusion that I was becoming too wild to ever be the accomplished young lady she wanted me to be. When we arrived in France in 1937, she promptly enrolled me as a boarder at the Convent of the Sacred Heart in Avignon.

It was a dramatic and difficult change, having to adopt a rigid, cloistered lifestyle after living freely in exotic lands. Abstinence, mortification, and chastity were everything at school. We were allowed a bath or shower once a week, and then only with the special permission of Mother Superior. Afterward we had to make a visit to the confessional in order to be absolved for having been naked in the bathroom.

Bedtime in the dormitory was also a production. Lights were turned out at eight P.M. sharp by Sister Marie-Thérèse. She was in her fifties, embittered and hateful, I had guessed, from her ascetic years in the convent. Once, I decided to play a trick on her. After curfew, I bombed her bed with the pits of various fruits I had saved. The lights came on, students sniggered and shrieked, and Sister Marie-Thérèse appeared in her long brown robe, her night bonnet tipsy on her head.

An investigation was conducted the next morning. I was finally fingered by one of my classmates. After appearing in front of a "tribunal" headed by Mother Superior, "corporal punishment" was decreed by Sister Marie-Thérèse. It was unusually cruel—for seven straight days, I knelt on the marble floor of the chapel, not moving for half an hour, reciting prayers under the supervision of both Sister Marie-Thérèse and Mother Superior.

A year passed, and my spirit finally became a little more subdued. My roommate, Jacqueline Bouquier, was of great help during this painful transition.

Jackie was pretty, vivacious, and always attentive. She was from a military family, stationed at the time in Morocco, and, like myself, had been sent to Avignon to finish her education and become a polished young lady. From the very first day, we bonded. We felt as if we had always known each other. I loved to watch Jackie sing and act, and she enjoyed my sense of adventure. We both approached life with the same unwavering, self-sufficient attitude. Through my newfound confidante, I learned to curb my appetite for rebellion. The tomboy in me subsided somewhat, and I became more or less the young lady my parents wished me to be. Still, more than a touch of defiance remained. It was a great influence as I grew older, and ultimately, it helped me to bluff an enemy and survive through the grimmest of times.

One morning, Mother Superior called me into her office. She was very strict, with cold, penetrating eyes. I delayed entering, practicing my curtsy outside the door, believing that I had been summoned, yet again, to be reprimanded for doing something wrong. Finally, I mustered my courage and prepared my entrance. I knocked at the door.

But Mother Superior was not stern that morning, and her

voice was unusually soft as she asked me to sit down on the narrow wooden bench facing her desk. She stood by me and patted my head lightly. Then, tactfully, fingering the crucifix suspended from her neck, she told me that my father was dying.

Vaguely, I could hear Mother Superior speaking of religion and trying to explain that all of us must go through great sorrow to earn a future life in heaven. But her voice came from a distance. It no longer seemed to reach me.

Father was dying.

Strangely enough, my first thought was of the daily schedule Father posted behind my bedroom door. During school holidays, everything was regulated at home, from seven in the morning until bedtime.

The day always began with an inspection. Philippe, Maurice, and I would stand in line while our father meticulously checked our appearance: Necks washed? Teeth cleaned? Hair combed and shoes shined? Beds neatly made?

We were afraid of him, for he had a no-nonsense manner. Yet he couldn't hide his deep love for us behind the soldierly strictness.

Mother was delicate and timid, always standing in the background of our lives. She was a gentle soul. Perhaps it was understandable that her husband intimidated her. She had been introduced to him a mere week before their wedding.

My thoughts focused back on the present.

". . . Hail Mary, full of grace, the Lord is with Thee . . ." Mother Superior was kneeling on a bench under a large crucifix. Her voice droned on, mouthing the ancient prayer.

A door slammed, shoes clattered on the tile floor in the hall, and voices came closer.

". . . Pray for us sinners, now and at the hour of our death. Amen." Mother Superior stood and took me by the shoulders. "You should get ready to go home, child."

At two that afternoon, Sister Marie-Jésus took her distressed student to the bus station in the convent's black, horse-drawn buggy. Once there, she handed me a little basket with sandwiches and a few dried figs. After giving me a token kiss on the forehead, she pushed me inside the coach, then hurriedly crossed herself and left.

What with the driver taking time to unload passengers and packages at several places, it was a three-hour trip from Avignon to Aix-en-Provence, a resort town near Marseilles. Upon Father's retirement he had purchased a lovely villa in a pleasant residential area.

Madame Giraud, our next-door neighbor, was waiting at the depot to take me home. She appeared agitated and was trying to hold back tears. I only felt numb.

As we walked home, we crossed the rue d'Italie and stopped at the parish of Saint-Jean-de-Malte just long enough to ask the priest to come to the house as soon as possible.

"This really is not happening," I kept telling myself as I entered the familiar hallway at home. The atmosphere was hushed, with a heavy silence hanging in the air, like an ominous weight.

I recall Mother kissing me and crying noiselessly. My brothers, looking grief-stricken and at a loss for words, were sitting in the living room.

I was pushed toward the stairs. I walked into Father's room alone, then closed the door and approached his bedside. All of my movements seemed precise and soundless, as if I were dreaming. I bent over and lightly brushed his forehead with my lips.

Father opened his eyes. They looked strikingly blue, and it seemed that all that was left of his life had taken refuge in them.

"I was waiting for you, *chérie.*" A faint smile appeared on his waxen lips. "I can go in peace now," he said in a whisper. He closed his eyes again. I waited for him to speak once more and stared down, lost in my grief. When he said nothing for a time, I raised my head.

He was gazing at me, this time with a frightful intensity. "Lock the door," he said in a faint but determined voice.

I obeyed, frightened, and filled with the icy knowledge that I was to be the only one to witness my father's final moments. Never before had I been close to death. I tried to swallow. My mouth was dry, and the lump in my throat was painful.

I returned to the edge of his bed.

He gave me a last glance, an *adieu.* I took his hand in mine, and he sighed. I understood. I accepted it quietly, alone.

He had been strict, even severe, and yet, I recalled, whenever I wrapped my arms around his neck, his stern eyes would turn as soft as a caress. I knew I had been his favorite child. People used to say that I was the very image of him.

I could hear muffled steps coming up the stairs. Father's face seemed strangely at peace. His arm had dropped away limply and hung by his side. I kissed his hand and placed it on his chest, and then I closed his eyes. I stood and turned off the lamp to shroud his form in darkness. After unlocking the door to let Mother in, I walked away without looking back.

A procession of mourners, dressed in black from head to toe, solemnly followed the horse-drawn hearse on foot. It was the beginning of May 1939, and the new leaves on the centenary trees lining the boulevard wore their prettiest, most tender green color.

The cemetery came into view.

With tears in my eyes, I could still imagine Father standing so proudly in front of his troops, seeming indestructible.

The cortege stopped at the great wrought-iron gate, and the altar boys stepped down from the draped black carriage. Six soldiers carried the bier to the family plot, trailed by family and friends meandering through small walks lined with cypress trees.

The grave had been opened, and the deep, dark hole gaped.

A voice rose, glacial and solemn. Words, in Latin, filtered into my ears slowly, somberly, without comfort. Prayers were said, and the holy water splashed the coffin like drops of rain.

Holding Mother's hand, I looked at the tombstones around me. Insipid paper flowers and photographs under glass were distastefully displayed over the headstones. A sad resting place, I thought, for a man with such strength and vitality.

The entire ceremony was like a film to me. I was totally detached from the event, as if I were watching from a distance. This was my last farewell to my father. I left a flower behind.

It was the end of my childhood.

A week later, Maurice returned to the army academy, and Philippe went back to his studies in Paris. I did not return to the Convent of the Sacred Heart to finish my school term.

Instead, I stayed at home with Mother. She was heartbroken. Having lived in her husband's shadow for so many years, it was difficult for her to understand his disappearance. Jackie, my dearest friend, who had joined us during the school holidays and vacations, had practically become a member of the family.

I was becoming an attractive, long-legged young lady. I did not look very much like my mother, except for the color of my wide-set, luminous brown eyes. My hair, which I wore shoulder-length and simply brushed in a large wave, was a brilliant copper color. I looked quite mature and had a shapely figure.

During a last family gathering, before my brothers went on their separate ways, it had been decided that I would enroll at an exclusive finishing school in Aix. The school was run by secular nuns, and upon my arrival, I was distressed to learn that it was dictated by the same spiritual austerities I had encountered at convent school. I was still the strong-willed, feisty adolescent I had always been. Though no longer a tomboy, I was a nonconformist, which was actually quite radical for young ladies then. My rebelliousness genuinely concerned Mother.

"Hélène, *chérie,*" Mother would lament, "what makes you so difficult sometimes? It frightens me!"

"I don't know, *Maman,*" I would say, contrite but not repentant. "I want so much out of life. I want to feel free!"

Often in the evenings, I would lie on my bed, soberly biting my lower lip in concentration, and would review myself—my merits and faults, my goals, my future, my hopes—all in desperate self-criticism.

I can't be who everyone wants me to be, I'd say to myself. I know I'm different from my friends, except Jackie. She understands me. Why can't I just be myself?

In 1939, my homeland was not prepared to face the challenge of events to come. Internal quarrels, petty party discords, and the perils of Fascism and Communism were weakening the nervous system of France. The public was divided—Rightists (Conservatives) and Leftists (Communists), Freemasons and Catholics, pacifists and militarists. France had not fully recovered from World War I. The French were tired and loathed the thought of more bloodshed, and the politicians willfully ignored the rise of Nazism in Germany.

On September 1, 1939, Hitler invaded Poland. Two days later, France and England declared war against Germany. Then, the next spring, the Germans struck in the West.

By the first of May 1940, exiles from invaded Holland and Belgium had begun trekking down the French highways. Endless waves of frightened and hungry people were determined to flee as far from their own countries as they could. They remembered the German occupation of the First World War and the horrible tales of torture and starvation.

Soon the French started to join the ranks, looks of desolation etched in their deeply sunken eyes. Approximately two million people streamed along the highways, paralyzing and glutting all southbound traffic. A combination of fear, hysteria, brutality, and human stench was everywhere. Women, children, and the elderly were crushed by this stampede. Pressed on every side and unable to reach the fields or the edge of the road, they would squat on the spot, defecating and urinating on one another, while being trampled by a relentless horde of bodies.

Endless waves of automobiles bulged with household goods. Even mattresses were roped to the tops of cars. There were lost children crying, exhausted soldiers unable to find their units, people on foot or horseback, others pushing wheelbarrows.

As soon as people heard the droning of a plane, a frantic charge would start. Thousands of bodies would tumble down on top of one another, like a deck of cards. The German Stukas clearing the treetops, fuselages gleaming in the sun, would strafe anything that moved on the road below.

The Battle of the Somme, France's ultimate effort to contain the German invasion, began on the fifth of June 1940. By the tenth, Italy had also declared war on France.

I observed the swift turn of events, which would change my life forever. Things were happening so quickly that no one knew from one day to the next what to expect. Though official reports came through the newspapers, they revealed nothing.

My brothers, Philippe and Maurice, had been called away to fight. Each morning, I watched the postman pedal by the gate on his bicycle, but no letters reached home. All we could do was hope.

By June 14, German soldiers manning machine guns positioned themselves around the Arc de Triomphe on the Champs-Elysées in Paris. The German flag with its swastika was hoisted above the arch. In a desperate attempt to save the country, Paul Reynaud, then the head of the French government, appointed Marshal Pétain his vice premier. Considered a national hero for his victory at the Battle of

Verdun in World War I, Pétain represented France's last hope. Pétain agreed with the head of the French army that they should surrender.

On June 25, an armistice was signed.

The conditions of surrender were harsh. France would be severed into two distinct zones: (1) The Occupied Zone, which took up three-fifths of the country, began at the city of Amiens in the north, arching down above Vichy. After passing the region of Haute-Savoie and the Alps, this zone reached Bordeaux on the Atlantic coast. (2) The Free Zone, free in name only, was to remain under the strict surveillance of German intelligence. Though this area was not occupied by the Nazis, the Germans appointed Marshal Pétain and his cabinet of ministers to run state affairs. This puppet government was set up in Vichy, which would become the capital of France.

The initial shock of a German victory left the entire country in despair. In less than three weeks, France had surrendered to the Nazis. Even worse, within ten days, more than one hundred thousand French soldiers lay dead. Though weary and bewildered by this sudden turn of events, few would accept that France had lost for good. Eventually, submissive heads lifted and eyes began to shine again with hope. With renewed spirit, the French people would wage a new battle. But this time it was a different kind of war, one without uniforms, medals, or pomp. It was a cunning and deadly war . . . a war of *Resistance*.

CHAPTER TWO

Resistance

The painful emptiness of life after the death of my father was dulled by the routine of daily life. The void was gradually filling when the International Red Cross in Morocco informed us that Jackie's parents had been killed in a car accident. Since all communications had been cut with the outside world, there was no question of her returning home. In any event, there would have been no one to take care of her.

Mother immediately asked her to move in with us, and she saw to the formalities of adoption. Now we were sisters in law as well as in spirit. After almost a month of mourning, she joined me again with my studies.

While France was still waiting for the conditions of surrender, I listened to General de Gaulle's appeal to the French population to resist the German invaders. De Gaulle, a colonel in the French Armored Division, had been temporarily upgraded to *général de brigade* during the invasion. He fled to London shortly before the armistice was signed. From there he rallied the French to fight on against the Germans. His speech aired on a BBC broadcast, the night of June 18, 1940.

The slow, calculated, perhaps overdramatic voice of General de Gaulle galvanized me. That very day, I decided that I would help my country in any way I could.

Following the surrender of the French government, I began listening to British radio reports, even though that was expressly forbidden by the Germans. They were our one remaining link with freedom, our only connection to the forces resisting Fascism.

One morning, I got up earlier than usual and was sitting in the kitchen having breakfast when Mother walked into the room. Her eyes were red from crying.

"Are you all right, *Maman?*" I asked, getting up and going over to her.

Mother shook her head sadly. "I don't understand what is going on any longer," she said, sobbing softly. "Now that the Germans have won the war, what more do they want? Your brothers should have been back!" She crossed herself in despair. "Oh, dear God! Please let them be safe!"

Bending over Mother's shoulder, I kissed her tenderly. "*Maman,* there is such chaos around us. Let's not worry so soon. Come and rest for a while. I'll bring you some hot tea." I took her arm and guided her back to her room.

With Father gone, I was the strong one in our home.

On the following Sunday afternoon, I went for a walk in the countryside, trying to gather my thoughts and make plans for the future.

I reached Le Tholonet, a hamlet at the foot of Sainte-Victoire Mountain, and took a path thickly overgrown with juniper shrubs. Staring through a web of pine needles, I saw a meandering dirt track to my left disappearing along the woods, and I realized I was lost.

Dragonflies were crisscrossing ahead, vibrating their rainbow wings in the sun. The silence felt heavy, disturbed only by the droning of insects and the silky sound of the breeze passing through the hissing pine trees. I breathed deeply, taking in the smell of pine and spruce.

I climbed the narrow, steep path. Hunters must have used it, because it was worn, the red clay churned where the weeds had been trampled over. Then, at the turn of a thick pine grove, I discovered an abandoned cottage, its stone walls cracked and discolored.

Shading my eyes from the blinding glare, I looked up at the faded tile roof, puckered with holes that gaped emptily, like the eyes of a blind man, at the boundless blue sky of Provence. A couple of pigeons cooed, fluffing their iridescent feathers in the searing sun.

With its lonely peacefulness, this seemed an ideal place to meditate. Wiping the sweat from my forehead with the back of my hand, I stretched leisurely in the grass, and took stock of my life. Thoughts, hopes, and doubts were raised from the depth of my soul. They had to be confronted in solitude. I knew I wanted to fight and perhaps help to save my country. I didn't know what the price might be. I was only certain that I no choice. I was a very realistic girl, and when I felt things as I did at this instant, I simply acted.

I reflected for a long time, distractedly watching tiny gray lizards with red, panting throats busily searching through the jagged stones, their long, gummy tongues, thin as a razor's edge, retrieving ants and small flies from the wild blackberry vines. My decision had been reached. I would fight for the liberation of France. I no longer felt oppressed, and I knew that for all the years to come, I would remember this decisive day, down to its smallest detail.

Now, how does one prepare to fight the enemy? I didn't know then. How could I? I was a seventeen-year-old girl who had had a sheltered life. Childishly, I imagined that it would be very simple and uncomplicated, almost like a game. Certainly I could not ask my mother for advice. She was not aware of my plans, and she would have done everything in her power to stop me. Determined nonetheless, I had to go my own way and find the people active in the still disorganized Resistance movement.

I will not involve Jackie, I decided. This is my own choice.

In my search, I had to put up with silent, stubborn faces, evasive or nervous answers, anger and even threats. Being young and naive, I sometimes found myself in dangerous situations. One close call nearly resulted in my arrest.

I had been directed to the house of a retired professor who, some friends had told me, was "dabbling" in the Resistance. Upon arriving at his doorstep, I was greeted by an aging woman who I assumed was his wife. I gave a fake name and, without the slightest hesitation, was led to the parlor. The professor was sitting at a small table, busily shuffling a stack of papers.

I should have known better than to trust a person who, upon my mentioning the Resistance, began talking about his entire strategy for the salvation of France. Even to my inexperienced ear, I knew something was wrong.

The door to the parlor was partially open, and I noticed that his wife had furtively passed along the corridor several times. My worst fears came true when I saw her throw a shawl over her shoulders and hurry out of the house.

Unconcerned, the professor continued to talk. Fifteen minutes later, his wife was trotting back down the street, accompanied by a man in military uniform, the two of them babbling excitedly.

I had heard enough to realize that this professor could not be taken seriously, and losing no more time, I got up. I left him in the middle of a sentence—index finger pointed to the ceiling, mouth open—and ran out the back door and down a side street.

For many people, denouncing others was the thing to do. It was surprising how many thought they were doing their duty by spying for the Germans. This first shock provided a good lesson for me: it taught me to be more cautious. That evening, as I curled up in bed, I reviewed the whole episode. What was I doing wrong? Surely there must be many people involved with the Resistance, I thought. I just have to be more careful.

My determination remained strong, and by the end of 1940 I finally located some of my father's fellow officers. Most of them were scattered outside of the city, and many were in hiding. None wore the proud uniform of France, but the old, brave spirit still burned, and I knew after talking to a few of them that I would soon be able to establish a contact.

Colonel Beaugard was the man I sought. He had been one of my father's closest friends, and I was convinced he would be among the first to start some kind of resistance, although at the time he seemed to be living quietly in retirement in his country home.

After calling to make an appointment, I sat in the sunroom. Suddenly uncertain of myself, I was surprised by my own audacity. What had come over me? What did I know about military matters? Most of all, what would I tell him? Despite finding no reasonable answers, I decided that it was indeed too late to change my mind. I would have to face whatever was to happen.

Dressed in a navy-blue dress, I tucked my handbag under my arm and, a stubborn frown puckering my face, knocked on Colonel Beaugard's door. I was admitted by an old servant who led me through the house and into the colonel's study.

Beaugard was a stern, martial-looking, sharp-tongued man of impeccable accomplishments. He greeted me paternally. "Hélène, my dear, what a pleasure to see you." He kissed my forehead affectionately. "How is the family? Any news from your brothers?"

"Mother and Jackie are fine, but there's nothing yet from Maurice or Philippe. We are very concerned."

He shook his head but made no comment.

"Colonel, I wish to speak to you about something personal," I declared without preamble.

Beaugard raised an eyebrow in surprise. "Sit down." He pointed to a leather chair across from his desk. "What's the matter, Hélène? Are you in trouble of some sort?"

I came straight to the point. "Colonel, I want to take an active part in the Resistance."

Beaugard momentarily stiffened, then resumed his normal composure. His clear, calm eyes gave nothing away. "Why come to me?"

"Because you were Father's friend, and I am certain that you would, like Father, start something on your own." He nodded slowly, reflectively, and smiled at me. Though usually precise, he was now evasive. "Even if I was involved in such a project, my dear child, you are too young to meddle in such matters. Leave it to the adults. I appreciate your enthusiasm, but shouldn't you go back to your studies?"

Forgetting my manners, I burst out, "Why shouldn't a girl of seventeen be able to fight the Germans just as well as any adult? Is my patriotism and determination of less value simply because I'm young? Study? What for? There's no future anymore, just submission to the enemy. I will not become like a marionette dangling from a string, at the mercy of the conqueror's fancy."

Beaugard listened to my tirade. As I was speaking, he reached for an old tobacco jar, then lifted the top off and fumbled his way to the bottom. His fingers reappeared with a large pinch of aromatic leaves, which he carefully packed into the small bowl of his pipe. He lit up, pensively watching the smoke drift to the ceiling.

"Can you explain more clearly your motivations in wanting to be with the Resistance?" he asked me when I had finished. "Isn't it a bit unusual for a girl of your age?"

I lifted my head and looked straight into his eyes. "In wartime, everyone should get involved. Don't you think so?"

Beaugard nodded. "Maybe, then, you should enlist in the Red Cross or the Civil Defense?"

"That's an excellent suggestion," I retorted. "However, it wouldn't be my idea of fighting the Germans."

He rustled a few papers and said rather abruptly, "Perhaps you want to join our ranks because you want to be with a friend. Or the idea appeals to you because you find it exciting."

I grinned at him. "I have no boyfriend, if that is what you mean, and I don't have a Joan of Arc complex either," I said, bursting into a clear gale of laughter.

Although my sincerity, brightness, and background spoke for me, Beaugard was still skeptical about using a female—never mind one of my age—as a prospective agent.

I kept on arguing with him, and gradually he recognized my absolute determination. I think he realized that if he did not accept me, I would work with someone else, and ultimately he decided that it was best I stayed with him.

He looked at me for a long time and then shook his head. My throat was tight with anticipation. The clock on the mantelpiece announced noon, and his reservations seemed to ease with the steady striking of the clock.

Nevertheless, after two hours, he was still reluctant. Pushing his chair back, he got up. His bearing was erect and his manner crisp as he paced the length of the room.

"Hélène, I don't want you to let your imagination run away with you. You realize that you are going to have to give up everything. It will be hard for you; I'm not hiding that fact. You will always be in danger, and you will receive no comfort from us."

Returning to his seat, he sighed and went on, "Better to forget the whole thing right this minute. You have to understand this is for volunteers only."

I would not back down.

"Very well. You will be part of my group. You are the first girl we've taken with us, do you know that? I am not yet sure what will come up, but I have to be frank. There will not be much for you to do at the beginning. As time passes, we will determine what you are capable of accomplishing."

"I'll do anything you want!" I said eagerly.

"Good."

He got up and came over to me, and placed both of his hands on my shoulders. Like most army men accustomed to wearing a military uniform, he looked awkward in his neat pin-striped suit. "For the safety of all of us in the network," he said, "you can no longer be Hélène Deschamps. We do not want your family involved in anything."

In order to fool the Nazis, supporters of the Resistance in the prefectures, police stations, and government offices provided fake identity papers and cards. These were an absolute necessity during the Occupation.

Recruiting, however, was difficult, since leaders could never be sure of the people enlisted in their ranks. They had to depend on their own judgment, recommendations, intuition, and luck. There was neither the time nor the facilities for checking the life history of each volunteer.

Beaugard turned to his desk and searched through a dossier. He stopped when he came to the sheet he'd been looking for, glanced at it, then paused for a moment. Raising his eyes in my direction, he said, "You will no longer be Hélène Deschamps. In our files you will be H-1."

"H-1," I repeated. I was suddenly nervous.

"Go home and don't worry. When it is time, we'll contact you. But remember, no one, not even your mother, should know about our activities. You must swear to that. Too many lives depend on it!"

I solemnly promised.

He embraced me firmly. "Your father would be proud of you, Hélène."

I could not answer. Too many feelings were overwhelming me. I left.

Walking home, I felt that there was a kind of challenge in the air, determining my destiny. I was scared, yet strangely thrilled. After continuing to walk for a while, I found myself in front of the Lycée Mignet, the town's largest secondary school. It was the students' lunch hour, and in an attempt to regain my composure, I sat on a bench and watched them play ball in the playground. Cheerful, lively children were dashing about the yard, and the air rang with their voices.

I tried picturing myself as a student. Had I looked like them when I wore the navy-blue uniform of the Sacred Heart, sailor collar flapping in the wind? Maybe. But that all seemed so unreal now. A new world, filled with dangers I couldn't even begin to imagine, lay ahead.

The idea of working for the Underground and defying the Germans was exciting, whatever the hazards might be. Arrogant with conquest, the Nazis ridiculed the idea that a French movement could be effective against them, and in a way, at the start, they were right. A handful of Frenchmen scrambling to organize guerrilla groups could not do much harm.

During this period, a transformation was taking place in French society. For centuries, French women had stood aside, bound to their homes, unable to take part in politics, not permitted to vote, and restricted from having a personal bank account. But because the war drew men away from home and into battle, women were forced to adopt less traditional roles. In some extreme cases, they even led men, fighting side by side with them, organizing networks and crossing enemy lines to bring back information.

And yet, after the war was over and France was liberated,

many of these women, who had shown just as much wit, strength, and courage as their men, found it more comfortable to go back to their usual feminine chores, delighted to return to being exclusively wives and mothers, satisfied with the mere knowledge that they had played a role in liberating France.

My earliest days in the Resistance were as Colonel Beaugard had promised they would be, straightforward and relatively easy, certainly nothing like the way they would become. I was a bike messenger. My chief job was to deliver messages from Colonel Beaugard to Paul Bouchon, at the prefecture of police in Marseilles. Other times, I would carry papers and pamphlets from Aix to Marseilles. These documents were simple sheets of paper that were printed or typed in secret one week here, the next somewhere else. Their message was essentially the same: Resist the *Boches*. They were distributed at night by teams of men, women, boys, girls—sympathizers of the Underground. Despite denunciations and the attempts of spies from the Vichy government to stop the flow of material, it continued to be disseminated, and in ever increasing amounts.

As the old colonel had promised, I eventually became more active, and my assignments grew increasingly intricate and even dangerous. I was sent on longer missions, carrying messages to Avignon, Nice, and Manosque. In between trips, Jackie would help me catch up with my studies. Facing Mother, however, was becoming more difficult. I was always inventing new stories about my whereabouts. It soon got to the point where she came to believe that her daughter had drifted from the family. Fortunately, Jackie was always there, seeing to Mother's needs and allaying her fears.

At any hour, under any circumstances, an agent had to be able to travel from one place to the next. I was quickly and inevitably caught up in the machinery of the Resistance. Soon I found myself doing my assignments with the total disregard for danger that only youth and inexperience allows.

One evening after dinner, Jackie came up to my room. I was sitting at my desk, trying to concentrate on some homework. My mind was traveling, though, thinking of new missions, new assignments.

Finally, after having stood at the door a few moments, she entered. I raised my head, surprised. "You caught me daydreaming," I told her.

With a hesitant look on her face, she said, "I want to be with you."

"What are you talking about? You are with us, and we love you."

"Oh, don't play with words!" Jackie pouted. "I've a pretty good idea of what's going on. I'm not blind, you know. I've helped you enough. Mother thinks you are tired of us. I know better."

"But, *chérie,* I'm not hiding anything from you!"

Jackie plopped down on the bed, where she ended up cradled among the pillows, like a bird in a nest. "Are you trying to impress me?" she asked, miffed at the evasive answer I'd given her. "Surely, you know you can trust me."

I didn't answer and started writing again.

"Do you want me with Beaugard, or do I look for someone else?"

I looked up from my homework and saw that she was genuinely hurt. Her eyes filled with tears. I felt guilty; after all, Jackie was making the same case I had argued to Beaugard. "I won't quibble with you, since you seem to know so much. I'll talk to Beaugard on one condition, though," I dictated. "You'll promise to stay with *Maman* when I have to be away."

Jackie's face broke out in an infectious smile, and she jumped from the bed, throwing her arms around me. "I promise! What do we have to do? Is it dangerous? Are you scared ever? I've been wanting to ask you for so long!"

"Yes, I'm afraid sometimes, but it's also exciting."

"Have you thought of explaining what you are doing to *Maman*? Maybe I should tell her."

"Don't!"

"Why not? She'll understand."

I shook my head. "No. She would try to stop us. It's not that I don't trust her. Poor *Maman*. It's for her own security, and besides, she's feeling bad enough not hearing from Maurice and Philippe."

✣ ✣ ✣

Early in November 1942, a number of important events occurred. On the night of November 7, 290 American and British ships, transporting 110,000 men and divided into three groups, reached the coast of North Africa.

The French Colonial Empire, which up to this point had stayed out of the fight against the Vichy government, was now entering the fray.

The Germans were, more or less, prepared. Their agents in neutral Spain had reported a heavy concentration of Allied troops at Gibraltar as early as October 23.

On November 8, Mother, Jackie, and I were about to start lunch when news of the Allied landing in North Africa was broadcast by Vichy radio. We were so emotionally shaken that we left the table without touching our meal and moved to the sunroom to hear the details of what was taking place. Immediately after this major Allied landing, the German Army crossed the Demarcation Line and invaded the Free Zone. No walls had been built between the two Frances, no barbed wire set, and almost no signs erected. The line simply bisected the country by following a road here, a bridge or a farm there, heavily guarded by German patrols, police dogs, and mines in some places.

The French people, on either side of the line, were only able to communicate with those on the other side with post-cards specially issued by the Occupation forces. All one could write was a few words about health, and even then, the mail was rarely delivered. Telephone calls were not permitted between the two zones. The Demarcation Line could not be crossed without permission, and to secure such a permit was anything but easy. Any violation meant arrest, deportation to concentration camps, and sometimes even death.

In such circumstances, people were separated from their loved ones and businesses came to a standstill. Spirits were broken and the general mood was one of apathy. The first phase of the total occupation of France had begun, and new and more intricate intelligence assignments began opening up for me.

CHAPTER THREE

The Italians

Whithe the Germans invaded the Free Zone, Mussolini received, as a reward from Hitler, permission to occupy much of southern France. Mussolini's Bersaglieri were stationed along the French Alps, while his Carabinieri (basically, his regular soldiers) took over the French coastal ground.

The Bersaglieri were a unit of the Italian army trained for special operations, and these duties gave them an air of glamor. They took their elite status so seriously that in order to distinguish themselves from the other troops, they ran, rather than walked, during military parades. Their gray-green uniforms, topped with conical headpieces and garnished with a couple of thin black cockerel's feathers, seemed more appropriate to yodelers in the Tyrolean Mountains than to an elite military unit.

Nice, the largest town on the fashionable French Riviera, was taken over by the King's Cavalry, a corps of officers composed mostly of Italian nobility. These cavalry officers, handsome to a man, wore expensively tailored olive-green uniforms and gleaming black boots.

The Italians were very friendly. They were definitely not war-minded, and it was indeed surprising to hear the enlisted men, as well as the officers, express their crude contempt for the Germans.

During the occupation of Nice, the Italians were so bent on gaining complete acceptance from the French that they were surprised and even offended by the jibes and jeers of Frenchmen. Despite the harassment and animosity of the people, who resented them simply for being there, the Italians sat on window ledges or stood on doorsteps singing, playing harmonicas and guitars, and waving at the girls.

"La vita è magnifica, però l'amore è sempre meglio!"—"Life is wonderful, but lovemaking is even better!"

The Italian occupiers of Nice seemed primarily interested in the flirtatious French girls, rousing music, and home cooking. They displayed no taste for acting as military conquerors. Any woman strolling on the streets was the object of close scrutiny. Their various opinions about her particular assets were delivered with an air which assumed that she could only be flattered by the attention she received.

One of the largest and finest hotels in town, the Ruhl, had been requisitioned for the King's Cavalry. Its salons were crowded with debonair Italians busily courting the young girls who flocked there in substantial numbers. The girls ranged from the adventurous daughters of good families to their more professional sisters. In addition to the customary boy-girl interests, there were many black-market activities afoot.

I was in Nice during this period, bringing some messages from Colonel Beaugard. I had arrived directly from Marseilles by train and checked in at the Hôtel de Berne on avenue Thiers, across from the station. I registered under the name Hélène de Champlain.

An agent from the network COMBAT was to meet me that afternoon. He had been notified of my arrival by a postcard sent from Marseilles, which simply read, "Can't wait to see you Thursday. All of my love, Suzanne."

"Patrice," the agent, knew in advance where the rendezvous was to take place. I was sitting in the hotel lobby reading an edition of *Marie Claire*. The magazine was the prearranged sign of recognition.

We greeted each other like old friends and left the hotel chitchatting happily. We stopped to enjoy a sherbet purchased from a street vendor, and I handed him the magazine, which contained a couple of sealed envelopes.

Patrice and I continued strolling leisurely down the street, and while talking, I gave him the contact name of a lawyer, Claude C., who had been of assistance to Beaugard on several occasions. The lawyer had relocated to Nice from Aix, and could be of help to Patrice's network. In return, I was given the names of two solid prospects for Beaugard's network.

Beaugard would also be interested in hearing about the Italian occupiers.

That evening, Patrice took me to dinner at a small brasserie near avenue Mozart and asked me to assist his network. They needed an update on Italian maneuvers in and around the city.

"Are you up to it?" he asked.

I was thrilled. "Sure," I replied confidently.

"Good," he said. It couldn't be anything terribly important, certainly not much danger. Be charming, flirt a little, and ask questions.

This was to be my first action assignment, and I accepted

promptly, without even consulting Beaugard, proud to show off my capabilities.

A room had been reserved by one of the men in the network at the Hôtel Méditerranée. It stood opposite the Italian officers' mess. Around three o'clock the next day, I started across the street for my first probe. It was rather early, but already the hotel lobby was quite crowded. I had barely been seated in the salon, at a tiny tea table, when I was addressed by two officers standing at attention. Catching my glance, they asked politely, "Would the signorina permit us to join her for tea?"

As I began to smile, they immediately sat down and showered me with exaggerated compliments, followed by an unlimited number of rich pastries, which were not normally available to the French in wartime.

One of them, Captain Umberto Alberti, was very handsome and probably the most perfect gentleman I had ever met. Tall and blue-eyed, as Romans can be, he was the picture of distinction in his uniform. He undoubtedly knew it and played the game of seduction to the hilt.

A friendly rapport soon developed, and our trio discussed many things, including American jazz, of which Umberto seemed to be very fond.

"Do you like jazz, signorina?" he asked, flashing a radiant smile while passing me a plate of pastries.

I pressed a finger lightly to my lips and said, "Shh, shh! The Germans forbid us to listen to or talk about it, or even pronounce the word! I could go to jail for doing so, you know?"

Umberto smiled and bent purposely over his cup of tea.

"Signorina, you are among friends. Can't we forget their barbaric ideas and express our feelings freely?"

I smiled back but didn't answer.

He continued the conversation as if nothing had been mentioned. Nonchalantly saying that Glenn Miller was his favorite band leader, he invited me to his room to listen to his records.

As coyly as possible, I declined the offer.

Our conversation continued, and in his single-minded quest of seduction, Captain Alberti inadvertently provided me with the information I needed. He was leaving, he said, with his men within a few days, on maneuvers to the Provence hills.

"Provence is beautiful in the springtime," I told him. "It will almost be a holiday for you."

"Not exactly." He grinned indulgently. "But it could be, if you would come and visit me."

I laughed, feigning delight. "Captain, I must say that you are most direct, but then, sometimes that is an appealing trait."

Pleased by my compliment, he beamed. "Then it's yes?" His blue eyes took on a dreamy look of great promise.

"We'll see when the time comes."

To avoid appearing too anxious, I left the hotel rather early, leaving Umberto intrigued and slightly disappointed. I knew he was not accustomed to women rejecting his advances.

For the rest of that week, I saw Umberto every afternoon. Faithfully, at four o'clock each day, I crossed the street to meet my gallant and eager officer. We flirted a little, danced, listened to American records with a group of his friends, or chatted about the good old days before the war, all the while enjoying Italian cigarettes and sweets.

Umberto was becoming more and more involved each day, and I had to ask him quite often, much to the delight of his friends, to restrain himself. I could not always avoid his inquisitive hands.

"*La signorina, Lei è così brutta!*"—"You are unkind!" he kept lamenting.

The day before his departure, Jackie came down for a surprise visit, planning to stay a few hours. She had taken the bus from Aix to Nice.

"Are you sure you are working for the Cause?" Jackie teased. "Pretty good excuse to stay on the Riviera."

I felt foolish all of a sudden. "I know this doesn't appear very serious, but I can assure you that the COMBAT group has asked me to get information on the Italians' whereabouts."

Seeing me bristle, Jackie put her arm on my shoulder. "Well, I believe you. We have many things to discuss, but first, I have very good news to give you."

"*Maman* is all right, isn't she?"

"She is smiling these days, and her mind would be at peace if you would talk to her heart-to-heart."

"Jackie, you know I cannot tell her what I am doing."

"Well," Jackie said, "thanks to Colonel Beaugard, we have received good news. Philippe and Maurice are safe in North Africa. They have joined the Free French Forces."

I felt elated. "Oh, Jackie, I'm so happy! We'll make it, you'll see. We'll make it!"

Jackie and I began talking of the Italians, the assignment, and all manner of things, and were so involved in our

animated conversation that curfew arrived before we knew
it. Even though she had not planned to stay that evening,
now she had to. Fortunately, since we were coming out of an
Italian-occupied hotel, we were not bothered by the soldiers
patrolling the streets for curfew violators. They did, however,
throw some crude remarks at us, something about liking
Italian lovers.

We went up to my room, which faced Captain Alberti's
suite across the way. His lights were out.

"Your handsome Italian has found a new girl," Jackie
kidded.

"It's all right with me, as long as I find out where they are
going."

We were famished, but could not go out without being
arrested. How stupid of me. I should have thought of it
sooner. Exasperated, I searched at the bottom of my purse
and found a few sugar cubes and cookies I had snatched
from the hotel. We sat on the bed, equally dividing the sugar
and cookies; still, we were starving. We tried not to think
about our empty stomachs.

"Let's do something constructive," Jackie suggested.

"Like what? We're cooped up in here until morning!" I
was in a foul mood.

"Just watch me," Jackie said, starting to prepare herself.

A clever actress, she began to mimic the Italians with their
accent, mannerisms, and overgallant behavior. "Signorina,
let me kiss your hand," she said. Taking my hand in hers, she
kissed it passionately all the way to the shoulder, sighing and
moaning. She was so funny that, forgetting my unhappiness,
I was in tears with laughter.

While clowning, Jackie had slipped on the bottom of my

pajamas. I was sporting the top. The heavy blackout curtains had been drawn in front of the window to hide the light, but apparently our shadows, moving back and forth, could be seen from outside, because in the middle of our performance, there was a loud pounding at the door.

Topless, Jackie jumped into the bed, instinctively drawing the sheet and blanket over her head. Quickly wrapping a towel around my waist, I answered the door. No sooner was it open than Captain Alberti popped into the room like a jack-in-the-box, dramatically waving a revolver in his hand.

"You have a man in your room!" he roared, staring at me so closely that we were nose to nose.

"I do not!" I retorted hotly. The towel slipped down, unveiling my slim body, and I quickly caught it and rewrapped myself with dignity.

At that instant, my sister started wriggling under the sheet.

"Aha! I was right!" cried the Italian triumphantly, grabbing the bedding to pull it down.

Scared to death, not knowing what was going on, poor Jackie moaned in anguish while holding the sheet.

"No! No! No!"

"Sì! Sì! Sì!" insisted Umberto, and in a single, pompous gesture, he jerked the cover off, unveiling Jackie's naked torso. She lay there petrified at the sight of the gun, her lovely, firm breasts pointing at him.

Umberto made a dramatic pause worthy of a player in a Shakespearean tragedy. With one hand over his face, the other hurriedly placing the revolver back in its holster, he retreated backward toward the door.

Keeping a serious face, with much difficulty, I announced, "Umberto, meet my sister, Jacqueline."

He only shook his head, and as I approached to close the door behind him, he grabbed my hand in a grand and contrite gesture. Kissing it, he asked, "Will you forgive my jealousy?"

I could hardly restrain myself from bursting out in laughter. "Yes, yes. I'll forgive you!"

He protested vehemently as I pushed him out of the room. I closed the door and then fell on the bed, sinking my head into the pillow to smother my laughter. It had been too ridiculous for words.

It took Jackie a moment to realize how foolish and harmless the situation had been. Then she, too, exploded into hysterical laughter.

"Some boyfriend you have there!" she shrieked.

We had forgotten all about our hunger.

✤ ✤ ✤

Jackie left the next morning at eight o'clock. She was late, and I rushed her to the bus. The folding doors shut quickly behind her before we could kiss good-bye.

"Take good care of *Maman,*" I told her through the window. I was left behind in a cloud of exhaust fumes.

Returning to the hotel, I found Umberto waiting in the lobby, reading the *Corriere della Sera,* an Italian newspaper. He folded the pages quickly.

Looking repentant, he asked meekly, "Are you still cross with me, *cara mia?*"

"No. I have forgotten all about it." I acted distant.

"Please," he insisted, "I'm leaving today. Can you come to the camp for a visit?"

I appeared mollified and smiled. "Oh, very well. I will come this weekend. Where will you be?"

"We will set up camp at Peille, in the hills." He beamed with pleasure. I walked him outside, to where his friends waited for him, piled up like sardines in an open car. Ostentatiously, Umberto held me in his arms and kissed me with passion. His friends applauded enthusiastically.

I felt as though I was onstage and almost bowed to the audience.

"Ah, *l'amore!*" sighed a young lieutenant.

"*Arrivederci, bella signorina,*" the officers chorused, blowing kisses in farewell as the car sped away.

The only way to get from Nice to Peille was in a tiny, toylike locomotive hooked to a half-dozen wagons. It departed every day at five A.M. and returned that evening. The Sunday after Umberto left, I got on board still sleepy but looking forward to a day in which I could complete the mission entrusted to me. I sat on the rigid wooden banquette in the third-class carriage, the only one available. Like clockwork, exactly at five A.M., the small engine, with its tall and wide funnel bellowing clouds of black smoke, started valiantly toward the hillside. The train was built to run at a maximum speed of thirty miles per hour on flat terrain, and its uphill speed could easily be matched on a bicycle.

As the train moved along, I could see an old Roman windmill in the distance, its sails immobile, entangled with vines, like the rigging of a ship. The fields were cluttered with lively poppies, and the hills had borne a green mass of saplings. Almond trees, burdened with their blooming of pink and white wings, filled the air with the sweet scent of their blossoms.

At one point as we approached Peille I became aware of a silhouette of a man on horseback coming toward us. Shading my eyes against the sun, I watched the rider curiously. Tall in the saddle, galloping smoothly, he came closer. It was Captain Alberti. I waved happily. In recognition of my greeting, he pirouetted his horse in my direction, removing his cap and placing it under his left arm with all of the gallantry of one of King Arthur's knights. He moved along with the train, staying just beneath my window until we had reached the station.

I was quite impressed with his manners and such a warm reception. I had to admit I liked Umberto a lot. It was with difficulty that I concentrated on my mission and stifled all personal feelings.

The day went by quickly. The entire group of officers tried to outdo one another, revealing to me the way the camp was run and what duties were expected of them. But I was disappointed. If it had not been for a few mountain artillery guns, some boxes of ammunition, and a number of rifles scattered around, I could have imagined the setting—with colorful laundry drying in the sun, the pack of mules, and the men trooping around the field kitchen, singing and whistling—to be that of a boys' summer camp.

Nothing much to report, I reflected, unimpressed.

A late lunch was served outside under the shade of the pine trees, and the whole atmosphere was busy and bright. Music was provided by a young soldier, who stood on a chair and sang, accompanied by an accordion. *". . . un po' di luna, un po' di mare, un po' di musica d'amore . . ."* The words were like honey from his lips.

Lunch was served by well-trained orderlies and the wine flowed freely, all very beguiling for one accustomed to Occupation rations.

Captain Alberti was at my side the whole time, passionate and attentive to my slightest desire. For a while, I almost forgot that we were enemies and joined the singing and merry conversation, setting aside the purpose of the mission. It was my first introduction to the art of flirting, and I found it easy to carry out with the courtly, handsome officer.

To my regret dusk came, and it was time to take the train back. I left the camp accompanied by the good wishes of the Italians and by the promise of endearing love from Umberto.

"Arrivederci, cara mia"—"Good-bye, my dearest."

He bent over for a farewell kiss and reluctantly left the train.

Even though I was bringing back the information we needed on the camp and its men, I couldn't help feeling a little bitter about life, and perhaps about myself, too. I was still young and naive in the "spy business" and had much to learn. Up until that point, I had seen my assignment as a game. I did not yet understand the danger awaiting anyone daring to interfere with the Germans.

Back in Nice that evening, I met two of the Resistance men at a café and relayed the few details I had gathered that day. They appeared pleased, even teasing me playfully.

"Just as we thought," one of them said. "Nothing to worry about. So don't fret."

Giddy at the thought of my "mission" accomplished, I decided to reward myself by taking a couple of days of rest, bathing and sunning on the flat pebble beach along the promenade des Anglais, before returning home.

✤ ✤ ✤

New Year's Eve 1943 came without celebration. Too much sorrow and too much distress laid waste the country.

On January 2, a communiqué from the Wilhelmstrasse in Berlin reached Marshal Pétain's Vichy government. The Führer was demanding 250,000 non-Jewish Frenchmen to be used as forced labor in Germany—150,000 specialists and 100,000 general workers, both men and women.

While this roundup took place, the number of people sent to jail increased from 18,000 to 50,000. That was not counting those poor souls already incarcerated in concentration camps. La Santé Penitentiary in Paris, built to house a thousand prisoners, was now crammed with four thousand detainees. In effect, one Frenchman out of every five hundred was deprived of his liberty.

French children were not spared, either. On July 31, the orphanages of Montreuil and Neuilly (towns outside of Paris) were raided by SS troops, and four hundred children were shipped to concentration camps in the East.

At dawn on the day of the deportation, the youngsters, between two and twelve years old, were awakened. They were so frightened that, in panic, they started running in all directions. The soldiers were called, and the children were dragged screaming in terror to the waiting trucks, not to be seen again.

During this period, I helped Jewish people escape across the Spanish border. I was never certain of the ultimate result of my missions, since the guides often handed people over to the Germans for an additional payment. There was nothing that could be done to stop this. It was a chance they had to take.

One group of Jews had gathered in an area on the north side of Marseilles, hoping to escape by boat. The Nazis, however, were watching this harbor closely. The only solution was to try to reach neutral Spain through the Pyrenees Mountains. To do that, though, they needed help: plans, a guide, shelter before the trip. Most of the time no one offered that aid.

Without knowing it, Mother initiated an undercover affair by agreeing to harbor a Jewish couple who were desperately trying to reach freedom. She had heard of the Meyers' misfortune through a friend, Madame Pochoy, who lived in Marseilles, and readily offered them shelter. But she did not realize how dangerous her kind gesture could be: harboring a Jew or helping one escape was punishable by death.

Strangers in our home would inevitably rouse the curiosity of neighbors, who might talk. Inquiries would then be made by the Germans. There were always people who, for a small amount of money, would be glad to denounce us. Extremely concerned, I discussed the matter with Colonel Beaugard. I had heard of an underground network that handled escapees, and I felt he might know someone who could be of assistance in this matter, even though all networks were understandably secretive.

Beaugard himself was concerned and wanted to help. To my relief, and after much effort on his part, he was able to arrange for the departure of the Meyers. No guarantee was given of the outcome of the venture, but it was a chance worth taking. Of course, the Meyers were warned not to mention a word to anyone about their upcoming departure.

The only catch was that I would have to accompany the couple to the city of Narbonne, where I would personally deliver them to an appointed agent. The agent would then take over details of the transfer.

"This will only take a couple of days, perhaps three," said Beaugard, who had provided funds for the journey.

Not a word was said to Mother. Jackie would stay with her. Quietly, the next morning, Monsieur Meyer, his wife, and I each took a different route to the train station in Aix. The Meyers had been told to take only one small suitcase in order not to attract attention.

On the train, where we all sat in an unoccupied passenger car, I deliberately ignored them most of the time. I knew my presence was enough to reassure them not to panic. At the appropriate time during the trip, I handed them fake ID cards prepared by two of Beaugard's men working at the police station. I was traveling under the name Anick Durand.

The meeting in Narbonne took place at a prearranged location, a Peugeot bicycle repair shop not far from the train station. All I knew about the owner of the shop was his name, Lucien. We waited cautiously at the entrance until he approached us, wiping his hands, black with grease, on a rag.

"Hello," he said, greeting us jovially. "What can I do for you?"

I smiled. "Marcel told me you could repair two bicycles for us."

"Not today, but certainly tomorrow," he replied, reciting the password.

We shook hands.

"They can stay here with me," Lucien said.

Knowing that the Meyers would be on their way to the border the next day, I wished them good luck and took the next train back home.

A week or so after my return, the mailman delivered a note from a friend of mine named Matthieu. It had been mailed from Marseilles. "I need to see you the day after tomorrow," it said. "Let's meet at noon at the bar at the Casino Municipal."

I was intrigued. Matthieu and I were only casual friends, but I could sense urgency in the few words.

When I arrived the next day at the casino, Matthieu was sitting at a side table with a young man, perhaps in his early twenties. I was introduced by my first name only.

"This is René Schurman," Matthieu said, giving an encouraging gesture to his friend.

René Schurman is one of the young Jewish men I remember most clearly, and I liked him right away. An artist, René romanticized life, and this made him totally vulnerable and incapable of seeing to his own survival.

After an initial hesitation, he looked at me with a desperate expression.

"I am a Jew, as you can guess by my name," he said timidly. He explained that he had heard of the Meyers' good fortune and thought that perhaps . . . I could help him, too?

"I would like to cross the border before the Gestapo gets me. My family has already been deported."

At first, I felt alarmed, even angry, upon hearing that the Meyers had chosen to discuss their escape, despite the advice given by Beaugard and myself not to divulge a thing. It could have jeopardized our lives, and I remained quiet for a while.

Matthieu broke the silence.

"The Meyers were so overjoyed that they called a family in Marseilles," he explained. "René happened to be there when the news came. Will you try?"

"I'll do my best." I turned to René. "You must understand that although escape could turn out to be simple, I can't ensure a journey without risks. We might be stopped and we may have to separate. I'll give you an address in case that happens."

René jumped from his seat and kissed me on both cheeks.

This time I took the route to Perpignan. I delivered René to an agent named Monsieur Pope at a small church, l'eglise des Augustins. I asked him to try to locate my brothers if he was going to North Africa.

After we parted in the Pyrenees, he wrote me a letter, which still is one of my most treasured keepsakes:

March 1, 1943

Dearest Hélène,

When you read these lines I will, if everything is all right, be ready to go. The expedition is set for tomorrow night, Tuesday. My letter will be posted on Thursday by the guide upon his return.

So there it is. You and I are going to live in a different world and my heart aches at the thought that perhaps we will not see each other again—and it is now that we have parted that I realize how much I loved you! I think of you constantly and will keep on remembering during the months ahead, when life without doubt will be hard and cruel in a strange land, with no way to make a living.

However, I have the will to pull through and hope to come back to France at the end of the war with the victorious Allies, and then I will try everything in my power to find you again.

In any event, you will always be for me, till the end, my dearest memory.

Farewell. I kiss you tenderly.

René

I never learned if he crossed the Spanish border or the border of life itself.

CHAPTER FOUR

Vichy

As my twentieth birthday approached, I was really becoming a seasoned agent. I realized this one morning after Colonel Beaugard asked me to come to his home. I arrived to find him puttering in the garden, a pair of clippers in hand, pruning his fruit trees. At my approach, he raised his head slightly, wincing at the sun's glare.

"Ah, Hélène, come, come. I was thinking of you just this minute," he said, gesturing for me to approach.

We sat in the old rattan chairs under the plane trees. He lit his pipe and let a few minutes pass, his eyes wandering around the garden. He was lost in thought and I waited for him to talk.

He was now observing me carefully through heavy, half-lidded eyes. "I have a new job for you outside this area," he said hesitantly.

I cleared my throat nervously, feeling an unfamiliar excitement. "A real mission? I'll do anything you want," I assured him with as much confidence as I could muster.

He smiled kindly. *"L'enfant terrible!"* He took my hand in his in a fatherly gesture. "Spirited! You remind me so much of your father."

I blushed with pleasure. It was a genuine compliment. "I

am trying to please you with my work. Am I doing a good job of it?"

"Of course you are. But you are also very young, and I am wondering if it is safe to send you away," he said softly, as if talking to himself. "What you have been doing up until now is just basic training compared with what you will have to face. This assignment will be new and different for you. It entails very real dangers, and you will have to watch yourself every minute. You must leave everything behind. Can you do it?"

The answer did not come easily. I thought of Mother. Suddenly I felt insecure, at a loss for words, and I was torn between love and allegiance.

"What exactly will I have to do?" I finally asked.

"We need someone to work undercover in Vichy. I realize this is quite different from what you have been doing with us, but what I need is someone who appears naive and unworldly. You will meet a man in Vichy you know quite well, and the main thing will be to appear believable when you talk with him. Your life will depend on it. Do you understand?"

I looked at him searchingly and felt a hard lump in my throat. He could sense my concern.

The colonel hesitated and took a deep breath. "Well, now, how can I explain it more clearly?" His brow furrowed deeply in concentration. I was still such a child to him.

"As an example," he began, choosing his words carefully, "you'll have to appear to be helpful but inexperienced, just as you should actually be at your age. Under all circumstances, lie, bluff, but whatever you do, be positive and decisive. The Germans and the Milice are good at spotting any sign of hesitation. Your life in Vichy will be a shadowy existence, a never-ending game of escaping detection. A flick of indecision in your eyes and you will be on your way to the nearest interrogation post, and you know what that means."

I stared at my feet, waiting for him to go on, but he paused for a minute longer to make me aware of the importance of what he was saying. It could become a matter of life or death. "When confronted by the enemy, bury your beliefs, Hélène. Lies must become real to you. You must convince yourself that you are one of them." He paused for a moment to look into my eyes. "Does this make sense to you?"

There would be no turning back if I accepted this assignment. I reflected for a moment before answering. In order to fight the enemy, I would have to make myself believe that I was a person who sided with them. I would no longer be Hélène Deschamps. Instead, I would have to become somebody else.

Finally, I replied, "Yes, I'll do my best." I felt as if a great weight had been lifted off my chest. "But you must tell me everything that is expected of me."

Beaugard rekindled his pipe. "In due time, Hélène. We will have a long talk before your departure," he said, getting up to indicate that the meeting was over. "By the way, Didier will accompany you."

I let out a sigh of relief. Yves Pelot, code-named Didier, was an old friend of mine from childhood. His father, like mine, had been an officer in the colonial army, and we'd lived in Africa and on the island of Réunion during the same time. We had shared many happy memories together.

"I'm so glad you chose him," I said gratefully.

We walked silently toward the wrought-iron gate.

I turned to the old colonel with a look of conviction on my

face and said firmly, "I have confidence. I know I will never
say anything to anyone about this mission. But, in return,
may I ask you to look after Mother and Jackie while I am
away?"

"You know I always do."

This mission would soon transform my life. I discovered
that leading a double agent's life was as lethal and treacherous as a double-edged sword. My assignment in Vichy was
to be very hazardous indeed.

On December 19, 1942, Hitler had demanded the creation
of a special French police force that he could rely on completely. A ceremony had taken place in Vichy on the first of
February 1943 to present a new institution, the Milice. Its
leader was Joseph Darnand, who had been given the title of
secretary general. Darnand's infamous Milice was directly
under the command of the Germans and was a subsidiary
unit of the Gestapo.

The men of the Milice wore SS uniforms, and the only
recognizable French element was the beret, which was worn
instead of a German cap. The *Miliciens* were notorious for
sweeping into the streets, highways, subways, stores, trains,
and churches to carry out local searches. They were trained
to suppress an insurrection and to protect the Germans
against any aggression from the French Underground or
other nationalists. The Milice was made up of volunteers,
and many of them were ruthless, sadistic mercenaries. Their
policy was one of sheer terror, using as their model their
bigger and more sinister brother, the Gestapo.

I was going to Vichy because I knew Jean de Simeon, one

of the chiefs of the Milice. He had been in college with my brother Maurice. Since my family knew him well, my orders were to get a job working for him and infiltrate his Milice unit. The ultimate goal was to pass on any valuable information I might learn. Meanwhile, my network would have access to rubber stamps, official Milice documents, and travel papers.

Jean de Simeon was the ne'er-do-well of a noble and distinguished French family. He was now in his early forties and had recently been promoted by the Milice to *directeur du service de répression anti-nationale* for the South of France. Small, sickly-looking, and filled with dreams of grandeur, he had a thin, pale face dominated by a sloping forehead. His eyes had a hard, metallic gleam. He drank a lot, perhaps to give him the kind of courage needed to fuel an inflated ego and the lack of conscience to be a full-time collaborator.

My first meeting with him took place in a black-market restaurant in Vichy, near the Hôtel du Parc, Marshal Pétain's residence.

I was sitting at a table with my friend Didier. I smiled at him, remembering our first year on the island of Réunion. The two of us would often explore the "citadel" along the shore, straddling old, rusty cannons on the ramparts, playing soldier, and defending the crumbling fort. And here we were together again, fighting in our own way this ugly, cruel war.

Didier was very special to me. He looked tough, and he truly was—but only when the occasion demanded. Very few people knew the kind heart behind the rough exterior. He was a wonderful, dynamic young man of twenty, with a shock of dark-brown hair, a high, intelligent forehead, and determined brown eyes.

We had been instructed to study de Simeon's schedule for several days before attempting to make contact with him. He followed his routine precisely.

At exactly twelve noon, Jean de Simeon made his theatrical entrance, working the room as if it was a social event. He table-hopped, kissed ladies' hands, and cold-shouldered those who did not meet his standards. I waved from my table and affected an expression of pleasant surprise. He spotted me immediately and appeared hesitant. I straightened up in my chair to hold his attention and delivered my most engaging smile.

De Simeon's eyes flickered from my head to my feet with approval. Finally he was coaxed over, an amiable expression filling his sour face.

"My dear Hélène, what a surprise!" He held my hand attentively, showing great interest. "You have grown so much. Yes, indeed, you are a young woman now. It took me a while to recognize you. And how is your mother?"

"Very well, thank you. May I introduce my friend, Didier Pelot."

The two men shook hands.

"How long have you been here?" de Simeon inquired, rudely turning his back to my companion.

"Only a couple of days. But I intend to stay awhile."

De Simeon readily accepted the invitation to join us for lunch. I knew he liked young women, and throughout the meal, I played a flirtatious game.

While sampling rabbit in wine sauce and polishing off a vintage bottle of Bordeaux, we chatted busily. Our conversation ranged from politics to the meaningless society chitchat de Simeon was so fond of.

Every so often he would take my hand or bend attentively

in my direction. I made a point of giving him warm, generous smiles in return.

When we were finished eating, the waiter arrived with a dessert cart, and I selected a chocolate éclair, a luxury I had not had in a long time. The men ordered coffee—real coffee—which was a rare extravagance but still available for an outrageous price on the black market.

"And your brothers, how are they these days?" de Simeon inquired casually. "I haven't seen them in Aix for a long time." He shook his head, reflecting. "Of course, I left town a while back."

My face froze. I was caught off guard, and in my confusion, I began fumbling with the stem of my glass, half raised it to my lips, and then set it down again.

Quickly Didier covered for me. Turning his body decisively in de Simeon's direction, he explained in a hushed tone, as if to avoid hurting my feelings, "They defected to North Africa. You didn't hear about it?"

It was safer to put the cards on the table, just as a precaution, in case he was already aware of the fact.

"No, I didn't know!" de Simeon exclaimed incredulously. At the mention of North Africa, a distinct change had come over his face. He put his cup down and his eyes narrowed.

"More coffee?" Didier suggested.

De Simeon declined, waving his hand. He appeared to be concentrating on his thoughts, his fingers distractedly sweeping the crumbs scattered in front of his plate.

I realized I had to distract him from further speculation; otherwise, it might endanger the entire mission. Taking his hand in mine and leaning closer, I confided: "You remember the outdated political ideas they both had in college? Royalists, of all things! They left home at the beginning of the war, and we never heard from them until recently through the Red Cross. Mother is assuming they still are in North Africa."

I forced my chin down sadly and pouted my lips with disappointment. "She is heartbroken over the whole affair."

De Simeon patted my arm in sympathy. "I remember all too well their foolish political whims. What a stupid decision they made. They should have known the Germans will win this war," he said grimly.

He took the bait so well, I thought prematurely. De Simeon wasn't through yet, though. He wasn't a man to be underestimated.

"But . . . you still haven't said what you're doing in Vichy," he insisted, searching my eyes for a glimmer of truth.

"Life has become difficult in Aix," I said. "Mother is so upset with everything and seems to have withdrawn from life. I came here with the hope of finding a job. There must be something I can do."

Didier coughed, timing his intervention carefully. "Just before you arrived, I was suggesting that Hélène apply for an office position in town. I'm sure, with her impeccable background, someone could use her as a receptionist or filing clerk."

"Didier," I interjected, with feigned embarrassment, "I told you. I have no experience."

He turned to look at de Simeon. "Perhaps she will listen to you more than to me. Among your friends there must be someone who could help her."

"Yes," de Simeon answered pensively, tugging the lobe of one ear. A long silence followed.

Panicky, I thought I had lost the match of wits, when

suddenly de Simeon looked at me with a thin, calculating smile.

This man was like a chameleon; his expression could change in seconds.

"As a matter of fact," he said thoughtfully, "I could use extra help in my office. Friends should help each other, don't you agree?" he added, directing an appreciative glance to my legs. "We'll see. Let me check. I'll give you a call in a day or two. By the way, where are you staying?"

"Well, I don't know the city very well. I've found a room at the Villa des Bains Lardy, rue Bardiaux."

De Simeon was smiling protectively at me, totally ignoring Didier. He drank the last of his coffee and dabbed his mouth carefully with a napkin. Pushing his chair back brusquely, he got up, saying, "I'll be in touch soon."

He shook hands with Didier and left the restaurant, trailed by an obsequious headwaiter, who apparently was attempting to get into de Simeon's good graces.

I felt jubilant and very proud of myself, but Didier wisely warned me to be twice as careful from then on.

"I'm going to find a place for myself in town," he said. "The only time you will see me will be after I receive instructions from Beaugard. I'll call him immediately and inform him the setup is on."

Two weeks later, I became Jean de Simeon's girl Friday and received my residence permit. (One had to have this paper issued by the city's police in order to stay more than a week in Vichy.) Didier received further instructions from Beaugard. He was to be my outside contact and courier for any information I might obtain. His orders were to report, not to interfere.

Each morning, I presented myself at the Hôtel Radio, the headquarters of the Milice. I would show my ID card to the two armed, dark-shirted *Miliciens* posted at the entrance and fill in the time, eight A.M., on the board.

De Simeon never arrived before nine o'clock, and this gave me ample time to perform what I ended up calling my "personal little duties." It became a regular routine, and I wondered many times why I didn't get caught by one of the eager staff members who were always on the prowl for something to uncover.

Promptly at eight-fifteen A.M., I would enter de Simeon's office, ushered in by his lieutenant. After casually checking the room to see if I was alone, I would walk to the metal filing cabinet, where hundreds of names of suspects and other important information was collected in alphabetical order. Taking a few cards at random, I would tear them up, put the pieces in my brassiere, and nonchalantly go to the bathroom with a comb in my hand. I would then flush the compromising papers down the toilet. It was my way of fighting back, and it became a game for me, a potentially deadly game. If I had been caught in the act, I would have been interrogated and tortured, and if I had survived that ordeal, I would have been shipped to a concentration camp.

That grim reality, however, did not change my beliefs. If the names of the unfortunate men and women had remained on file, these people would have been arrested, thrown in jail, or worse, shipped like cattle to the death camps. I saved many lives by destroying those papers.

The Milice had collected the names of people of all faiths

and all walks of life. Sometimes the unfortunates were denounced by their own families for personal gain!

When I would overhear plans for a raid by de Simeon's office, I would contact Didier as soon as possible and give instructions to notify the persons in danger. It was easy for me to know when such activities were arranged, as de Simeon made a sadistic and gruesome game of it. He was always in a good mood before the kill. De Simeon would call his aide, a tall, trim lieutenant named Goeth. The Alsatian was vain and distant, his blond hair slicked back like a shiny helmet. His looks should have given him a certain presence, but the fixed, stony stare from his pale blue eyes made one feel that he was not looking at you but through you. Goeth occupied the outer office of de Simeon's personal bureau at the Hôtel Radio, and the two worked hand in hand.

A sadistic team, they would carefully open the ominous file cabinets, and de Simeon, dwarfed by Goeth's height, would ask casually, "Now, which letter of the alphabet shall we choose today?" Playfully, they would select the unlucky letter to which blind fate guided their fingers, and the next victims would be chosen. Their papers would be processed immediately. Often, the poor souls were condemned to death for no particular reason.

On occasion, my plans to warn the targeted individuals did not work. It sometimes took days to locate the right person, and help would sometimes arrive too late.

In retrospect, I wish I could have saved all of the faceless people on file. Though I never had the opportunity to meet them, I do know that I helped many of them cheat a cruel and untimely death at the hands of the enemy.

By this turning point in my life, I had begun to shed many

of my childish expectations. I had to mature too quickly, too fast. But I could not yet erase the thought of personal danger from my mind and continue my mission without looking back.

I would write to Jackie when the burden of events became unbearable, and I found strength in thinking of home. . . .

> *Dearest Jackie,*
> I miss you so much! But, I promised our friend I would remain here, and I must keep my word. How are you? *Maman* is well, I hope. Take good care of her. I wish I could hold both of you and live the quiet, happy life we once had.
> Remember the holidays at Saint-Ange? The lazy days in the sun? Perhaps, one day soon . . . who knows? Give *Maman* a big kiss for me and try to cheer up.
>
> Love,
> *Hélène*

During my normal office routine, I was able to whisk away blank forms marked with the official Milice stamp, which the Resistance used to get supplies or safeguard their travels around the country.

For a time, everything went smoothly, too smoothly. My intuition told me something was wrong. I couldn't explain the nagging, unsettling feeling that began to twist my stomach. But I listened to the inner voice, waiting for a sign.

In June 1943, de Simeon decided to lead a raid on the town of Grenoble, and everything about my dangerous double life changed.

CHAPTER FIVE

The Raid

De Simeon had been after one particular Underground leader for a long time. In June, the Milice figured out who he was. As usual, I passed the information on to Didier during lunch so that the Partisans would be forewarned.

The day of the raid, de Simeon summoned Goeth to his office. I was there working, but naturally lent an ear to the details of their plan. It was about two o'clock in the afternoon, and the team was to set out by five. The room quickly filled with cigarette smoke, an overpowering odor of brown Gauloises biting at my throat.

De Simeon began making arrangements. "First, we will take care of the leader in Grenoble. We'll make him talk in no time. He'll be more than happy to spill the names of the rest of the band." He smiled grimly and chuckled. "We'll use Werner. He's good at interrogation."

Sitting behind my typewriter, I attempted to appear busy when de Simeon sauntered across the room and passed my desk. He was gathering papers, which he carelessly stuffed into his briefcase.

"Is there anything I can do while you are away?" I suggested engagingly. "Should I sort out your files?"

De Simeon suddenly raised his head in surprise, not answering immediately. "No, thank you," he said at last, mouthing his words carefully. He sat quietly at his desk. His swivel chair gave a faint squeak of rusty coils.

His laughter broke the awkward silence, laughter that held no humor. He leaned back nonchalantly, his eyes hooded as if he was contemplating a new idea and at the same time sizing me up. His skinny, white hands were resting lightly on the arm of the leather-worn chair. He paused, tapping his fingers, then when the silence was almost unbearable, he announced, "You're coming along! Yes, I'll enjoy having you keep me company."

I felt as if my heart had stopped. The last thing I wanted to do was be part of one of de Simeon's infamous raiding parties. I remained silent and tried to appear pleased with this turn of events.

De Simeon loved feeling important, and traveling with a full staff inflated his ego immensely. He especially liked having a girl by his side.

"Come on," he said. "Hurry home and pack. I'll pick you up in one hour. Be ready when I arrive."

We had been driving all night. De Simeon, myself, and five *Miliciens* were on the main road in two separate cars. Afraid to think too far ahead, I gazed blankly into the distance. The gray crags of the mountains appeared misty and forlorn on the horizon.

We passed a tiny hamlet at sunrise, and across the lush fields, a small boy whistled at us cheerily as he herded a flock of goats homeward for the morning milking. The rising sun splashed the awakening land with gold-laced streaks.

Around eight o'clock, de Simeon declared abruptly that we would stop at the village of Villard. "We are going to have a little entertainment while having our breakfast," he announced, a cruel smile curling his thin lips.

Noting the inquisitive glance I threw him, he patted me on the shoulder, explaining, "I have been notified that there is a large group of Jews hiding out here, but for the moment, they are out of our reach since this area is under the Italian Occupation. Still, we can have a little fun."

He poked his head through the window and, after a few minutes, told the driver to stop at the door of Le Relais, the only inn at the end of town.

Startling the night clerk by clanging the bell at the front desk, he commanded that all the guests gather in the dining room immediately with all personal identification papers.

"Give me the list of all the transients. No excuses," he demanded. "I want everyone downstairs now!"

The hotel proprietor and his staff were terrified by the Milice uniforms, the guns they carried, and the arrogant, overbearing manner of the group. They also feared being imprisoned for harboring illegal guests who were fleeing the Occupation authorities.

A table was quickly set for de Simeon and his entourage. Coffee and buttered bread were promptly served, as the hotel guests, young and old, entered the dining room, some still wearing their night clothes. A stony expression of fright swept over their faces as they contemplated their arrest.

De Simeon took a few sips of his coffee, taking his time

and relishing his sense of power. With a sway of his hand, he ordered his men to collect all identification cards. They began circulating among the tables and gathered up the papers, which were docilely handed to them.

Thoroughly disgusted but unable to reveal my emotions, I excused myself and left for the bathroom. There I found a woman, in her thirties, hiding behind the door, timidly peeking through the slightly opened panel. I attempted a smile. She was so frightened, she was shaking under her robe.

"Don't be afraid," I told her. "We won't be long. Nothing will happen to you for the moment, but tell your friends they will have to move as soon as possible. These men will be back."

I splashed some cold water over my face, and without looking back, returned to the table.

De Simeon and his crew were already preparing to leave. He had barely looked at the identification papers, but was pleased that he had scared the defenseless group. Lifting himself up with great aplomb, he began passing between the tables, stopping at random and lifting a chin here and there with his gloved hand.

"Look at them!" he exclaimed. "They're shaking in their boots. Aren't they pitiful?" The *Miliciens* laughed derisively.

Munching on my slice of bread, I followed his steps without a word as he passed among the tables. It was not the time to irritate him in any way. I gave an imperceptible nod of recognition to the young woman I'd met in the bathroom, who had gathered her courage and joined a couple of other guests. The shadow of a grateful smile illuminated her tired face.

"Let's go," de Simeon ordered. "We'll see you soon, I

hope," he warned the terrified hotel guests, taking a final glance at the room.

I walked out the door without looking back.

As our cars left the village, an old man, smoking his pipe placidly in a doorway, saluted us politely, a man obviously at peace with himself and the world. From the chimney, pitched on the thatched roof of his hovel, eddied a blue spiral of smoke, slim as the poplar trees by the edge of the road. Somewhere a silvery bell began to peal.

We entered Grenoble through the old walled town, where the swollen current of the Isère River plunged past. Our caravan stopped in front of the Milice post, a small station located near a church, and we all got out. The street was empty except for a man on his bicycle, pedaling leisurely in our direction. He had a shopping basket strapped across the handlebars, and he wore his beret cocked to one side.

"Bonjour," the man greeted the *Miliciens* amiably as he passed by.

Without replying, de Simeon walked ahead. I trailed behind him. Four local *Miliciens* were ahead of us in the small building.

Without warning, an object flew through an open window, rolling across the floor and stopping in the middle of the room. I could see men inside the office scrambling for safety. One threw himself under a heavy oak desk, while two others straddled the windowsill, then desperately made their way out. A fourth man froze, staring at the small, dark object on the wooden floor. Then the explosion came, shattering the quiet of the morning.

Standing behind de Simeon at the station's entrance, I felt the blast travel through my body. It knocked me to my knees, blood sputtering from my nostrils.

Everything in the room was chaotic. Smoke and fragments of metal and wood flew in every direction. Then . . . total quiet.

Staggering, I attempted to stand up, but my legs gave way under me. I could see the *Miliciens* opening their mouths, but no sound seemed to escape their lips. I was deaf!

A grenade had been tossed through the open window of the office by an FFI—French Forces of the Interior—man on his bicycle. The Underground had left its calling card.

De Simeon was standing near me, his back against the door. The sleeve on his right side was torn and bloodstained, and his face was a deathly white. A nervous tic was making the cuts on his right cheek twitch awkwardly.

I felt nauseous. Holding on to the wall, I finally got to my feet and made my way to the men's room in the small hall facing the entrance. After throwing up, I splashed cold water over my face and arms, which were pitted with small, open wounds from the shattered glass.

When I came out of the bathroom, de Simeon was leaning against one of the station's walls, mumbling incoherently. My hearing was beginning to return, but I felt a terrible pain in my head, as if tremendous pressure had been applied to my temples.

"The bastards! The damn bastards!" de Simeon kept screaming. "I'll get them, all of them, one by one!"

He squinted at the *Milicien* who lay sprawled in a pool of blood. His left arm had been blown off, leaving an ugly, jagged, bloody wound. The two men who had escaped through the window were coming back in, unhurt. With sweating faces, they moved toward their comrade, who was crying out feebly. It was a hideous sight, and the sickly sweet smell of blood was heavy in my nostrils.

With crushing glass and plaster beneath my feet, I wobbled closer to the wounded man. For me, he was a collaborator, but he was, after all, still a human being. In the presence of death, antagonism melts.

De Simeon stopped me in my tracks, holding my arm. Gagging at the carnage, he pulled out a handkerchief from his pocket and held it over his nose.

"Come. They'll take care of him," he snapped, adding to the men who had been outside, "I will contact you in a couple of hours. It will give you time to clean up this mess and reach the German authorities. My men will help you. From now on, I strongly suggest you post a guard outside."

The five *Miliciens* who had traveled from Vichy with us were still unwilling to enter. De Simeon started to leave, then turned around abruptly. Pointing a gloved finger at them, he ordered, "I'll need eight men ready for action by noon. We have an arrest to make."

They saluted smartly. "Yes, sir!"

The street had filled with neighbors and curious townsfolk. Some of them wore expressions that registered a range of emotions from horror to fear. Others had a gleam of triumphant revenge in their eyes.

Ignoring the crowd, de Simeon pushed through and walked to his car with me in tow. I wrapped my handkerchief around my wrist to stop the bleeding.

"Someone will take care of us at the hotel," he told me.

Looking at my own blood, I suddenly felt the gravity of the

deadly game I had become involved in. I was not merely stealing passes and stamps; I was a spy who could be killed at any moment, and by either side.

I was taken to a nearby hotel and was left to recover from the morning's events. De Simeon was still keyed up and eager to seek revenge. He rounded up several of his men and left without muttering a single word.

I never did find out what actually happened. After our return to Vichy, the details of the expedition were discussed only once by Goeth, who said that de Simeon had reached the Underground leader's cabin, located in a nearby wood, and the only thing he found was the man's unfinished meal. I did not dare ask de Simeon myself. His dark, foreboding expression discouraged any queries. In the days following this incident, he was intolerable. It was extremely difficult to cope with him during working hours, and he drank more than ever.

I felt so tired and scared at this point that I had a hard time doing my job. De Simeon was often furious, and lashed out at everyone around him.

But after a week, life returned to the same normal routine as before. Still, I was wary. It was only a matter of time before de Simeon's rage would resurface, and I could not be sure of the consequences.

CHAPTER SIX

PT Boats

The explosion changed everything for me. I longed to be home and safe again, if that was still possible. I was starved for affection and often wished I was still the same Hélène Deschamps I used to be, bicycling or basking in the sun, playing mischievous games with my brothers and friends from school, or maybe going to university.

"Why don't you quit before it's too late?" I asked myself more than once. But already it was too late. There was no turning back. I had chosen a path that could very well lead to death. I did not want to die, and yet my pride wouldn't let me give up.

One morning a couple of weeks after the explosion, de Simeon showed up early at the office in the Hôtel Radio in Vichy, sporting a grin on his face. He was in one of his rare benevolent moods. During a meeting that day with Goeth, he announced his intention to take a week off to visit his wife and children and leave all responsibilities to his lieutenant.

I hadn't missed a word of this and waited until we were alone to approach him.

"Will you let me go with you?" I asked him. "My home is not far from the château de Simeon."

He looked at me with his heavy-hooded eyes and, as usual,

took his time to answer. Finally he nodded his assent. "Why not? It will be nice for you to see your mother."

In the pleasure I felt, I actually was grateful. "Thank you, so much. When are we going—tomorrow?"

"Next Tuesday," he said brusquely, closing the subject, and he went back to his papers.

Because of the important position Jean de Simeon held in Vichy, we were allowed a private, first-class compartment on the train. The trip turned out to be tediously slow. By late afternoon, the train had stopped in the middle of nowhere to let a convoy pass. German trucks, ammunition, and cannons rolled by interminably.

It was seven o'clock in the morning when the train entered the gare Saint-Charles in Marseilles.

Impatient, I slid up the window, glancing at the platform. A smile came over my face when I stared up at the blue sky of Provence welcoming me. The temperature was already in the seventies, a warm draft sweeping across the platforms. Loud-speakers announced the arrival and departure times, and there were commands in German for soldiers getting off incoming trains.

A car was waiting for de Simeon at the exit to take him to his ancestral château in the nearby countryside.

He handed me a small envelope containing an advance on my monthly salary. "Have a good time," he said. "I'll contact you in a few days." Then he gave me a boneless handshake and turned away.

I opened the door with my own key and tiptoed to Jackie's room, where I found her, chin in hand, head bent over a book, reading. The slight creak of the floorboards made her turn around, and she let out a cry of surprise.

"*Mon Dieu!* You scared me!" She got up and ran to kiss me.

"I didn't mean to. Didn't you receive my letter?"

"No!" She began talking a mile a minute. "How did you manage to get away? If I had known, I would have come to the bus, and—"

"Relax." I laughed softly. "I'm here for a week. Let me go see *Maman*."

"I took her two days ago to visit a friend in Cannes. It'll do her good. Oh! I'm so happy you're here."

Suddenly, I felt how lonely I had been.

"I'm glad to be here! Believe me. Sometimes I feel like running all the way home." After a pause, in an effort to change the subject, I asked casually, leafing through the open book, "How are you doing at school?"

Jackie shook her head, pouting. "Not too well, I'm afraid. I'll know soon enough at the end of the year. Beaugard often keeps me quite busy, but *Maman* doesn't suspect anything."

"I'm glad you are being careful," I said dully.

Jackie knew me too well not to feel the uneasiness right away. Bouncing back to her usual cheerful self, she took me by the arm. "Come. Let's go to your room. I'll make the bed while we talk." When we got there, she kept on chatting and began tidying up the place.

"I have been quite active as a courier for the past month," she announced proudly. "Will the colonel be glad to see you! He's up to something, and he's being very secretive about it."

Silent, I kept unpacking my bag. "Listen," I said without looking up, "for your own safety and *Maman*'s, I wish you wouldn't get so involved with all of these matters. I don't want to hear about what's going on with Beaugard. I have enough to handle in Vichy, I can assure you. I came to rest and to be with you. I'm sorry *Maman* is away." My voice had taken on a sharp edge.

Jackie looked at me closely and saw the feeling hidden behind my eyes.

"Something happened to you in Vichy. Do you want to talk about it?"

I moved my hand as if chasing away a bad dream. "I'll be all right. Let me recover. I just went through a bad time, that's all."

Respecting my wishes, she left the room.

Left alone, I stood by the window a long time and watched Madame Giraud next door watering the flowers in the garden. It was so nice to be home, I thought. To be in my own room, to think of a million things and nothing at all, to remember the good days and be able to forget the future. I lay on the bed and closed my eyes.

At lunchtime, I went down and found Jackie in the kitchen, preparing our meal. I approached her and smiled, putting my arms around her shoulders. "Let me help you set the table."

I busied myself until we sat down to eat, sharing the small meal Jackie had been able to put together.

"I'm sorry I was so abrupt with you," I apologized. Though I didn't want to alarm her, I couldn't hold back any longer. I began telling her about Vichy, and soon I was talking about de Simeon's madness, about the Milice and the dangerous game I had to play each day, and then finally, about the violent mission in Grenoble.

"You cannot imagine how terrible it was, with the blood spattered all over, and de Simeon so cold as he looked at the dying man!"

Tears running down her cheeks, Jackie threw her arms around me. "*Ma pauvre chérie!* You must have been horrified. Were you hurt?"

"No, not really, only a few cuts and bruises. I was lucky."

I rested my head on her shoulder and felt comforted. "You know, there isn't a day when I don't think of what could happen to me if de Simeon discovers what I am doing. He can be so violent. I never realized it until that moment."

"Please, Hélène, don't go back. Stay home. Beaugard will find someone else."

I raised my head slowly, looking at my sister with eyes that were now brimming with tears. "I was chosen for this job because I knew de Simeon personally. It was the only way to have an inside contact. Beaugard warned me of the danger. I went anyway. You see why I can't quit now?"

Jackie protested vehemently. "I understand very well, but I don't want you to be killed!"

"I'll be more careful. I promise. I feel better already to have been able to talk to you."

Jackie got up and turned her back, tinkering in the sink to hide her fear. "Well, I won't try to dissuade you. You wouldn't listen anyway."

"I only feel guilty to have dragged you into all this."

"You're wrong!" Jackie insisted. "I'm the one who wanted to be a part of it."

That afternoon, around five o'clock, we took a stroll arm

in arm along the Cours Mirabeau and stopped at the Café des Deux Garçons.

While sitting at our favorite table, Jackie said, "Like before, isn't it?"

"Almost." I smiled.

That night, in my room overlooking the rose garden, I finally let myself rest—the familiar scent of the flowers reminded me of the past.

When I awoke, I looked at my watch and realized I had slept for ten hours straight. I wrapped my robe around me and went down to the kitchen to make a cup of ersatz coffee. Sitting in the garden, under the linden tree, I let the peace that surrounded me mend my wounded spirit.

Around eleven o'clock, the phone rang. It was Beaugard. "Hélène, dear, I heard you had come for a few days. You couldn't have come at a better time."

"I would have called you, but I'm not feeling well, and—"

"I understand," he cut in. "You need to rest. I must see you for a short while, though."

The war had caught up with me. I didn't say anything. I only heard the colonel's voice: "It's important. Come around two o'clock this afternoon. I won't keep you long."

"I'll be there," I said quietly.

According to the rules of the Resistance, secret discussions were to take place only between two people. Furthermore, agents were to have as few contacts as possible. In this instance, however, three men and a woman were in the colonel's study when I arrived.

Anne-Georges Loudes, Beaugard's girlfriend and companion, whom I'd met before, was sitting next to him. She came forward to shake hands. A tanned, attractive brunette in her forties, she wore her black hair short, combed behind the ears.

Anne-Georges was the ex-wife of a navy captain. Back then, divorce being virtually unknown in France, the divorcée had found Beaugard's home and gallant hospitality quite comfortable. Through Didier, I had heard she was trying to form her own network. (She eventually succeeded. The network was called Franc-Croix.)

I sat next to the three men. I didn't know them and Beaugard had purposely not introduced us. They simply nodded in my direction and remained silent. The youngest one, in his early twenties, had wavy blond hair and the shadow of a mustache. The other two seemed ill at ease and in a hurry to go.

"I'm sorry to hear you are not well," Beaugard commented. "Did you see a doctor? This won't take long. Listen to what I am about to explain. It's extremely important, and in the days to come, if you get any leads—anything at all—let me know at once." He turned to the others. "This goes for you, too, my friends."

He then told us that late at night, German PT boats had been harassing American and British convoys on their way to North Africa. During the day, the PT boats disappeared, and no one knew where they were hidden.

Studying the stem of his pipe, Beaugard slightly tilted his head. "I need a lead as soon as possible. The PT boats' hiding place has to be in our area. I realize there are many coves and caves along the coast, but with all of us working on it, we should come up with something concrete soon. I'm counting on you."

The three men looked at one another, then nodded. On this note, the briefing broke up. The men left, one at a time, heading off in different directions. I had just listened, waiting, knowing we'd have a chance to talk afterward, as Beaugard would want a succinct report on the Vichy enterprise.

Anne-Georges excused herself and left us together. In a flat voice, I gave him all the details I could recall. The colonel observed me closely as I spoke. "Go see Doctor Latil," he said when I had finished. "You need to gain some strength and have a good rest. You will be called back from Vichy in a couple of months. You and Didier have been of great help; however, the Underground is growing, and I need as many passes as possible so our people can circulate in restricted areas."

"I'll do my best. They are being very cautious lately in Vichy. Things are not going well for them. Goeth is the man to watch. He would love to catch me doing something wrong."

"Then be most careful. Remember what I told you at the beginning—always show that you are sure of yourself. Well," he added, "see what you can do for us. It's good to have you home."

His pipe was dead. Laying it in the ashtray, he got up and held me away, at arm's length, then kissed me on both cheeks and took me to the door.

The occupying forces had requisitioned many buildings and private homes in Aix and had installed their officers' club in the villa of Robert Thierrot, a student friend of Jackie's and mine. Everyone knew that when a house was requisitioned the owner could do nothing but go along or go to jail. Robert's parents had left for the country, and he had stayed behind to look after the property. Robert now lived in the gardener's house, while the officers enjoyed the lovely villa. But he did have permission to use his own pool at sundown, when the Germans were not around.

Being in such a strategic position, Robert, who was a sympathizer to the Cause, was sometimes of much help. He was constantly on the alert and passed along information about conversations between his "guests" on various military moves.

One afternoon not long after I spoke to the colonel Robert showed up at our house, ringing the bell impatiently, looking flushed and out of breath.

I came out running. "What's happening? Are you in trouble?"

Robert looked quickly around to make sure we were out of earshot. "Listen to this," he told me while I led him inside. "This morning a *Kriegsmarine* officer came up to my house."

"Are you sure? How do you know he's with the German Navy?"

Robert laughed. "It wasn't hard to guess. A sailor drove him to the door, and he wore his dark uniform. He's staying overnight. I heard him give the order to the driver."

Jackie, who had been listening from the dining room, said excitedly, "We have to work fast!"

The three of us sat together, like the young conspirators we were, turning over possibilities, trying to come up with a strategy. Finally I decided, "The best thing is to find an excuse for me to come to your house tonight without looking suspicious."

"You could be my girlfriend." Robert beamed genially.

"On such short notice? They are not fools, you know."

Jackie, who had been silent, suddenly jumped from her chair. "I've got it!" Looking at me with a twinkle in her eyes, she declared, "Today is the eighteenth of August. Don't you know what day it is?"

Robert and I looked puzzled. The eighteenth of August had no special meaning for me.

"It's your birthday, silly!" she cried with delight, nudging me with her elbow. "Robert could arrange a little party for you, ostensibly to celebrate the event. After all, you are school friends."

It was, in fact, a very good cover, and we decided that I would drop by the villa and, while visiting, try to talk to the navy man or overhear a conversation. Germans were always pleased to meet an adventurous French girl.

Looking prim in a blue cotton dress bought with my clothing coupons earlier in Vichy, I showed up around eight o'clock at Robert's villa, bringing along my old two-piece bathing suit. Robert had prepared a small decorative plate of fruits from the garden and a few leftover sweets from the Germans' dinner.

While sampling a few cookies, I took my time changing in the guest house. Then, intentionally playing the flirt, I slowly walked around the pool, joining Robert, who was already in the water.

Before long, a group of officers had gathered out by the pool, sipping wine, smoking cigars, and exchanging remarks about my anatomy. Among them, I recognized one with the navy uniform. The man, a handsome fellow in his thirties, was the perfect image of the young Aryan, complete with intense blue eyes, fair skin, pale blond hair, and a bearing so erect it seemed affected. He appeared quite interested in my gyrations in the water, and gave me a hand each time I came out of the pool. Naturally, I did my best to attract his attention.

In the midst of the eager attention shown by the men encircling me, one of them, rather drunk, fell in and ended up holding me in his arms. Then a rather stout colonel made an off-color remark in French, which I could not fail to overhear, and spontaneously, probably in response to the anxiety I was feeling, I burst out in deep, husky laughter. "Come join us for a drink," the colonel said, his heavy hand resting on my waist.

Moonlight, coming through the tall cypress trees, reflected on the placid pool, like stage lighting. Delicious peach wine was served, tongues began to loosen, and jokes sparked back and forth in both French and German.

"Let's sing," one of the men suggested. He began, and they all followed with one tune after another, clanging their glasses in rhythm.

After a while, they got tired of singing, and the drinking resumed. Most of the men present were speaking rather decent French, and Robert mentioned that it was my birthday. They all drank to that, even though I stressed modestly that, with the war, there could be no question of celebration.

"It's the eighteenth of August, isn't it?" the navy man asked. His companions nodded. Steadying his walk on his way to the terrace, he swept all of the flowers off the tables and brought them back in a bunch.

Handing me the bouquet, he declared, "It is also my sister's birthday. Accept these flowers for reminding me of it." He bowed, clicking his heels.

For an instant I was speechless. The man was feeling mellow, no doubt because of the alcohol he had been steadily consuming, but he seemed genuinely sincere in his action.

It was getting late, and the Germans started to leave a few at a time for their quarters. I had not been able to get anything out of the navy man. I needed information, perhaps a good lead, and I began flirting openly. Between enticing smiles, I kept on filling his glass; he was becoming very intoxicated. At my suggestion, we moved into the garden.

"You will excuse us," he gleefully told his envious companions, passing his arm around my waist. "We are going for a little stroll," he added, and winked slyly in their direction.

Obviously, he liked me, and I played along. He had taken a full glass with him and kept on drinking while we sat on a bench near the pool. When he finished the wine, he tossed the glass over his shoulder, then placed both arms around me.

I started to play coy. "You are wearing a uniform I have never seen before. Is it army?"

He was looking for action more than talk. "*Ach!* Not army," he replied with disdain, caressing my face. "I'm navy."

I giggled inanely. "I'm not familiar with military branches. You must excuse me." I paused for a minute, as though puzzled. "I don't understand. Aix is not a harbor. Why is the navy staying here?"

The man was really drunk, his tongue getting heavier and his French more difficult to understand. Somewhat incoherent, he kept on repeating himself. "You see, *Liebchen,* we're not stationed here . . . no, we're not stationed here," he blurted out.

"Oh, I see. You are just visiting?"

He was stammering, and he struggled to utter the words in French. "Yes, visiting, but I can come back soon, if you are nice to me. I can bring you some food and silk stockings. Cute little French girls like gifts." He smiled vacantly.

"How about tomorrow?" I enticed him.

He let out a chuckle and, tightening his grip, started nibbling at my neck, trying at the same time to slip my bra off.

His foul breath nauseated me, and I became jittery, wanting to get the game over with.

He squeezed me. "Don't be concerned, *Liebchen*. I'll come back. I can make it easily," he bragged. "*Ja!* We are stationed at the canal du Rôve, and I have a staff car."

At last, I had my tip—the PT boats were in the canal du Rôve, an underground canal connecting the Marseilles canal to the Rhône River. As quickly as possible, I slipped away from the now-passed-out officer and left the party.

When I arrived home, Jackie called me from her room and told me, "De Simeon wants you to meet him tomorrow afternoon at gare Saint-Charles in Marseilles at three o'clock."

As I was cramming my cardboard suitcase, Jackie was insisting that I stay until morning. "It's only eleven o'clock. You can give your information to Beaugard on your way to Marseilles."

"No. It's better for both of us if I leave now. I don't want to involve you any more than you already are."

"Yes. I know." Jackie's eyes were filled with tears. "Write, will you?" she asked sadly, kissing me good-bye.

I looked back uneasily, for I was leaving behind the security and peace of home, to return to my uncertain life of lies. I headed in the direction of Colonel Beaugard's new hideaway. I was not questioned by the German patrols because I had a Milice pass. By morning I had passed the news to Beaugard. The colonel permitted himself one of his rare smiles.

"Good job!" he said, wincing, as he got up from his chair. His old war wound must have been acting up, but he forced himself to walk. Passing me across the large room, his hands clenched behind his back, he limped a little. With his back slightly rounded, he looked, all of a sudden, much older.

"Damn good job," he grumbled again. And from him, it was indeed a great compliment.

CHAPTER SEVEN

Dear Didier

Routine life in Vichy resumed. Late one afternoon, as I was getting ready to leave the office, a Milice agent by the name of Garçin arrived from Marseilles with an important document.

Garçin and I knew each other. He came from Aix and was something of a hanger-on at de Simeon's place. He was hardly one of my favorite people, and I had tried to avoid him as much as possible. Seedy-looking, with ugly cross-eyes, he made a profession of informing on his compatriots. From looking at de Simeon's private files, I knew that he had even denounced his own brother.

De Simeon had left earlier that day for a meeting with German officials and members of Marshal Pétain's cabinet, so I took the envelope from Garçin. As he started to leave the room, he looked back again as if wondering whether he should have given it to me. Sensing his hesitation, I calmly placed the document in the filing drawer reserved for urgent matters. Garçin followed my move carefully and, satisfied, left the office.

I acted swiftly. I had noticed that the envelope was the same kind we used, with the Milice insignia. I ripped it open and examined the contents. There were two sheets of paper.

One had a crude map with red circles around the towns of Manosque and Aix. Under the map were three addresses. The second page had a list of names, some of which were underlined in red pencil, so that the most important ones were highlighted. As I read the page, I recognized several names of people involved in the Underground, including Anne-Georges Loudes and an ex-captain in the colonial army named Bacchieri.

I carefully folded the torn envelope into my brassiere, then sealed the message back into a new envelope and filed it in the drawer. Leaving the office, I only stopped long enough to chat with Goeth and Garçin in the anteroom.

As soon as I arrived at my hotel room, I called Didier from the hall phone, asking him to come as soon as possible. While waiting, I wrote down the names and addresses that I had memorized. Within thirty minutes, Didier rapped at my door. I pushed the lock open to let him in.

"Something special, am I right? I knew from the tone of your voice."

I nodded while handing him the note. He read the information I had scribbled down several times. Then he lit the paper with a match, holding it over an ashtray. It blazed for a second and dissolved into black ashes, which he then dumped into the sink. The running water pushed the cinders down the drain, leaving a charcoal film behind.

"This is a rush job," he told me, heading for the door. "I'll see you later." He went off on his bicycle to call Beaugard in Aix.

By the time de Simeon entered his office the next morning, it was well after eleven o'clock. There was a good excuse for his tardiness. The night before, he had attended one of those lavish parties given by the Germans in Vichy. The results of his debauchery were clearly printed on his jaded face.

When he opened the inner door, I greeted him with a cheery "Good morning." Then I took the document out of the drawer and placed it on his desk.

De Simeon pulled off his coat and hung it carelessly on the hook against the wall, his gaze moving unhurriedly to the envelope. After walking over, he sat down and inspected the paper. He finally unsealed it and, after reading the contents, became alert in a matter of seconds. He shoved back his chair and shouted for Goeth.

The door opened and his lieutenant entered the office, a sheaf of documents in his hands.

"Read this," de Simeon told him, throwing the papers across the desk. Goeth looked at them without a word.

De Simeon was observing his reaction. "What do you think of it? Do you trust Garçin?"

"Yes, I do. We have to act quickly, if we want to catch them. They are constantly on the move."

De Simeon was annoyed. "I have some unfinished business here with Hermann. I'm counting on you."

Goeth nodded and left the room.

Three days later, de Simeon received word from Manosque that once more the raid had proved futile. Though a couple of men who had not received Didier's warning soon enough had been arrested, none possessed any critical information about the network.

Since he had been in charge of this affair, it was Goeth's turn to be upset. He remained at his desk, sullen and brooding. Around three o'clock that afternoon, a team of three uniformed *Miliciens* asked to talk to de Simeon in private.

I was ordered to leave the room at once. As I went by Goeth's office to sit near the window, he sent a stack of papers crashing to the floor. The three officers remained with de Simeon for a couple of hours. After they left, de Simeon poked a rather deflated face from his office and asked Goeth to come in. The door was shut tightly behind them.

Unsure of what was happening, I left work as usual, stopping at the grocery store on my way to the hotel to pick up some things for dinner. I had established a habit of cooking a meager dinner in my room on a small kerosene burner. The entrance of the Villa des Bains Lardy was dark as a mole hole. I walked up the dimly lit stairs, lugging my shopping bag, and arrived on the third floor near my door. To my surprise, Goeth was waiting there. With a sheepish smile, he followed me inside my room.

I should have realized that his smile could mean no good. He paused inside the doorway, waiting for me to close the door, his eyes surveying the room. Without warning, he slapped me hard across the mouth, knocking me off balance. The back of my head crashed into the wall, and I dropped my groceries to the floor. The attack was unexpected. I straightened up cowering, waiting to be struck again. I could feel blood oozing down the corner of my mouth.

"What have I done?" I whimpered.

He looked at me for a moment, those colorless eyes staring with calm brutality. He jerked his head toward the bed and ordered, in a low, bullying voice, "Sit down."

This is it, I thought. That's why those men were there to talk to de Simeon. He knows! My stomach turned over. I didn't want him to see the fear in my face, so I tried to lower my head as he stared at me in silence. Since I was not obeying fast enough, he struck me again across the face.

He proceeded to search the room, starting with the drawers of the night table and going through my belongings systematically. Constantly pushing me aside, he looked through the dresser, under the mattress, shook the pillowcases, removed the blanket. Nothing!

With all my will, I tried to prevent myself from collapsing, glad at least that I had learned not to write anything down. I had made sure to leave no traces of conversations and reports. I felt slightly relieved.

Goeth rummaged through my purse, then went to the closet. My wardrobe was skimpy: two skirts, a white blouse, a raincoat, a blue crepe dress, a pair of shoes with heavy wooden soles, walking shoes, and slippers. My nightgown hung on a single nail behind the door. One by one, he searched all the pockets.

Finally, he stood in the middle of the room, looking around. He bent down and fumbled under the armchair. Thinking he had found something between the material and the woodwork, he ripped it out, but ended up with only a handful of stuffing. Angrily discarding the wad, he moved back toward the bed. He pulled a chair from against the wall and set it down with a bang.

I was sitting down now, and I passed a hand over my forehead. The pain in my head was becoming so sharp that tears were running freely down my face. I found the courage to ask, "What on earth are you looking for?"

"Let's stop playing cat and mouse. Obviously Jean trusts you, but he is blind to your act. I know what you are up to."

I cried louder. It was not difficult because of the fear that twisted inside of me. Through my tears, I managed to sound innocent. "What's that?" I begged.

"About the leak in the outfit," he replied nastily. "I'm sure you have something to do with it. I want all of the details." Then, in a low, almost caressing tone, he added, "Tell me everything. Who knows, there may be some extenuating circumstances that might help you."

With horror, I thought of tortures! Yet a little voice inside kept telling me to deny everything. That was the only way out. I forced a thin smile to my lips, knowing that they were already so distorted, I must have looked very odd. "I don't understand. What are you trying to tell me?"

He raised his fist once more, and I let out a howl before he even reached me.

I began to sense that Goeth was fishing, because if he wasn't, I would have been arrested on the spot. It was only a guess on his part, and I said nothing. After watching me for a while, he shook his shoulders. He was angry; his entire visit had turned out to be futile.

Taking advantage of this, I struggled to steady my voice. "I've done nothing wrong and know nothing about the activities against the Milice. I can't see why you are holding me responsible!" I could hear myself talking, but I wasn't sure what I was saying. I was making it up as it came into my head. I closed my eyes to concentrate. "I'm Jean's friend as much as you are. If the Milice are looking for a guilty party, search in the organization. People like Garçin are more likely to be guilty than I am."

Goeth had been rifling through my grocery bag, perhaps hoping to find a message or note of some sort. When I was through talking, he turned in my direction and gave me a long, surprised glance. "Have you discussed this with anyone before?"

"No. Why should I?"

"Where did you go after leaving the office today?"

"I only stopped at the grocery store."

"Did you talk to anyone there? Did somebody approach you, perhaps?"

"No. No one. You can check with the owner. He'll tell you." Goeth was unsure of himself. My story would do, for now. "I only mentioned Garçin because he is denouncing lots of people. You know that. He might be working for the Underground and be trying to infiltrate the Milice. Why should it be me? I'm only a clerk!" Goeth paused.

"Let's go back to the day when Garçin arrived. What happened to the papers he brought from Marseilles?"

"He gave them to me in a sealed envelope."

"Yes . . . ?"

"Well, I took it and told him that Jean was at an important meeting."

"Did he make any calls from Jean's office?"

"Yes," I lied. "Only one. I didn't pay much attention at the time, since he is a friend of yours . . . I thought."

Goeth's eyes narrowed. "Hmmm, why not call from my office?" Suspicion had been planted.

"You see," I insisted. "Now that you mention it, I think the same thing. Why not call in front of you, if he had nothing to hide?"

"Was there any conversation between the two of you afterward?"

I swore there was none, which was the truth. "But I've noticed that each time he has been here," I added, "he's always trying to find out what's going on, and what Jean is planning." This was also true, but I knew that the man was only trying to look important.

I started to cry again, playing my part fairly well and making so much noise by sobbing and talking at the top of my voice that I could tell Goeth began to worry that other members of the Milice, who were staying at the hotel, might report him to de Simeon. Quizzing me was his own idea. De Simeon didn't like his men to act independently. Now he could get in trouble.

Goeth made a move toward the door, saying as he passed by, "Not a word to Jean about this. Just don't come to the office for a few days. It'll give you time to think things over. Try to remember who else could be undermining our work. I'm not convinced yet about Garçin. So let's forget about this evening for the time being."

I didn't complain, knowing that I was pretty lucky to get out of the ordeal so easily. Goeth turned quietly and left.

I sank onto the bed, crying until I could cry no more. A splitting headache added to the terrible fear tearing at me and shattered my nerves, and I went numb.

Unable to sleep, I got up and bathed my red, swollen eyes. I looked at myself in the mirror above the washbasin and saw a most miserable reflection. I consoled myself with the thought of how lucky I had been up to now.

"Oh, my God!" I exclaimed out loud, remembering Didier. He couldn't visit me in my room any longer. He had to be warned quickly.

I went to the door and opened it, waiting long enough to calm my breathing and to listen. All was quiet. A light breeze sighed through the shutters, ruffling the thin lace curtains. It was one A.M.

There was a telephone on the wall near the stairs. I knew it was not safe, but I couldn't afford to have Didier come to see me. We would have to find another way of communicating. I was about to slide out of my room when I noticed that the door next to mine was slightly ajar. Someone was listening. I stepped back inside.

After swallowing a couple of aspirin, I went back to bed and, strangely enough, fell sound asleep. I awoke the next morning around seven o'clock, more rested than I had the right to expect. Dressing quickly, I left my room and walked along the shabby carpet down the hallway to the phone.

Holding the receiver close to my mouth, I spoke in a low tone, giving Didier's number to the operator. The phone rang several times at the other end before he answered.

"It's me." I forced myself to think of what I was going to say.

Didier took so long answering that I wondered if I had been disconnected. "*Allô! Allô!*" I pressed.

"It must be good news to call so early," he remarked sleepily.

"Listen, *mon ami*," I said. "*Mon ami*" was our emergency phrase for getting in touch with each other, but I couldn't speak clearly. My voice was weak and still shaky. He didn't understand me.

"*Mon ami,*" I insisted, raising my voice into the receiver. "I had a nasty conversation with one of Jean's colleagues."

"Do you need help? Shall I come over?" the now-anxious voice asked urgently.

"No. I'll be all right. I prefer not to see you for a while. It's better that way. You understand, don't you?"

"Yes, but . . ."

I placed my hand over the mouthpiece, afraid the hotel manager might listen. Actually, it didn't matter too much, for our conversation had been rather insignificant and no names had been exchanged.

I hung up on him.

I felt a little faint and rested my head against the telephone. The metal was cool and felt good. A few minutes later, I exited the hotel in search of the nearest drugstore.

"A nasty bruise," the man noticed from behind his stand.

"I fell down the stairs," I told him. "Should I put something on it?"

He gave me some ointment and advised that I take more aspirin. "You'll be all right in a few days. You had better watch your step."

When I returned to work a few days later, I found my office closed; de Simeon had been transferred to another post in the organization because of the many failed missions. Colonel Labat, the new man in charge, notified me that my association with the Milice was over. I didn't ask him for my pay, even though it was nearly the end of the month. As I left the building, I noticed that Goeth was not there either.

I called Didier from a nearby café and asked him to meet me as soon as possible at the train station. I had talked to him only a few hours earlier that day to explain in detail what had happened with Goeth. When I called again, he thought I had run into more trouble. Nervous, I fidgeted on the hard wooden seat in the third-class lounge.

Facing me on the wall was a picture of Marshal Pétain, looking down benignly at me. Only a few passengers were sitting; some were reading, others lost in their own personal thoughts. No one paid much attention to the girl impatiently waiting at the door.

I caught sight of Didier as he pushed his way through the revolving door. His face was anxious.

"What's up now?" he asked as soon as he reached me.

I explained that de Simeon had been fired, and as a result, I had lost my job. We talked over what to do next.

Didier checked the railway timetable. "There is a train leaving for Marseilles at five-fifty this afternoon. I think we should pack and go home. Anyhow," he added, "we were supposed to return soon."

"Perhaps I should try to contact de Simeon," I suggested without enthusiasm.

"No. It is better that you lie low for a while. You've done enough. Going home is the best thing to do."

I didn't need much coaxing, for I couldn't agree more. I had had enough of Vichy's deceitful life.

"I'll come with my bicycle to carry your suitcase," Didier said.

"What? Oh. Yes, I'd appreciate that," I answered distractedly, still thinking about de Simeon and the Milice.

He shook me by the shoulder. "Hey! This is me, Didier. Are you listening?"

"I'm sorry. I'm still not myself."

"I'll see you as soon as I pack my bag."

We parted, Didier on his way back uptown and I to the Villa des Bains Lardy.

I had a violent headache. With three hours to kill before Didier could rejoin me, I decided to rest for a while. The deep sound of a church bell finally woke me. I looked at my watch and jumped out of bed. It was four-thirty P.M. I got dressed again and gathered the last of my possessions. As I was closing the suitcase, there was a knock on the door.

"Come in," I said over my shoulder, thinking it was Didier. A heavyset man in civilian clothes was standing in the doorway. I froze in my steps.

"Mademoiselle Deschamps?" he inquired in a guttural French.

I felt as if the floor was collapsing. There was no doubt in my mind. The man was Gestapo!

I forced a smile and stepped aside to let him in. "Yes?" I began, broke off, gulped air, then took a long breath that gave me time to steady myself.

The man handed me a paper with the German Eagle engraved at the top. It was an order signed by Hermann, one of the *Kapellmeisters* in Vichy and a good friend of de Simeon's. I knew the signature, having seen it many times on official correspondence.

"A car is waiting downstairs," the man said.

I had often considered the possibility that I might be arrested, but had never faced the reality. At that moment, the deadly fear of torture literally shook my body, but at the same time, terror made me think at an incredible speed and I tried to come up with a plausible story.

Had there been some dreadful slipup somewhere? Perhaps Beaugard had been arrested. If so, he might have talked. He was getting old and had not been feeling well lately.

"Are you ready?" the German asked.

Throwing a jacket over my arm, I gathered up my bag. "Let's go." We moved toward the door.

My next-door neighbor at the hotel, the one who had been listening when I almost left my room to call Didier the night of Goeth's visit, was an old maid who had worked at the Vichy post office long before the war began. She was curiously watching from her door as we headed to the stairs. The woman shook her head disapprovingly when I went by, as if to say, "I knew it!" Then she slunk back into her room.

As we emerged from the hotel, I caught a glimpse of Didier bearing down on his bicycle.

I knew the rules: never acknowledge a comrade. Not a word passed our lips. Our eyes met for a split second, and a distressed smile spread across his mouth. In answer to his mute appeal, I gave him the cold glance of a stranger. To be so close to a friend and not be able to call for help is real agony! I wanted to run toward him.

Suddenly, he bent over his wheels as if engrossed in putting air in the tires with a small hand pump.

The Gestapo messenger opened the car door for me. I blindly climbed in and we drove off.

Didier gave a single, desperate look in my direction as we passed by.

We went by the Hôtel du Parc and entered the residential area of Vichy, slowing down as we reached a charming villa, nestled in greenery and enclosed by an elegant wrought-iron fence. The house had a substantial, warm appearance, but this impression quickly vanished at the sight of a *Feldgrau* (a German soldier) posted at the gate. He wore an iron necklace, a large crescent held by a chain hung around his neck. He reminded me of a bulldog guarding his domain.

I listened to the rapid flow of German words exchanged with the driver. The guard came forward.

I stepped out of the car, my stomach tightening, and waited for the gate to open. I was now in the hands of the Gestapo.

Feeling lost, I went up the three steps leading to a large door, which opened in front of me. Two men in civilian clothes were waiting there. "I am Hélène Deschamps. I'm supposed to see Herr Hermann," I told them, showing them the letter.

One of the men led me to the living room and opened an inner door, letting me in. It was then that panic hit me. I felt I had no strength left. Dizzy, I tripped on the edge of the Persian rug, and I reached the corner of a table just in time to prevent myself from tilting over. I then sat on a small settee, upholstered in an expensive brocade, and waited.

I didn't know what to make of it. Were they suspicious? Was I arrested? If so, why were they being so polite?

The house had nothing to suggest the presence of the Gestapo. It looked like the house of any peaceful family. A few magazines were spread on a stool by the chair. I reached for one. I was so frightened that I stared vacuously at several pages before realizing that I was holding it upside down!

It seemed like ages before the inner door opened again, and a short, beefy man entered. He was roly-poly, from his bald head to his slightly arched legs.

He approached me with an engaging smile, but I couldn't miss the icy, calculating glare behind the gold-rimmed glasses. His suit was freshly pressed, his fingernails polished.

"Mademoiselle Deschamps," he cooed, "how nice to meet you. Jean de Simeon has told me such nice things about you."

I felt a ray of hope, and I smiled timidly at him. "Yes, I

have known Jean for a long time. He is a friend of my eldest brother."

"Hmmm!" Hermann angled himself into a chair close to mine, and after opening a cigar humidor on the end table, he carefully selected a long Havana. He bit off the end and lit it slowly, surveying me from the corners of his eyes.

"I have been told that your brothers are in North Africa with traitors."

I sank into my seat and said nothing. He appeared amused at my embarrassment, and this angered me. I remembered Beaugard's advice: "Lie, bluff, but whatever you do, be positive and decisive."

"As you know, Herr Hermann," I said, "not all Frenchmen have the same political opinions. I happen to like winners and do not share my brothers' views. That is why I served with Jean in the Milice."

It wasn't a perfect explanation, but it was a plausible one.

"Your loyalty to us is commendable." The irony in his voice was stinging. The fleshy, bespectacled face frowned. He was visibly pleased with my quick reply and shook his head appreciatively, with the clumsiness of a walrus.

His lips pursed as he proceeded to switched the subject. "You are out of work at the present, I understand?"

I nodded in agreement, not quite knowing where the conversation was going.

Hermann drew deeply on his cigar and then exhaled. "I thought perhaps you would do a little job for us." He peered at me through the thick cigar smoke.

I couldn't help staring at him, wondering what he was after. Perhaps he was testing me.

"I'd love to, if I can. However, all I know is clerical work. Is this what you had in mind?"

"This has nothing to do with secretarial skills." He patted me on the knee in a fatherly manner. "All I want you to do is to go to the town of Royat and get some information. For a clever girl this shouldn't be a difficult task. Get friendly with the townspeople and try to obtain their trust so that you can get a lead on the location and whereabouts of the men involved in the Resistance in that sector."

He paused and took several puffs at his cigar. "We presume the Partisans' hideout must be somewhere near the town, and it's up to you to find out—just get a few names so we can close the net." Hermann smiled benevolently and clamped his teeth onto his cigar.

I shook my head uncertainly. "I'll try and do my best, but I've never done this type of investigation before," I apologized, trying to look at a loss.

Hermann raised my chin with one finger. "I'm confident you can do it. Act as a tourist would act. It will be a pleasant stay for you. Be back in a few days with good news."

He got up and took me to the front door. After searching through his wallet, he handed me a wad of French bills. "For your travel expenses and food," he added, smiling.

I stepped out into the sunlight, greatly relieved to get out of this house and away from the ominous atmosphere. I went off on foot in the direction of Café Lucien, east of town, where I knew Didier would be waiting to hear from me. This was the meeting place we had arranged in case of an emergency.

Didier stood when he saw me arrive, and swept me off my feet. He held me tightly against him, then kissed me passionately. "*Chérie!*" he exclaimed loudly, loud enough to be heard all around. "I thought you were still mad at me!"

"Of course not, *mon amour,*" I purred.

For the patrons sitting around us, we were a young couple making up after a quarrel, and they appeared to indulgently approve of our demonstration of affection.

He nuzzled against me playfully. I leaned against his shoulder and he whispered, "I was out of my mind thinking you had been arrested! I almost spoke to you at the door, but I saw the expression on your face."

"If you want to know the truth, I was so scared that I even lost the ability to think straight. But when they dropped me at Hermann's house, they treated me more like a guest than a prisoner."

"Hermann's house? The Gestapo?" he interrupted me, bewildered.

I nodded.

A waiter passed by. "Two Cinzanos," Didier ordered.

I told him the details of my strange meeting with the German and his unusual offer. I felt panicky and did not want to get involved with the Germans, but Didier shook his head. "You'll have to go through with it. If you leave for Aix, it really would be an excuse for them to start investigating not only you, but perhaps to arrest your mother and Jackie."

"I'm scared, Didier. I'm very scared!"

He placed his arm protectively around my shoulders, bringing me against him.

"Strong people survive. We are survivors. For your sake, just play along. Go to Royat, stay for a while, and then come back. Show Hermann your train ticket. Tell him that you couldn't find any leads. Act stupid. After all," he tried to joke, "you are not supposed to be a secret agent!"

"Please, don't make fun of me," I said. "I want to go home."

"Not for now. It's too dangerous after the incident with Goeth. You know I'm telling you this for your own good."

An insecure smile formed at the corner of my mouth and, relieved, he suggested, "How about merging our ration tickets and having something to eat?"

My spirit was starting to perk up. "On one condition. I'll pay for it. After all, I have money now."

Soon we were strolling arm in arm on one of the main streets, searching for an inexpensive place to eat. On our way, Didier even splurged and bought me a corsage. The flower woman, dressed in a man's jacket with a crocheted shawl over her greasy hair, waved a fat hand. "Beautiful flowers, mademoiselle. Choose," she simpered. I took some violets from the small wicker basket.

"I'd like these," I told my companion.

Didier gave the woman some small change while I pinned the posy on my blouse. Then he kissed my lips. "I love you, you know!"

I felt silly all of a sudden, for I had never imagined he had any special feelings for me. I had been so engrossed in our teamwork that, for me, he was always simply "dear old Didier."

"Let's go," I said, breaking off the thought.

We ate at a brasserie, enjoying some potato salad, a slice of cheese with bread, and an apple. Didier took me halfway home, then we parted.

"See you soon," he said, and started walking, but then he stopped and turned toward me, looking concerned. "Don't forget to call me as soon as you come back. I'll miss you."

My trip to Royat was without incident. During my few days there, I deliberately did very little. Some mornings, I hiked in the surrounding wooded hills. Afternoons were spent in the town park, where I watched a German military band play Viennese waltzes and martial songs.

At the end of the week, I returned to Vichy. It was with much apprehension that I presented myself at the gates of Hermann's villa.

I was received this time with a trifle more grace and was even treated to smiles from the two civilian guards. Hermann joined me directly.

On hearing that my "efforts" had been in vain and that I had collected no information concerning the whereabouts of the Secret Army, he became angry. He hurled a volley of curses at me, his face turning red and his voice becoming vicious as he slammed his fist on the table, upsetting a pile of papers. The paternal attitude displayed at our first meeting had completely disappeared.

I tried to act intimidated and embarrassed, wiping real tears from my eyes, for underneath I was frightened and wondered if any retaliation would follow.

"I don't know what to say," I apologized. "It was difficult for me going about asking questions without being noticed. They were on their guard."

Deportation entered my mind, and I could already picture myself being hoisted into a cattle car on my way to Germany.

Hermann crossed the room with measured, brusque steps and, after a few minutes, stopped in front of a painting, which he seemed to examine pointedly.

"We won't need your services any longer," he stated coldly. "You are fortunate to be a friend of Jean's. I can't imagine what he ever found in you besides your looks!" He grinned, amused, it seemed, by his own comment. "Yes, he is good at that." Without warning, he barked, "Get out!"

My first instinct was to run to Didier. I turned and rushed out into the street. Within minutes, against all safety rules taught by Beaugard, I arrived at Didier's flat.

Still shaken, I downed a large glass of water and collapsed on the sofa. He held me for a while, without talking, while I had a good cry.

He seemed preoccupied when he finally leaned toward me and said firmly, "I can't see you going through this any longer. It is not a task for you. I think you should tell Beaugard that you are quitting at once."

I raised my head so abruptly that I bumped his chin. "Quit! After all I've been through? Are you serious?"

"Absolutely. I'm taking you back home."

"Yes, a break will do me some good. But I'll only go for a while, and you might as well do the same. For right now, though, just hold me," I said, snuggling up against him.

He hugged me tightly and the warmth of his body filled me with a new sensation I had never before experienced. I would have liked to prolong that feeling indefinitely.

CHAPTER EIGHT

Caught

I t was late afternoon when I arrived in Aix, feeling the fatigue of the long train ride home. To my surprise, the house looked deserted. The shutters were tightly secured, and the plants in the garden needed watering. Still tense from my encounter in Vichy, I worried that both Mother and Jackie might have been arrested.

"I was a fool to leave them! They have been taken away because of me!"

I put my suitcase down, sat on the doorsteps, and wept. I was so upset that I did not hear Madame Giraud approaching.

"Hélène, dear, you are crying! What are you doing here alone? Your mother left with Jacqueline two weeks ago for your country home."

I felt no joy on hearing the news, only profound relief. I knew they were safe.

Madame Giraud took my hand. "You should make up with your mother," she said gently. "Misunderstandings can be mended, and she misses you very much."

What could I say? I had promised Beaugard never to reveal my activities. Madame Giraud, like everyone else, believed that I was gone so much because Mother and I simply didn't get along.

"Well, be sure to stop by if you are in need of anything," she added. She was a childless woman in her middle years, devoted to nursing her husband, brother of the famous General Giraud, who had escaped German jails to join the Allies in North Africa. She had always been extremely kind to our family.

I entered the house with my key and began to open doors and windows, feeling lost, looking about, peering into each room, leaning over Mother's balcony to look at the garden. As I moved from one place to another, touching familiar things, I realized how empty my life had become. Moving to the sun lounge, I sat in Mother's chintz-covered chair and allowed myself the rare pleasure of a moment's nostalgia.

Later I telephoned Beaugard. I learned that it was on his advice that Jackie had taken Mother to Saint-Ange, where the food restrictions were not so severe and she could be taken care of by the housekeeper.

"Your mother is safe. I have always kept an eye on her."

We talked for a while, and I explained as best as I could, without giving too many details, the reasons for my return.

"I've just finished talking to Didier," Beaugard told me. "You should get in touch with him. I think you should go somewhere for a while, until things calm down."

"Very well. I'll see him tomorrow. I'm very tired now."

After sleeping through most of the next day, I awoke in total darkness. I stretched into a faded sweater, then vigorously brushed my hair.

It was pitch dark as I moved across the garden on my way to the gate. The stars, as bright as they were, failed to give enough light to guide me.

I began to hurry, for I wanted to arrive at Didier's before

curfew. As I closed the gate, I was instantly alert, a trait that had been sharpened by my experience in the service. Something had moved, I was certain of it. The scrape of a shoe on the gravel told me that I was right. A shiver ran down my back.

I sensed motion near me and, without warning, the hard muzzle of a gun bore into my ribs. Then a voice spoke. Fear tightened my chest. My throat had gone so dry that I had the urge to cough.

The man, with the gun tightly pressed against my side, knew exactly what he was doing. I wondered frantically if I could use my bag as a weapon but dismissed the thought almost as soon as it entered my mind. He would have plenty of time to fire at the first hint of resistance.

"Let's go back inside," he urged.

He took the latchkey from my hand and put it into the door, then turned the brass knob. Without releasing the pressure of the gun, he pushed me inside and fumbled for the light switch.

We were in the hall. The irrational desire to see my assailant made me pivot on my heels. Eyes blinking to adjust to the bright light inside, I recognized him and let out an involuntary cry of surprise.

It was Garçin, de Simeon's stool pigeon from Vichy. He leered at me nastily, and the laugh he let out made me sick inside. He reminded me of a snake.

"Surprised?" He smirked.

I only stared at the gun, wondering when it would fire. I moved toward the living room and slumped on the edge of a chair, speechless, waiting. My teeth were clenched so tightly they ached.

Had he been sent to get rid of me? Frantically, I tried to reconstruct my last days in Vichy.

Garçin caught me glancing in the direction of an open window. "It won't do you any good," he said. "No one is around. I checked."

He shut the window tightly and sat down on the green sofa, resting against a cushion. He was staring at me, holding his revolver, shaking his head like someone who has heard a good joke. His mood then changed abruptly, his face hardening.

"After being fired by the Milice," he started, "and on hearing what you said about me in Vichy, Goeth and I decided that you should come back to clarify a few things for us. I am here to fetch you—unofficially, you understand, since we are not in the service anymore. There are some questions we would like you to answer. By the way, Jean will not be there to help you."

I couldn't speak. There was nothing to say, for I knew with a depressing certainty that I was caught in a trap. My silence irritated him. He probably wanted me to beg and plead.

Without warning he leaped from the couch. "Aren't you going to say something?"

Before I could answer, his fist struck my cheekbone. Pain shot through my skull, and it felt as if my head was splitting open. I gave a cry and wrenched away from his reach, holding my arm over my face, which now was trickling blood.

"So, you think I am the one who betrayed Jean!" he spat. "Well, let's see what your story will be after a thorough interrogation." Like all weaklings, having a gun made him feel strong.

I tried to get up from my chair, but his hand pushed me

back. My heels got caught in the legs of the chair, and I stumbled full length, taking the chair with me as I hit the floor.

His face convulsed, and the veins swelled on his neck. His hatred was now in the open, and he kicked me in the back.

I tried to avoid his blows as best I could. I opened my mouth to protest, but he yelled, "Shut up! Shut up!" accompanying each order by a kick.

His laced boot found my shoulder. A sharp, intolerable pain flashed through the bone like a knife blade. My head began to spin, and I passed out.

I was still on the floor when I came to. One eye was swollen shut, and through the other I could see the back of Garçin's head.

My God! I have to get out of here, I thought, but all I could do was lie still and stare blankly at the ceiling.

Garçin came into view again, bending over to see whether I'd come back to life. Reassured, he started fidgeting around the living room and stopped in front of the copper serving cart. Putting down his gun, he poured himself a Dubonnet, capped the bottle, then set it aside.

I tried to avoid looking at him. He was obviously deranged. I had to get out of his hands before we left Aix, or it would be the end of me.

Garçin had calmed down somewhat. "With the curfew on," he said, "we have to wait until six A.M. before going to the station. I do not have my Milice pass any longer."

I tried to muster some strength. With hands shaking and holding on to the chair, I painfully hauled myself upright. "Garçin," I said, "I can understand your anger toward me, but I have nothing to hide."

"You'll have time to prove that in Vichy."

I was speaking with difficulty, as the left side of my jaw ached where his fist had struck. The swelling was starting to distort my face. It was as if I had a big swab of cotton in my mouth.

Sliding his hands into his pants pockets, Garçin leaned against the door, seeming amused.

I shook my head dejectedly. "Don't believe me, then! But I cannot take the train like this. My sweater is stained with blood, and my face needs to be tended to. People at the train station may ask questions. At least let me go to my room and change."

There was a calculating slant in his eyes, and a deep frown creased his forehead, but there was no answer. His face had set into a mask. "All right," he finally conceded, "but don't try anything. I'm going to watch, and don't forget that I have a gun."

Instead of going to my room upstairs, I went to Jackie's bedroom on the ground floor. I calculated that I could perhaps make a move from there since it was near the garden.

Garçin sat, gun in hand, in the hallway, so that he could see me through the open door. Making noises to fool him, I rummaged through Jackie's closet in search of a sweater.

I was starting to feel dizzy, as spasms of pain mounted. "I can't start to feel sick now! I can't!" I told myself. Ignoring the pain, I passed the window that was out of his view, noiselessly pushed a chair to the ledge, and carefully unlocked the latch. Scooping up my wallet, I shoved it into my coat pocket. My left shoulder ached so badly that I could hardly move it. Sheer determination kept me going.

From his chair, Garçin demanded, "What are you doing?"

He mumbled something to himself about teaching me a lesson.

I had no time left. He was approaching the bedroom door.

Stepping onto the chair, I flung the window wide open, jumped over the ledge in a single leap, and landed in the flower bed below.

Caught off guard, Garçin fired several wild shots in my direction as I ran toward the locked gate. It was so dark that he couldn't aim properly, and I clambered quickly over the low gate just like a gymnast—an exercise I had practiced many times as a young girl with my brothers. Spurred on by fear, I felt neither the pain in my shoulder nor the splintered point of the wooden gate cutting into the calves of my legs. I just kept on going.

Garçin was now in the garden, and I could hear him swearing as he came nearer, "Goddamn! The bitch!"

A light shone at the Girauds' house. Its glow crossed the yard, then quickly disappeared, but no one came out. These days, most people thought it unwise to get involved in anything.

Fright gave me wings, and I was quickly lost in the night, running from one enclosure to another. Using a side road, I passed a large field, moist with early dew. I soon found myself on the bank of a stream that flowed a couple of miles or so from my home. Kneeling down, I cupped some water with my free hand to cool my face. I started shivering all over.

Spooked by the surrounding darkness, I said out loud, "I have to get away!" I moved unsteadily toward the highway. The determination to make it to safety gave me the strength to go on.

⚜ ⚜ ⚜

Dawn was barely breaking when I reached Didier's house. I had tried not to move my left arm, for the shoulder throbbed painfully at the slightest movement. I pulled myself up the stairway and rang the bell. Receiving no response, I banged the brass knocker.

It took a long time for Didier to answer the door. His hair was spiky and unruly, as he had just crawled out of bed. I was panting, holding on to the wall, ready to pass out.

"Hélène!" he exclaimed. He carried me into the living room and sat me down in a chair. As he poured some brandy into a glass, he turned and asked apprehensively, "What happened? Who did this to you?"

I was incapable of answering. He brought the glass carefully to my lips, and I swallowed the alcohol. With my mouth open, the pain in my jawbone became excruciating. Garçin's fist had probably cracked or partly dislocated it.

I forced myself to take another sip, fighting to get the liquor down. I felt a hot flush spread through my body.

"I was not followed," I assured him, explaining with difficulty my brutal encounter with Garçin.

"We must take action before he talks," Didier said. "You'll have to get out of circulation until we get him. He has to be eliminated at once. I'm calling Beaugard."

I only nodded approvingly.

He stepped out into the hall and called for his mother, who came running, wrapped in her dressing gown. Seeing the painful bruises, she cried, "My poor child! What happened to you? You look awful."

"She fell from her bike," Didier said, avoiding his mother's eyes.

"At this time of the morning? I—"

Didier made a gesture, and she stopped short. Taking my arm, she led me to the sofa. Then she left the room and came back a minute later with a small jar containing some salve. It was brown and had a nauseating smell, and as she rubbed my cheek with it, I became ill. After several retchings, I fell back on the couch, sapped of what little strength I'd had.

Didier went to the phone, and after a short conversation, he came back and sat next to me.

"Everything has been arranged," he assured me, stroking my hair. "You'll leave for Paris in a few days. A friend will take care of you. Beaugard wants you to be courageous. Within a few months, the Milice will have forgotten about you. He's tracking Garçin. We'll get him."

Didier's mother brought a pan of water and washed my face and hands. I let her nurse me, for I dearly needed to be comforted and reassured. Cautiously placing my arm in a scarf that she knotted around my neck, she said, "I hope it won't hurt too much. You realize that we cannot call a doctor without arousing suspicion. He might talk."

I moved my head weakly.

She fluffed the cushion under my head. "Rest for a while longer. I'm going to get a bed ready."

Even though Didier's mother asked no questions, I felt certain she knew what was going on. Perhaps she was also helping the Cause, but I could not be sure, because in the Underground, you only knew those few people directly associated with you.

"We have to change your appearance," she declared on the third day, "particularly your hair. It must be combed differently and dyed black, to make you look more mature."

With Didier's help, she cut my hair and darkened it. The transformation made me look ten years older.

I could walk freely within the confines of the house during the day, but only when the charwoman was out. She lived in town and might mention my presence. Didier's mother would come up after her departure and unlock the door. She prepared liquids to feed me, because I could not chew or use my jaw.

On the sixth day, after treating my face, she applied makeup with the lightest touch and, laughing with satisfaction, commented, "Now, look at you. It hardly shows! You are, shall we say, a new woman." Then, suddenly serious, she added, "You are leaving today. Didier will come early to fetch you. Be prepared."

I waited until she left the room, then washed and got ready. After putting aside the few articles given to me for the trip, I went downstairs to the living room. No one was around.

I thought, How much longer can I go on like this? Until now, I've helped others to escape, and now it's my turn to be on the run. The anxiety was insufferable, and I found it difficult to catch my breath.

At eleven o'clock, a black van stopped in the gravel driveway. Didier's face appeared at the window.

His mother emerged from her kitchen with a small package of food. She handed it to me with a smile. "Just a little something to eat on the train. Take small bites and chew carefully," she advised. Her concern reminded me of Mother. "Now, don't forget to take the sling off your arm; otherwise it might attract attention."

She hugged me tightly. "God be with you. One day we will have peace again."

Didier said in a huff, "Hop in. Hurry!"

Before stepping into the vehicle, I double-checked my identification papers once again. I was now officially Anick Seignon. Yes, everything was in order.

"All set," I declared, looking straight head.

Didier let down the heavy tarpaulin to screen the opening at the back of the van.

The driver was wearing a police uniform. Leaning heavily against the front compartment, he acknowledged me with a wide, toothy grin, and told me his name was Sabatier. He was a policeman but also worked for Beaugard. They were using the police wagon from Aix.

I received instructions for the trip and also the name and address of the person to contact in Paris.

"Memorize everything. I can't write it down," Didier told me.

I assumed that by now my description had been given to the German authorities. That meant I could not afford to be recognized. Didier had not heard a word from Beaugard since my encounter.

Upon entering Marseilles, we heard the shrill of whistles, and the van jolted to a halt. I quickly hid under the bench in the back, pulling the rags that were scattered on the floor over my body.

Sabatier answered a battery of questions. His voice reached my ears as he gave his destination and explained that he was on his way to pick up a prisoner. The officials asked for his papers. Then, after a long pause, the magic words came: "Drive on!"

The van proceeded without interruption, but I was now more wary of detection than before and continued to lie under the bench until we reached the train station.

A stream of passengers were flooding the station, clogging the passageways. Didier swiftly moved to join the line forming at the ticket window. Pushing and shoving impatiently, people lined up aggressively behind him.

At the sight of the unruly line, a German *Feldgrau* left his colleagues and came over to enforce order. Making a point of proving his authority, he ordered all suitcases and bundles to be opened on the cement floor in front of him.

It was fortunate that Didier possessed so much self-control. His calm demeanor and cool exterior made me feel safe.

For a moment, I was distracted by the arrival of a freight train at a platform lined with a column of German soldiers standing ten feet apart, guns in hand. The wagons, which were normally used to transport animals, were sealed. Horrifying screams filtered through the vents—human screams. I turned to my companions with an expression of horror and disbelief.

His eyes avoiding mine, Didier said, "They are Jews going to concentration camps."

A foul odor reached our nostrils, a mixture of warm urine, human sweat, and decaying flesh. The repugnant smell made us gag.

From inside one of the wagons echoed the pounding fists and desperate cries for food and air. A woman's ghostly hand surfaced, the rigid fingers gripping a baby's bottle. A sepulchral voice rose above the hell, begging, "My baby is hungry!"

A feeling of total helplessness engulfed me.

If any civilian dared to move, he or she would have immediately joined the death cargo. Several Red Cross women dressed in uniforms were strolling along the platform in search of refugees and lost children. One of them hesitated, then, obviously regaining confidence because of her neutral status, raised up on tiptoes and took the bottle from the forlorn hand. Instantly, a guard rushed toward the Red Cross worker and broke the glass bottle with the butt of his gun. The woman stepped back, a look of disbelief on her face as she was led away. The blood gushed from her wrist.

A few minutes later, the moaning convoy departed, moving inexorably toward its deadly destination. Hypnotized, I watched the train enter the tunnel and disappear.

Revolted at what I had witnessed, I finally boarded my train. Sabatier handed me my bag through the window as the train pulled out.

"Anick Seignon!" Didier called out.

I hesitated. "Yes?" I finally replied, poking my head from the open window. My code name sounded so strange to me.

Didier smiled at me reassuringly. "Anick, don't forget and don't worry. Everything will be all right."

CHAPTER NINE

Paris

As the train from Lyons came to a halt, passengers flooded the platform. The huge gare de Lyon was jammed with troops. Harsh German voices were everywhere. Dissonant commands echoed loudly across the vast dome.

It was a strange experience for me, having a new identity. I felt as though I was onstage, an actress trying to give her best performance yet fearing the consequences of forgetting the part. Swept along, I became happily anonymous in the waves of soldiers and travelers walking, nudging, and pushing in all directions.

Outside was Paris, a watery sky, stark gray buildings, bridges and trees far and near.

Following the instructions given to me, I took the subway in the direction of the metro station. The safe house was located in the square du Roule, only a few minutes from the Champs-Elysées. I was to stay with a young man named Helier Beaurillon, who would give me shelter, I had been told, until the coast was clear. He could be trusted implicitly.

Going through the metro entrance, I noticed the posters plastered on the walls. I understood enough German to see that they were warnings to the occupying troops against fraternizing with Parisians. One notice, larger than the others, read in bold black letters: DO NOT WALK ARM IN ARM WITH FRENCH WOMEN! Naturally, I found this ludicrous, for who (besides a prostitute) would *want* to be seen with them?

I carefully mingled with the flow of metro passengers exiting the station. Taking the stairs leading to the platform at the Arc de Triomphe, I stopped for a few minutes to get my bearings, then walked across the avenue des Ternes down to the square du Roule.

I soon arrived at what I believed to be the home of Helier Beaurillon, my new host. Not fully convinced, though, I timidly rang the doorbell. To my surprise, the door opened immediately; Helier was expecting me. He was a tall, personable young man, with a thin, black mustache. His apartment was extremely elegant and was furnished with authentic antique furniture—a bachelor pad deluxe.

After supper that evening, Helier came to my room and sat at the foot of my bed. "I have to give you an idea of my schedule," he told me. "I leave at eight in the morning and return at six. I would prefer if you didn't go out often, because the authorities might ask for identification papers on the street. I'll do the shopping for both of us. During the weekend, I'd appreciate it if you stay in your room until I call for you."

"Am I being punished?" I asked, peeved by his dictatorial attitude.

"Not in the least. My girlfriend, Sylvie, is a ballerina at the Paris Opera. This is the only time we can see each other. You understand, don't you?"

This arrangement worked out amicably, and it appeared

that artistic tradition was maintained, as their passionate
trysts were accompanied by the romantic melodies of De-
bussy or Brahms.

Time went by peacefully for a while. I looked forward to
getting the mail that arrived through Helier, though letters
from home were rather short. My mother and Jackie had to
rely on trivial events to be on the safe side. I read a lot and, as
part of the agreement, cooked the meals and did the house-
work.

My stay at the square du Roule turned out to be a short
one. The sudden appearance of a strange young woman at
Helier's bachelor place, and the comings and goings of our
friends in the Resistance, eventually aroused the curiosity
and comments of the neighbors, as well as the concierge.
Once, I caught the old man peeping through a window.
Another time, Helier opened the door and found him much
too close to the peephole for comfort. When that happened,
I moved out within twenty-four hours. I took it philosophi-
cally, since this was the life I had accepted upon joining the
Underground, to be constantly on the run or in hiding.

From there I took refuge at Konstantin (Kotia) Levtiev's
home. Kotia was a Resistance sympathizer and a good friend
of Helier's, a White Russian exile of about twenty, tall
and very blond, with eyes as blue and transparent as glass
marbles.

He fed me using his own ration coupons, watched over me
like a brother, and became my world and family in Paris. I
didn't dare to venture out often, for identification papers
were demanded constantly in the streets, shops, trains,
buses, metro, restaurants, and even the churches.

On Sundays, the occupiers would turn into tourists. On

that day of rest, they became art connoisseurs and took the traditional sightseeing tours of the City of Light. Invariably, their destinations were Notre Dame, the Arc de Triomphe, or Sacré Coeur on the Butte Montmartre. Naturally, being a nation of warriors, what impressed them most was the Musée des Invalides and Napoleon's Tomb.

Each day the Germans paraded along the Champs-Elysées. We could first hear the rumbling preceding the cavalcade, the military riders stopping all traffic. Then came the German troops, headed by a marching band, and followed by a single cavalry officer on his mount, saber raised. A Nazi flag would appear followed by flanks of soldiers, three or four per line, all marching to a hallucinating rhythm. All of this was done in an effort to destroy the French spirit and pride.

One morning, having nothing to eat at home, I decided to head over to the open market, which was used by the public on Wednesdays only. I had made an arrangement with a woman at one of the stands: she would save whatever she could for me—a few vegetables too old and wilted for the Germans or, if I was lucky, a rabbit or scrawny chicken too unappetizing for the occupiers' taste. These were great luxuries.

I followed the riverbank and crossed the Pont Mirabeau in a light fog. A slight drizzle and an unexpected gust of wind swept over the bridge, emphasizing the unpleasantness of this murky day. Shivering, I told myself how foolish I had been to leave my heavy coat at home. My step was brisk as I continued toward the market.

After passing rue George-Sand, I crossed the intersection and reached avenue Mozart. Neighborhood cafés were al-

The Deschamps family in Tientsin, China, 1923. FROM LEFT TO RIGHT: Maurice, Hélène, Gabrielle, Gaston, and Philippe. *Photo courtesy of author.*

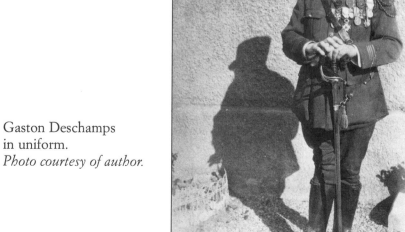

Gaston Deschamps in uniform.
Photo courtesy of author.

Hélène Deschamps, age 17. *Photo courtesy of author.*

Nazis occupy Paris, August 1940. *Photo courtesy of AP/Wide World Photos.*

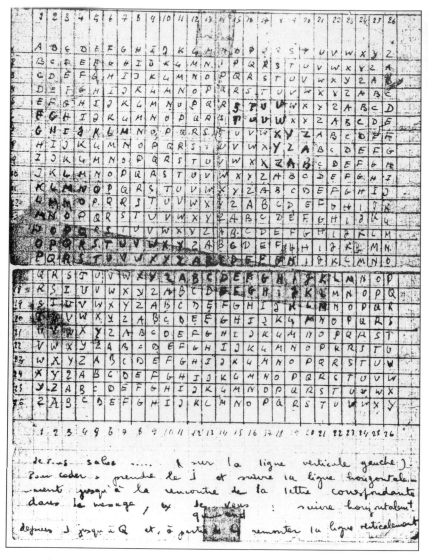

Codes, like the one above, were used by *Miliciens* to write secret messages. Hélène managed to steal this one out of de Simeon's office. *Courtesy of author.*

Petit-Jean. *Photo courtesy of author.*

CARTE D'IDENTITÉ

Nom: **BOUQUIER**
Prénoms: Jacqueline
Profession: Serveuse
Née le: 24 Février 1920
à: MÉKNÈS
Département: Maroc
Nationalité: Française
Domicile: à AIX-en-Provence
18, Cours Gambetta

SIGNALEMENT

Taille: 1 m 70
Cheveux: châtain
Moustaches:
Yeux: marrons verts
Signes particuliers:

Nez: Dos, base
Dimensions: recti-
Forme de visage: ovale
Teint: mat

N° 6373

Empreinte digitale   Le Titulaire,   Les Témoins,

All French citizens had to carry identification cards at all times. This phony identification card was given to Jackie by Petit-Jean. *Courtesy of author.*

BELOW:
Jacqueline Bouquier. *Photo courtesy of author.*

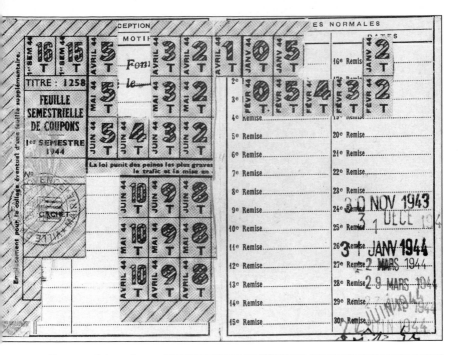

ABOVE: Counterfeit ration card given to Jackie by Petit-Jean. *Courtesy of author.*

One of several leaflets given to OSS agents indicating enemy insignias, ranks, battalions, artillery, and armor. *Courtesy of author.*

OSS agent Hellops.
Photo courtesy of author.

Anne-Georges, leader of
the network Franc-Croix.
Photo courtesy of author.

ready open, some with empty tables obstructing the pavement. A bistro with a tattered awning had its lights on. I walked in, past the stacked-up chairs and tables. Workers stood at the old zinc bar drinking wine. I ordered a cup of bitter ersatz coffee, which I sipped at the steamy counter, and watched the people passing by. It struck me how drab and shabby so many looked—how *weary*. Perhaps they were thinking of a son or a missing father, the lack of food, illness, or the Occupation. Nothing was cheerful anymore.

With no apparent warning, sirens began to howl. The Allies were getting bold these days, bombing even in daylight. The café emptied rapidly, and I rushed to the nearest shelter, the Jasmin metro station. A wide, black arrow on the wall indicated the entrance to the air-raid shelter, which was on the train tracks. The ramp going down was only dimly lit, and I moved cautiously. Others, more accustomed to this route of safety, rushed by me.

A pale bluish light in the tunnel gave out a phosphorescent glow. I pushed my way into the crowd. There were loud complaints in the dark and shouts, coughing, and screaming children. I was rudely jostled by people looking for space.

From way back, a woman wailed, "Keep your hands off my ass!"

"You asked for it, *ma chère,*" jeered a man.

In the distance, I could hear the thump and rumble of explosions.

"God have mercy on us," a bleating voice implored next to me.

I felt a rough hand reach beneath my skirt, moving upward between my thighs. I got away from it and pushed my way deeper into the crowd.

"The nerve!" an irate woman barked at me. "Watch your feet, you idiot. Where do you think you are going?"

I stood quietly, pressed on every side by others. After what seemed to be hours, the distant explosions diminished and then ceased. The sirens bellowed their long all-clear signal, and the shelter began to empty. We had only a short time to get off the rails before the electricity would be turned on again. I joined the rush upward and finally felt the cold air on my face. It felt good to be alive! The daylight made me blink as I started down the street, my eyes yet unaccustomed to the glare. Suddenly I was stopped by a sudden shriek of whistles. Germans, in uniform, were encircling a small group of people. A dull knot formed in my stomach. I was trapped.

With barked commands, we were shoved with the snouts of machine guns. In a desperate move, I turned away from the human rope encircling us. A gun, held by a tall, skinny man dressed in a dark Milice uniform, pinned me to the spot. I felt the cold metal against my back, then on my chest, as I turned around. The man looked at me unwaveringly. "You there. Move!"

We were herded toward a truck waiting at the intersection. It was black with a tarpaulin roof. None of us protested. It would have been pointless. We let the soldiers prod us like cattle going to the slaughterhouse.

There were three women, eight men, and a small, sickly boy. The guards got in behind us and sat flanking the opening of the rear of the truck. Two cars, Citroëns, filled with heavily armed men, followed closely. We rocked back and forth on the hard seats as we went along the cobblestone streets until we reached a police station. I hadn't even paid attention to where we were going, my mind concentrating on only one thought: *Escape.*

No one spoke until we stopped, each of us too stunned to react. The chain holding the back panel was unlatched, and using the butt of their weapons, the soldiers motioned for us to step down.

A dowdy housewife lost control. She began crying, "What are you going to do to us? *Mon Dieu!* Have pity. My children are alone at home."

Once we entered the sad, dirty hall, though, she calmed down.

One of the men started coughing nastily, his neck and face turning blue. His misery became the center of attention. The others watched him with dull interest, his trouble momentarily distracting them from their own. His hacking cough increased until he finally spat. He looked around to see if anyone had noticed and then bent his head to stare at the floor.

I leaned against the wall and closed my eyes. Usually, under such conditions, my mind was alert. I'll have to tell them something, but what? I thought. I felt empty.

Two men had already been called into the interrogation room and had not reappeared. My false identification papers and ration card gave no security. It would not take long to prove that they were fake.

"Anick Seignon," came the call.

"Yes?"

"Come along." A guard gestured for me to enter.

The door grated as it closed behind me. Two men were waiting inside. The elder one, a man in his fifties, had the self-important air of an inspector. He had grayish hair and sad, flabby cheeks. The desk in front of him was cluttered with dossiers, old dirty ink pads, and assorted rubber stamps. The second man was in a police uniform.

I stood before the inspector, my arms behind my back, waiting to be interrogated. He looked at my papers and photograph.

"Mademoiselle Seignon, what is your profession?"

"I am a salesgirl at the Samaritaine department store," I lied resolutely.

"Indeed," he said, raising his head. "This is a working day. It is almost noon. Shouldn't you be there?"

"I am not well. I have an appointment with the doctor."

He stood up and walked around his desk, stopping purposefully in front of me. "You are a member of the Resistance," he announced with conviction, pointing a menacing finger at me.

"Dear God, no!" I fought back unreasoning panic.

The man's lips curled in a cynical smile. "No? Why were you arrested, then?"

"I don't know!" my voice whined. "I was coming out of the shelter when some men pushed me in with a group of people. I don't even know them."

He seemed utterly bored, and I relaxed slightly, realizing that this must be the customary tactic used in grilling Parisians picked up at random in the streets.

It was with a low, almost enticing tone that he inquired, "Do you know anyone subversive to the government?"

I looked at him stupidly. "What?"

After almost three years in the Underground, acting had become second nature to me.

"Are you going to cooperate or not?"

"I don't understand. What do you mean?"

The inspector shrugged in a gesture of annoyance and stubbed his cigarette out. His thick eyebrows lifted. "We won't get far with this one," he told his uniformed attendant. "Very well," he added, nodding in my direction. "You will be held until your identification papers are verified." He took a gold watch from his waistcoat pocket and opened the engraved cover. It was his lunchtime, and he couldn't be bothered any longer. "We'll take care of the others this afternoon. That'll be all for now," he told the guard.

"Come along," said the policeman, who had been standing silently during the interrogation.

He took my arm, directing me out and down to the basement through a low-ceilinged passageway. Slime from rusty water pipes was dripping down the walls. The steps were worn smooth and slippery.

We came to a small rectangular room, bare except for a wobbly wooden table in the center where four guards were playing cards. Several large key rings hung from rusty nails in the wall.

One of the men, with a gold stripe on his sleeve, got up and came over to me. He was short, with a chalky, puffy face, which obviously saw little sunshine.

"We've got a cute one this time." He grinned, running his hands over my body, supposedly in search of weapons. He stopped at my breasts and groaned, like someone weighing plump chickens at the marketplace.

"Got anything for me, *poupée*?" he questioned, squeezing my nipples. His breath reeked of wine.

"Hey, hey," his companions jeered, "look at him frisking the doll."

The man snatched my handbag and opened it, spilling the contents on the table in front of him. "Well, what have we got here?" he asked, sorting through the scattered objects. My money, so carefully saved for the market, was swiftly divided among them. He then took one of the key rings from its hook and fastened it to his belt.

I was pushed down a dim hall. We passed several locked doors. A weak lightbulb covered with wire mesh hung from an electric cord every twenty-five or thirty feet. Halfway down the passage, the jailer stopped, opened a door, and motioned me in with a resounding slap on the rump.

Total darkness. A strong, musty smell assaulted me, making me cough. Gradually, I became aware of a faint beam of light filtering through a grill inset in the upper part of the door. It shone on a single spot on the floor.

Like a blind woman, I groped about, feeling my way by touching the damp stone wall. Inching along in the gloom of the cell, I went through an instant of uncontrollable fear. There was a corner. I continued probing with my hand.

The stench of vomit hit me, turning my stomach. I stumbled over something.

"Who is there?" My voice was barely audible. There was no answer from the darkness.

I bent down and my fingers touched a thick mat of hair. Suddenly a hot, clammy hand grabbed my ankle. I was terrified. My mouth gaped open, but instead of a wild scream, no sound came. I could only gasp for air, kicking, trying to back away. My foot finally came loose, and I staggered backward, scraping my thigh against a protruding piece of metal. In shock, I didn't even feel the pain.

I stood in the dim ray of light from the door, not knowing what awaited behind the screen of darkness. The silence was so thick, I could hear drops of sewage water dripping from the ceiling, landing on the uneven floor. As my eyes dilated, the outline of a man emerged through the haze, like a photograph gradually appearing in the developing tray. From his slurred voice and the swaying of his body, I knew he was drunk.

He lurched at me, mumbling suggestive filth. In a panic, I smashed into the clammy wall like a cornered animal. His arm shot around my neck, his calloused hands tearing at my blouse. He was trying to pull me down to the floor, the trail of his nails digging into my skin. His short, fetid breath smothered me.

"Let me go," I gasped, choking, and bit savagely at his bare arm. The armlock loosened. I spun to one side, and the man lost his balance. Taking advantage of his sudden vulnerability, I swung my right leg up and aimed the tip of my wooden-soled shoe viciously at the man's groin.

He let out a hoarse, cackling wail as he stooped down. He was now kneeling, moaning, while clutching his private parts in torment. He then fell backward and retched.

I could feel my throat pulsating furiously. Leaning against the door, I struggled to reclaim my sanity and wrench my mind from this nightmare. Terrified of the darkness around me, locked up in a cell with this brute, I wanted to cry but couldn't. I stayed there paralyzed—how long, I couldn't tell. The only sensation I felt was that of a warm liquid along my thigh. I touched it with my fingers. It was blood.

I let my body slide down to the floor. The underground jail was cold, but I was bathed in perspiration. I felt pain and terrible thirst. I swallowed, and my tongue stuck to my palate.

The man was still inert a few feet away, stretched out cold in his own stinking excretion.

An incomplete thought that had been playing at the edge of consciousness finally started to take shape. An idea was trying to emerge, but I couldn't make anything of it: *"I'm not well, I'm not well..."* The words kept dancing in my head, but I couldn't recollect when I had heard them before. "I'm not well!" I screamed.

The cold numbness that had enveloped my body eased, and a door seemed to open, clarity creeping into my mind, cooling my feelings, casting my perceptiveness. After a last shudder, I remembered telling the inspector that I'd been on my way to a doctor. The idea, crazy as it appeared, was totally logical and feasible. He had failed to ask the reason for my visit to a physician. I was about to produce one.

I rested for a short while. Then, staining my fingers with the blood oozing from the deep gash in my thigh, I rubbed them on my cotton panties and stockings. I repeated the motion several times, then, keeping my hand blotched with blood, I started screaming again at the top of my lungs.

An interminable moment passed. It was now, or perhaps never again.... "Please, God! Please!"

A guard poked his head in the door's open grill. "What's going on here?"

"Help! Help me!" I pleaded, rolling myself on the dirt floor. "It hurts so badly. I'm having a miscarriage!"

The keys rattled, the door was unlocked, and the jailer came in, pointing a flashlight in my face. Blinded by the beam, I instinctively moved my bloody hands to screen my eyes. Glaring at them, the man stepped back, emitting a long, low hissing sound through his lips. He lowered the light and saw the blood on my legs. "In the name of God!" he swore in annoyance. "What's next?"

He quickly left and soon returned with his superior. They were whispering. "She was complaining of being sick this morning and needing to see a doctor," said one to the other. There was more muffled talk. The sergeant finally declared, "We have no doctor here. We'll have to take you to the general hospital."

"I can't walk. I just can't!" I lamented, doubling up in a fake spasm. I was acting with the convincing air of a seasoned actress. A great performance wasn't needed, however. The terror generated from being imprisoned and nearly being raped was convincing enough.

Moaning and complaining, I let them support me up the stairs, down a long corridor, and, at last, out to a waiting paddy wagon.

A sudden sense of relief came over me as we pulled away from the jail.

My mind raced ahead, trying to figure a way out. The first step had been fairly easy. I was out of jail. Attempting anything during the ride would probably be futile, I realized. *From now on I must remain alert, play it by ear, and grab at the smallest opportunity, perhaps maybe even manage to escape.*

The van stopped. A policeman stood in the middle of the street directing traffic, black cloak folded over his shoulder, white stick in hand. Through the grill of the window, I could see Parisians furtively glancing in our direction, then rapidly moving away from the feared vehicle. I read apathy in their faces.

We began moving again. The palms of my hands were wet.

Dejectedly, I slumped back on the bench, jolting at each bump along the paved streets.

Our arrival at the hospital caused much commotion. After I was registered, a guard was placed outside the glass-paneled door of my room on the third floor.

A young woman was in the bed next to mine. Ignoring her, I grabbed a water jug from the table between the two beds and drank several full glasses.

Within a few minutes, a nun, from the order of Saint-Vincent de Paul, entered with a basin full of soapy water. She helped me undress and washed my body thoroughly. The sponge bath made me feel alive again. She then toweled me dry and put a rough cotton hospital gown on me. I felt very refreshed and thanked her. She slid a bedpan under my bed and left without uttering a word.

My roommate had been watching the whole exercise, frightened, and as soon as the nun left, she whispered, "What happened to you? Why are the police guarding the door?"

I turned toward her and noticed that she looked very pale and sickly. Brushing the questions aside, I asked, "What is your name?"

"Jeanine Lesueur."

"My name is Anick Seignon. Which ward are we in?"

The woman looked baffled. "The maternity ward, of course. Didn't you know?"

I hadn't noticed her swollen belly. I weighed my next question carefully. Jeanine was my only chance, and I took it. "Is someone coming to visit you tonight?"

"Yes, my husband. He works late."

"Listen, then," I pleaded, "and listen carefully. Please help me; otherwise, I am on my way to a concentration camp."

Jeanine Lesueur's eyes widened with fear. Concentration camp meant death. She kept silent. "Tell your husband to telephone Etoile 17-60 for me and ask for Helier."

I stopped to reflect and reassure myself. *He'll know what to do. He is very resourceful. He will find some way to get me out.*

Hesitantly, like a child reciting a lesson, Jeanine repeated, "Etoile 17-60. Helier."

"That's right. Tell him that Anick is being held at the general hospital, and she must leave as soon as possible."

Jeanine shook her head. "I want to help, but I'm not sure my husband will do it. You see, I'm ill." Placing a hand on her belly, she gave me a weak smile. "With the baby coming and all . . ."

"I understand." I turned my face to the wall. The harsh hospital gown chafed my skin. I hated the ward I was in. I was a prisoner, and the four walls of the room made this another jail. I had been a fool to think that by coming here, I might find freedom. Helpless and scared, I started to cry.

Jeanine reached from her bed, bending as far as her bulging stomach would permit her, and touched my hand. "Don't cry. Honestly, I'll try."

A doctor marched in, his white coat wrinkled and unbuttoned. He was a rather old French man, with a trim salt-and-pepper Vandyke beard. A nun followed, pushing a trolley filled with bandages, instruments, small bottles, and swatches of cotton. "So, you are the girl they brought from jail?" he asked gruffly. I turned my bruised face, wiping away the tears.

He pulled the sheet down all the way to my feet and raised the gown to my chin. The policeman came forward and stood next to him, craning his neck to get a closer look at me. One must adjust to anything to survive, I thought indifferently. I gazed straight ahead.

The doctor first gave me a cursory examination, noting the bruises and deep gash streaking my thigh. "How did you get that?" he inquired, his brows lifting with concern.

"The guard could tell you." My glance met his. "His superior thinks I work for the Underground."

"Hmm, well . . ." The doctor adjusted his glasses carefully while clearing his throat. He appeared to be debating the options. "I hear you are having a miscarriage," he said, poking my abdomen.

I winced and tried to move away.

"Hurt there?" he inquired calmly.

"Of course it must hurt," protested Jeanine Lesueur from her bed.

I squinted at him. "Yes."

He knew I was lying. For a few interminable moments the old doctor seemed to be on the verge of saying something but hesitated.

The guard's question forced the issue. "Is she faking or what?"

I must have looked as if I had the weight of the world on my shoulders when I turned my head to look up at him. The doctor kept a poker face, but I saw a sparkle in his eyes that hadn't been there earlier. He realized I was in trouble with the German authorities. In his own way, he was fighting them, too.

Irritated at the guard's insistence, he made a brusque gesture with his hand, dismissing him. "Move aside," he ordered.

The doctor began bending over me again, as if he was diagnosing, feeling here and there, looking concerned, taking his time. Then, turning to the policeman, he announced, "This girl is in no shape to be moved. We have to ensure the bleeding has stopped. A miscarriage is a dangerous thing."

He exchanged a knowing look with the nun who had accompanied him on his rounds and nodded. "Tetanus," he mumbled. She handed him a syringe, and he set to work, patting the gash and bruises with alcohol. He pressed around the cut, mumbling to himself, then looked at me over the rim of his wire glasses. "It'll need a few stitches."

I didn't cry as he laced up the wound but thanked him with a thin smile. I felt safe for now.

After bandaging the wound, the nun started cushioning my bottom with a thick swatch of cotton. Then she wrapped me in cloth, securing each side with a large safety pin, as if it was a diaper. A bag of ice was placed on my abdomen for visual effect.

Convinced by now, the guard reluctantly pulled away. "I'll notify the inspector of her condition," he announced.

"I think you should," the doctor replied sharply.

I let out a sigh of relief. The immediate danger alleviated and the anxiety subsided, my body demanded food.

"I'm hungry!" I pleaded.

The doctor summoned his nurse. "Sister Marie-Joseph, please see that this girl gets something nourishing and warm to eat." He patted me on the head. "Good luck," he said, then exited the room to continue his rounds.

The nun trotted past the policeman, who was arguing on the telephone with demonstrative gestures, and soon returned carrying a steaming bowl of stew, which I began to wolf down.

"Not so fast, my child," the kind nun admonished.

I finished my plate and placed it on the night table.

The sister tucked me in. "Close your eyes and rest," she ordered.

By then my body was throbbing. I turned painfully to one side. Between the fatigue and the shock, I was asleep almost before I'd stretched my stiff legs out on the mattress.

Visiting hours were over when I awoke. The cut on my thigh was a blunt pain, and I ached all over. I hadn't heard a thing and wondered if Jeanine had passed on my message to her husband. But she kept her back turned as if to avoid me, not wishing to be involved. I remained silent, nervously chewing my lip.

There was only a dim light in the room. Through the panes of the glass door, the hall seemed brightly illuminated.

My panic grew. Had I been abandoned and left to my fate? Forgotten? My face sank into the pillow. My heart was racing, and I couldn't catch my breath. How long will I be kept here, before they discover my real identity? I wondered fearfully. Beads of perspiration began to form along my forehead.

Turning over onto my stomach, I felt a presence next to my bed and brusquely turned my head. Sister Marie-Joseph was by the nightstand, quietly filling the water pitcher for the night.

I reached for her hand and squeezed it hard. "Sister, they are going to kill me!" I whispered with a sob.

The old nun bent forward, her wrinkled face softening as she fluffed the pillow. "Hush, girl. Say a prayer, and everything will be all right very soon. You'll see," she mumbled, raising a finger to her lips. "I'll turn off the light now." The room went dark, and she was gone.

For a few seconds, I thought I had been dreaming, but the pitcher was full and the door had slowly closed.

Suddenly, exalted by the idea that something was really going to happen, I rolled to one side and sat up in bed. I reached for the shelf above my head and grabbed my soiled clothes, slipping them noiselessly on, and waited.

From my bedside, I anxiously watched the strange behavior of three civilians in overcoats and felt hats, talking to the police guard. Their backs were turned to me, and I could only wonder, Friends or foes? Gestapo?

One of the visitors was showing the guard a paper that he'd extracted from his inside pocket. The guard inspected it carefully. Handing it back, he appeared to be arguing fervently. He shook his head while making an attempt to unstrap his revolver.

Everything seemed to move like clockwork. One of the civilians made a move, distracting the guard's attention. It took only a second for one of the other ones to hit him at the base of the skull with the butt of his gun, and the guard collapsed on the linoleum floor.

I almost cried out and brought my hand up to muffle the choking gasp trying to escape my lips. I didn't want to scare my roommate any more than she was at the present. I could see the frightened woman's head hidden under the blankets.

His back turned to me, the tall man, who had taken charge of the assault, paused for a few seconds. His companions had already grabbed the guard's body, and he bent down to lift the feet. The dark silhouette of Sister Marie-Joseph glided like a shadow, leading the way to the nearest hall closet. The guard was shoved into the cramped space without decorum and locked in. The nun disappeared.

Fearful but hopeful, I could feel my body shaking. I froze when the glass door burst open. The civilian facing me was Helier.

I threw myself into his arms.

"Come, quickly," he said, hurriedly disengaging himself.

Still shaking, I leaned over the pregnant woman who was still hiding under the bedclothes. "Jeanine, *merci.* You saved my life."

Jeanine Lesueur poked her head out and gave a frightened little smile. "Will they suspect me and Sister Marie-Joseph?"

I put my hand on Helier's arm and looked at him imploringly.

He shook his head. "Don't worry," he said gently to the woman. "All I ask of you is to wait for twenty minutes or so. Give us the time to leave, then start screaming. No one will suspect you that way."

We rushed along the empty white hall. When he reached the stairway, Helier peered over the banister. It was quiet below. He led the way, followed by the two men who were supporting me by the arms. He gave the night clerk a confident smile.

"Everything under control, inspector?" she asked as we passed by.

"We're taking this girl to the prefecture of police for interrogation," replied Helier.

The four of us walked to the main door at the entrance. It was painted with a large red cross. Opening the panel, Helier looked around, then suddenly his face stiffened and his eyes grew hard as he made an abrupt gesture of retreat in our direction.

A four-man German patrol, large metal crescent badges shining around their necks, was ambling in the direction of Helier's escape car. The crunch of their heavy boots resounded on the cobblestones.

One of the soldiers stopped to take notes, while another, after inspecting the vehicle, turned suspiciously in the direction of the hospital. He began crossing the street.

Helier and his companions, who were still holding me, withdrew to the desk, acting as if they were engrossed in an animated conversation.

"Is the girl giving you trouble?" the night nurse inquired.

Bluffing, Helier replied curtly, "Don't be concerned; this is a police matter."

From the sidewalk, the German NCO was calling his man back, laughing. "Come, Otto, someone's being taken to emergency."

"Okay with me, if you say so," the man grumbled reluctantly.

They proceeded to march on, taking rue d'Arcole.

Helier pushed through the heavy front door, tugged the collar of his coat tightly around his neck, and walked purposefully to the muddy car. The black Renault had its windows smeared with fine, wet slush, which clouded the view from outside. We rapidly piled in. The driver turned the key, and the motor started, coughed, and died.

"Hurry," said Helier, nervously urging the driver.

The man turned the key again and the engine fired up. The parking lights were switched on. We were in second gear when a couple of nurses came out screaming for help.

"The patrol will be back in no time," one of the men mumbled.

With sputtering sounds, the Renault rolled off past the square Charlemagne and, upon reaching the river, followed the meandering of the Seine to boulevard Sully.

"Where are you taking me?" I asked.

Helier answered laconically, "To Kotia."

I looked at him pitifully. "I'm scared."

Obviously feeling sympathy for me, Helier leaned over and patted me on the knee. "It'll be all right. We've gotten through the most difficult part. But, please, no more carelessness. You see what can happen. You must stay put and do exactly as I tell you from now on. You'll get fresh identification papers in a week or so." His voice was sharp and pressing.

"I only wanted to buy some food, because there was none in the apartment," I said, trying to explain.

Helier did not answer.

Trying to calm down, I asked him for a cigarette. He silently handed me one, along with his lighter, but my hands were shaking and he had to light it for me. The tobacco tip glowed brightly as I took a long drag.

The streets were empty, and there were no cars on the road. Under the low lights, the pavement glistened. After we'd been driving for a while, a few drops of rain splashed on the windshield, and by the time we reached porte de Saint-Cloud, rain was pounding on the Renault's hood, the tires sliding over the wet pavement.

Helier and his comrades remained stonily silent.

Rue du Général Masse lay squelched in silence when we reached our destination.

"I won't be long," Helier told the driver.

Taking me by the arm, he led me into the long stone structure. Inside the dark hall, a low-wattage bulb let out a faint glow, vaguely illuminating mailboxes along the left wall, some with tattered calling cards, others with names carelessly scribbled across in white paint.

The sound of our footsteps clapped up the dark stairway. Kotia had apparently been waiting in the poorly lit kitchen. We entered and found him sitting there, his head low. Judging from his gloomy expression, he must have been depressed. The table on which he leaned heavily was covered with a floral-print oilcloth. A meager dinner lay untouched on his plate.

His head quickly snapped up when the door opened, and he jumped to his feet. "My God! Where have you been? It's . . ."

Suddenly speechless, he stared at me, frightened at the sight of my disheveled appearance and bloodied clothing.

"I had to rescue your roommate; she was in jail," said Helier, without detail. He knew Kotia and I would have plenty of time to discuss the ordeal after his departure.

"A drink will warm you up," said Kotia, slowly regaining his composure.

Helier gave him a friendly slap on the back. "No thanks. Take care of her, *mon ami*. She's been through a lot today." He was in a hurry to go, explaining, "We'll have to ditch the car a few blocks from here. The *Boches* took the license number at the hospital. With this damn curfew, it will take us some time to reach home on foot."

I kissed Helier on the cheek. "I had no more hope!" I exclaimed.

He shook his head and gave me a tight smile. "I must say, it wasn't easy getting the papers and the car. It was fortunate Jacquin was at the prefecture of police this evening. From now on, be more cautious. You might not be so lucky next time. *A bientôt.*"

He disappeared into the dark hall.

Solicitous, Kotia took me into his arms. Using his pet name for me, he said, "*Darogaia,* you need rest. We'll talk tomorrow."

I cradled my head in the hollow of his shoulder.

"Now, you must have something warm to drink and go straight to bed," he chided as he felt my chest heave fitfully against him.

He lit the gas under the stove in the kitchen's alcove, and when some water had boiled he poured it over a bouillon cube. I drank all of it, savoring the salty taste. I then went to the bathroom to remove the fake padding and filthy clothes.

The mirror on the wall reflected a ghostly face with hollowed-out eyes. I didn't think anyone could change in so short a period of time. There were bluish marks on my neck where the man in the cell had choked me. Fortunately, the scratches on my shoulders and chest were not deep. After washing, I applied iodine on the cuts and went to bed. Kotia came in a few minutes later to say good night, then he turned off the light and left me to my thoughts.

Painfully stretching my body, I told myself I wanted to go home, to rest and forget this whole episode. But then, it was too late to change anything. And besides, did I really want to stop my work with the Resistance?

I raised my head from the pillow and sat up. I lit a cigarette, trying to concentrate. Why had I become involved in a profession that was usually considered a man's job?

I thought for a long time. Finally pushing the cruel picture of war out of my mind, I got up and stood in front of the window, watching the coming of dawn. Birds were chirping happily in the chestnut trees. Yes, I reflected, there had been a time when I, too, had led a carefree, happy existence. It was now part of a distant past.

To obtain a train ticket for Marseilles was difficult, almost impossible, at this point of the Occupation. Most of the trains were being used to transport troops, and the Allies were bombing the railroads heavily.

Kotia's cousin was an interpreter for the French at the SNCF (Société Nationale des Chemins de fer français), the Paris railroad office, and he promised that he would do his best to get me a seat on the express. I didn't hear from him for several days, but then, early one morning, the phone rang.

"Everything has been arranged," the voice said, "but the ticket will have to be picked up right away, before questions are asked." The departure was for the same day.

I had waited for Kotia's return, with my tote bag at the door, impatient and ready to go, wrapped in my warmest clothes. I couldn't help thinking of our strange association.

When I had met Kotia, during one of the meetings at Helier's apartment, he had clearly displayed his attraction for me. His Slavic handsomeness fascinated me; yet, if I had found another alternative, I probably wouldn't have taken refuge at his home—because of the magnetism I felt for him.

After moving in with him, there had been a great formality in his courtship, even though we shared the same roof. Later, I discovered that while he had taken me under his protective wing, as a brother, he really wanted to become my lover. However, the life I led as an agent did not allow me the luxury of falling in love.

I saw him from the kitchen window as he hurried across the street before entering the building. Once more, he had eased the obstacles by providing some cash for my fare. I had received a small amount of money from Jackie every two weeks, and it had been just enough to buy food.

We took the metro to the gare de Lyon, using my *carte d'identité* with the name Anick Seignon for the last time. It was a cold but clear day. The vast steel-domed train station was absolutely jammed with German soldiers. After getting the ticket, Kotia eventually found the right track.

It was a madhouse. Not only was the express loaded with regular German troops, but there were also platoons of Mongolian soldiers, looking fierce and savage. Kotia tried to find a place for me as far away from them as possible.

The Mongolians had initially been press-ganged into the Russian army and later on taken prisoner by the Germans on the Russian Front. Now they had been incorporated (under the supervision of German NCOs and officers) into the German army.

Two compartments ahead was the officers' car. The German officers peered down at me through grimy windows and, upon seeing an attractive young girl, lowered the glass. After inquiries, they let me have a seat with them.

The entrance leading to this particular coach was so congested with soldiers and their equipment that I was unable to get through the human barrier the conventional way, just by walking in.

Kotia lifted me onto his shoulders so I could reach up to a window, and I was unceremoniously hauled into the compartment by the officers, who appeared to savor this unusual exercise.

A few piercing whistles, several announcements of *"Attention au départ,"* and the express began to gradually jolt forward in the midst of grinding metal and wafts of hissing steam.

I leaned out the window and reached for Kotia's hand. "Kotia, *merci.* I will never forget you."

His fingers grasped mine tightly for a few seconds, his blue eyes studying me for the last time. *"Darogaia,"* he said. "Farewell and good luck!"

His voice faded in a screen of black smoke.

A big lump tightening my throat, I whispered, *"Adieu, cher Kotia. Adieu."*

He stood there motionless, the train gradually picking up speed. Soon, I could no longer make out his form.

I stepped back into the coach.

One of the officers indicated an unoccupied seat and offered me something to read. He himself was engrossed in the *Pariser Zeitung,* the German newspaper printed in Paris.

I thought of Kotia for a while longer, recalling all he had done for me.

Every once in a while, one of the men would glance in my direction and try to carry on a conversation. Fortunately, their French was limited, and I felt grateful for that. I spent most of my time worrying, wondering what was awaiting me at the end of the line.

Several hours elapsed, and I felt the need to exercise my legs. I got up and walked to the end of the coach in search of a toilet, stepping over men reclining in the aisle and stacks of guns and equipment.

The bathroom door was open, but was occupied by a trooper with a large, round face, like a moon, who sat comfortably on the lavatory stool. He was eating sausages.

I made my best efforts to make him understand my immediate need, but he remained sitting, shaking his head, chewing.

"Nein, nein!"

He slid his free hand into his trousers and scratched his buttocks.

I gave up and returned to my seat.

Later, in the afternoon, I went back to the rest room. Once again, I had no luck in persuading the overbearing trooper to get off the stool.

My unhappiness must have been written on my face when I returned once again to my seat. The officer sitting next to me inquired, *"Was ist denn?*—what's the matter?"

"Keine Toilette ist frei!"—"The toilets are occupied!" I replied with urgency.

"Ach, ein Moment," he said, getting up and adding, *"Bitte kommen Sie mit mir"*—"Please come with me."

I tagged along, and we walked in the opposite direction to another toilet. At his approach, the men moved swiftly to let us pass, pressing themselves against the wall, with their rifles at their sides. The toilet in the next car was genuinely occupied.

"Kommen Sie." The major gestured with a hand. We reached the third compartment.

The Mongolians were standing everywhere, and they did not move aside as readily for the officer as the German soldiers had. They were making obscene gestures with their hands and were laughing uproariously.

The major rasped a sharp order. *"Raus!"*

"Jawohl!" They let us pass by.

The piercing sound of the train whistle resounded. We were being attacked by Allied bombers.

The locomotive's engine stopped slowly, and the carriage doors burst open. Men jumped from windows, some crushing others in the melee, trying to exit faster.

The German major was hustling me in front of him toward the nearest exit. Still in shock, I began walking, entangled in this human wave, my mouth gaping and gasping frantically as I was almost lifted off the floor.

The train appeared to vomit these struggling men, who carried their rifles, ammunition belts, or nothing at all. They were all running madly, as fast as their legs could carry them, away from the train.

I found myself outside, sprinting in the direction of a ditch. Then it was hell on earth.

The ground raised, trembling, as if ready to split open and burst. Bombs were falling along the tracks, and the ground shook, as if seized by a powerful earthquake. Again and again came that horrible approaching whine. Out of the corner of my eyes I saw one of the carriages, black against a background of mounting flames, cut in two like a broken straw. Stones, mud, and shrapnel flew in all directions. A rain of gravel chips pummeled my head.

The droning of the planes slowly receded. I remained inert, completely numb. I could taste blood slowly dripping down my throat from the blasts, and I raised my head above the ditch for air.

There was a deadly silence, and an unhealthy smell filled my lungs.

Wearily I looked up. It began to snow. A fine, dry, almost imperceptible downfall, of which I was barely aware. Yet when I looked up at the sky, the air was filled with millions of beautiful swirling snowflakes.

The serenity of this eerie calm was rudely shattered as my vision focused on the edge of the tracks, farther along the divested slope of vineyards. Steam was still wafting from the locomotive's engine, and most of the carriages remained intact. Huge craters yawned along the rails.

It was an unearthly scene, with huge pieces of crumpled metal twisted into strange sculptured shapes, pointing to the heavens, like headstones in an old, abandoned graveyard.

I clambered out of the ditch, the cold gnawing at my bones.

The NCOs barked angrily at their men to organize first-aid and work crews. The few civilian passengers, who had escaped from the train, were huddling near a knoll, their faces covered in mud—scared.

The Germans were sending a platoon to the nearest village to telegraph for help and get a rescue team to replace the damaged rails.

The sky had cleared, but the harsh, penetrating wind still whirled fine, stinging crystals across the road. The passengers followed the soldiers like sheep and arrived at a hamlet—a few dull houses, with narrow windows reflecting the winter sky.

Hearing of the ordeal, its inhabitants offered the civilians lodging until the train could continue its course once again. The troops camped outside.

It took two days to remove the wreckage and make repairs. The work was rudimentary, but the tracks were reinforced well enough to let the train pass through.

The Germans used the Mongolian soldiers as forced labor and treated them as beasts of burden, prodding them with the butts of their rifles to make them work faster. The train was, at last, on its way again.

By then I was in a state of total exhaustion.

Finally we reached Marseilles. Reunited! I couldn't believe my eyes. There, by the train, Jackie and Didier, who had been notified by Helier, were waiting. To see them, with tears of joy on their cheeks, brought a weak smile to my lips.

Their demonstrations of affection overwhelmed me. Until then I could not believe the ordeal was over. I was too weary to react.

I believe what helped me to recover was the news that Garçin, the man who had so brutally attacked me in my house, had been found hiding at his mother's house in Aix. After a short trial conducted by Beaugard's men, he had been executed as a traitor in the woods behind the Château Noir. For the moment, I was safe.

PART II

1943–1944

CHAPTER TEN

We Join the OSS

November 1943

Colonel Beaugard's health had been declining, and he was not well enough to maintain a firm hand over his network. The carelessness in which things were run could put us all in danger. Anne-Georges, his lady friend, was now in charge of the network Franc-Croix and had incorporated most of Beaugard's agents into her group.

By the end of November 1943, Jackie and I had become disenchanted with the political turn taken by the Underground. There was the regular Underground (FFI), the Communist Underground (FTP), the Secret Army (SA), the Maquis (guerrilla fighters), the pro–de Gaulle and pro-Giraud forces, and a large number of independent networks (or *réseaux*), all functioning on their own, each trying to outdo the others.

Through Colonel Beaugard I was referred to a man code-named Arnaud, an FFI leader in the Nîmes area. I asked him to introduce Jackie and me to an agent of the American OSS (Office of Strategic Services) who, I had heard, was operating in our sector.

Arnaud was far from enthusiastic the first time we voiced

our desire to work for the Americans. Hard-headed and pro–
de Gaulle, he could not understand our growing dissatisfac-
tion with the infighting and petty squabbling we felt existed
in the Underground. After much reluctance, however, he
agreed to arrange a meeting. Pleased by his change of mind,
Jackie and I traveled to Nîmes and took a room in a modest
little inn run by sympathizers. Though the innkeepers had
been recommended as "safe," we remained cautious and
made no special effort to be friendly. The term "sympathizer"
did not necessarily mean that they were devoted to the
Cause, and we had learned by experience that villagers
quickly grew wary of strangers. Jackie and I kept to ourselves, waiting for the American agent.

That evening, just as the sun was setting, the sound of
droning engines drew us to the window. The sky was still
light enough for us to see a fleet of Allied bombers proceed-
ing toward their target—probably railways or some ammunition depot.

Quickly removing their camouflage netting, the German
antiaircraft batteries came into action with high-pitched
whines. The thud of flak from the guns broke the silence and
small white puffs dotted the sky, bursting with a subtle pop
and exploding with a wisp of black smoke.

One bomber was hit and fell away from the last squadron
overhead. Its engine screeched and burst into flames. The
big B-17 was crashing, rolling out of control, leaving a trail of
darting tongues of light and black smoke. Eventually, a single
mushroom blossomed in the sky, and an indistinct figure
began to descend, the wind carrying the chute toward the
hamlet.

We heard the spattering of machine-gun fire and saw the

crumpled body fall not far from the inn, near a knoll dominated by large sycamores.

A few country folk raced down the dirt road but were
immediately stopped by the gunfire of German soldiers trying to prevent them from approaching the body. The spray of
bullets scattered the people like a flock of sparrows.

The following day, the German authorities forbade anyone
to bury the unfortunate airman.

"This will serve as an example for anyone trying to help the
Allies," stated the notice.

Some thirty-six hours passed while the body lay there, no
one daring to do anything. The cords of the chute had been
removed by the German soldiers. The corpse began to bloat
and flies swarmed over it in a thick cloud. The man's arms
were extended as if crucified. His head rested in the dirt, his
blond hair was matted with dust and dried blood, his eyes
were glazed, mouth ajar.

Sickened at the sight, Jackie and I brooded over the matter
all that morning. We had learned to live by our wits, and we
quickly made our decision: we would remove the body during the night and give the man a decent burial.

That afternoon, we went to the small countryside cemetery
at the foot of the hill and contacted a gravedigger, a gray-
bearded Provençal named Eustache. He must have been fat
in his younger years because his body was now skinny with
age and sagged like a sackcloth. Sitting with his back against a
tangle of withering vines at the entrance of the burial grounds,
he considered our words cautiously, smoothing his chin.

Finally, he gave a cautious cough, then shook his head in
disagreement. "I'm very old," he pleaded in a feeble, quivering voice.

However, as is often the case, money did the trick. After some parlaying and the promise of a substantial bribe, he said, "I'll help you. Come around ten o'clock tonight. I'll be through digging by then. The gate will be unlocked."

"That's good!" we told him, and began to leave.

The old man's eyes suddenly came alive, and he grabbed Jackie by the arm. In a surprisingly strong tone, he demanded, "Where is my money?"

We gave him part of the bribe. "You'll get the rest tonight."

Eustache closed his eyes and, once again indifferent, resumed his midday siesta.

We returned to the inn early in the evening and retired to our room, having spent the intervening hours searching for a wheelbarrow with which to transport the body.

The evening turned out to be gray and cold, as the pale winter sun descended behind the slope of vineyards. At curfew, the road emptied, with no lights visible anywhere.

Awaiting total darkness, we sat at the end of the bed. Jackie was silent, lost in her thoughts. All was still now. Restless, I moved about, pacing the room a few times, then said in a detached tone, "I hope the coast is clear. I'll go out and check."

Jackie didn't answer.

Unlocking the front door, I glanced outside. It seemed peaceful enough. I went back into the room. Jackie's somber mood had lifted, and she was dressing. "I think it's time," she said, checking her watch.

I felt hesitant at the last minute. "Do you think he'll be there?"

"I'm sure! He's greedy!" replied Jackie.

It was a little after nine o'clock when we started out, pushing the wheelbarrow we'd finally found in the garden next to the inn. The rusty wheels made an annoying squeak as they rolled down the road. The Mistral, the angry wind of Provence, had suddenly sprung up in whips and gusts, sending shutters creaking against walls, shaking the trees near us, and blowing flurries of dead leaves around our feet.

As we moved along, the beam of a flashlight probed across the street, exploring the walls. It shone on a discarded mound of broken tiles.

It was a German patrol. We could hear the pounding of their boots coming closer. Dropping the wheelbarrow against a tree, we jumped over foul-smelling garbage and dashed up the road.

A pebble rolled under Jackie's foot.

"Who's there?" shouted one of the soldiers, flashing his light around.

Jackie and I squeezed into a narrow alleyway between two houses.

"Come on, it's nothing!" mumbled another one of the soldiers.

Our hearts were beating so loudly that each of us thought the other could hear it.

The soldiers passed without seeing us. The clatter of their heavy nailed boots faded into the distance. We didn't dare stir until silence encircled us again.

I could feel the sweat running down my neck, and my blouse clung to my breasts. We groped our way along the dark road to fetch our gruesome burden. Although we knew the location of the body, we had to fumble for a while in the darkness, straining to make out the dead airman's form.

I rubbed the palms of my clammy hands against my coat to remove the sweat.

We attempted to load the corpse in the wheelbarrow together, but as I lifted him by the armpits, the cloth from the upper right sleeve, which was riddled with bullet holes, ripped apart. The body was putrid, the stench making me gag violently. Nauseated, I dropped the body.

"Grab him!" pleaded Jackie, still clinging to his feet. We dragged the body into the wheelbarrow.

Slowly we started down the road, each of us holding a handle of the wheelbarrow with both hands. At the crossroads, we turned left. The small burial ground, surrounded by a low stone wall, was just ahead. Its rusty iron gate was difficult to pry open. We found Eustache among the dark wooden crosses in the tall grass.

"You certainly took your time!" he cackled through his toothless mouth. He was nervous as a cat, standing beside a hole he had been digging since nightfall in the paupers' corner, where the earth is for everyone and no one in particular. The wind, blowing a cloud of dust around him, looked like an eerie black cloth.

We couldn't make ourselves touch the corpse again. I did not even have the courage to remove the dog tag hanging from the airman's neck. We tipped the wheelbarrow sideways, letting the body fall into the grave.

Using the shovel and our hands and feet, the three of us pushed the dirt over the airman's body, then arranged handfuls of dead leaves and branches to hide the new grave.

When we were finished, we gave Eustache his money, which he quickly counted. "There's some missing," he grumbled angrily.

"Well, that's all we have left," I told him. "What are you going to do about it?"

He faded into the night.

After abandoning the wheelbarrow in a shack on the way out, we snuck out of the cemetery like grave robbers. In their glossy whiteness, the lime-washed houses along the road seemed like ghosts standing at attention.

Back at the inn, we slept a bit, but it was far from restful. The night's escapade had upset us, especially after we had time to realize how dangerous it was to have acted on impulse and sheer emotion. It could have been disastrous. By five A.M., we left the inn, avoiding the owner, who was already at work in his kitchen, and headed for the Café Modern to find Arnaud.

As we were finishing breakfast, Arnaud showed up at the front door. He was wearing a shapeless sweater with a high turtleneck collar, an old pair of corduroy trousers patched at the knees, and army boots, which had just about walked their last mile. A youthful-looking man wearing glasses, not very tall, with light brown, wavy hair, followed Arnaud in. He was introduced as the key OSS agent for the southeast sector.

The young man lit a Caporal cigarette and peered at us through the smoke. Speaking softly and carefully, he said, "I am Petit-Jean. I'm told you want to join my network. Arnaud says you have been in the field for some time. I'm sure you have contacts. I can use people like you."

"My name is Anick, and this is my sister, Jackie," I said.

Then Jackie and I began speaking at the same time. "We were so anxious to meet you" . . . "Yes, we were afraid you wouldn't come" . . . "At last the Americans are here to help, and—"

Cutting us off, Petit-Jean said, laughingly, "I'm glad to see such enthusiasm!" As we spoke and explained why we wanted to join the OSS, he kept watching us with steady, serious eyes, as if trying to read our thoughts.

We stared back as he settled in his chair, realizing how mistaken our girlish speculations had been about our first American. The last thing we imagined was an American speaking flawless French. But was he really an American?

We stopped talking, our attention suddenly attracted by a crowd gathering outside, near a World War I monument in the village square. Small groups were talking feverishly, pointing toward the knoll where the airman had been shot down.

I recounted the previous night's events to the two men and briefly gave the details of the flier's humble burial.

Arnaud's eyes narrowed as he gazed around the room. "It was foolish of you to do that. Don't you want to live?" he asked flatly. There was a touch of scorn in his voice that rankled. His face was set, insensitive to the incident.

Petit-Jean said nothing. Obviously, he knew how to keep control of his emotions and thoughts. But I noticed a slight twist, almost a smile, curling his lips.

"Let's leave on the double," grunted Arnaud, getting up. "We can't continue our conversation. We are strangers here, and it's not healthy for us to be seen in this area."

Taken aback by Arnaud's selfish, scornful attitude, Jackie blurted, "We can't go very far. We're broke."

"Yes," I snapped, "the gravedigger was expensive!" I was irritated that Arnaud was more concerned with his own safety than with ours.

Petit-Jean stamped out his cigarette while pushing his chair back. He stood up before he turned to us. After searching inside one of his pockets, he produced a few French bills and handed them to me. "This will keep you going until we meet at Arnaud's farm near Avignon. Be there in a couple of days. You will get your instructions then."

Then he added, "I appreciate what you did for the pilot last night." Giving a final look around, he left some change on the table's marble top and walked to the front door to join Arnaud, who was already on his way. Little did we know then that Petit-Jean would play such an important and decisive role in Jackie's life.

Jackie and I headed for the open fields. A few women, working the soil, were starting their day and lifted their heads curiously as we went by.

Our hasty enlistment in the OSS made Jackie and me feel very special. Recruiting a field agent during the war did not require paperwork or oaths of allegiance, investigations or background checks. One's word and an introduction by a known Resistance leader was sufficient; patriotism and proven ability provided the initial recommendation. It was a chance we all had to take.

We had no special training and had not undergone any schooling. Our espionage skills were self-taught. All we knew came from the dangerous encounters we'd had with the enemy. Our new activities with the OSS, Petit-Jean told us at the farm, were to be different from our previous ones. We were to provide details on troop and ammunition movements and their destinations; targets for bombing; locations of fuel depots, minefields, and antiaircraft positions; and information on the strength of enemy troops in the area.

The name of our OSS network was Penny Farthing, and its leader was Jacques I. We were instructed to pass our messages, at predetermined locations, to an agent code-named Hellops. If Hellops could not be reached, another agent, code-named Naf-Naf, would replace him. If our station was burned, we were to fall back to an alternate under the direction of Jacques II, near Clermont-Ferrand.

As we were about to leave on our new venture, a young man showed up at the farm, who we later learned was Hellops himself. He was quickly admitted and warmly greeted by Petit-Jean.

Hellops was slim and not very tall. One had to see the mischievous glint in his deep-set eyes and catch the devilish expression of his grin to realize that he was an irrepressible, friendly rogue. He trained us in our new enterprise and initiated us into many missions. He became our most trusted friend.

Since Jackie could work only occasionally, and mostly in the Aix surroundings, Hellops and I covered the territory of Avignon-Montpellier-Marseilles, reporting on the strength and movement of enemy troops, transportation equipment and ammunition, drawings of fortifications and defense work, and evaluations and results of Allied bombings.

We also covered the location of airfields in the Marignane-Istres-Miramas area. We bicycled along the coast, between Martigues, Marseilles, and La Ciotat, as well as from Toulon up to Nice, detecting coastal defenses and reporting on German mines, antiaircraft, and camouflage nets. We even spotted a 380-millimeter railway gun in Peyrolles, which the Germans had hidden in a tunnel during daylight hours.

All of this, Hellops and I managed to do within a 200-mile radius of Aix-en-Provence.

So began my work for the OSS.

CHAPTER ELEVEN

The American Fliers

On January 20, 1944, I received orders from Petit-Jean
to escort two American fliers from the city of Avignon to the Spanish border. The two pilots had been
shot down somewhere in the North and were scheduled to
arrive on Tuesday. They were to be entrusted with maps and
sketches, which were to be given to the Allies in North
Africa.

Jackie wanted to come along, but I was adamant that she
not. "One of us has to stay behind," I argued. "You promised
to be with Mother. I don't know how this trip will turn out.
The Germans are watching the entire Pyrenees Mountains
area. You have to stay behind, in case something happens
to me."

"But Mother is safe with friends. This won't take long."

Petit-Jean intervened. "Anick is right. She has more experience."

At the bus station, just before I left, Jackie and I held each
other and she started to cry.

"Look at you," I tried to joke. "You'd think I'm abandoning you!" I stepped quickly onto the bus without turning
back.

During the ride to Avignon, I tried to remember all of

Petit-Jean's instructions. "It will be necessary to use a Basque guide," he had told me, "even though they can't always be entirely trusted. Still, they know their way over the hunting trails and are able to avoid German patrols. They also have contacts across the frontier. Our people in Barcelona have already been notified of the arrival of the pilots. They'll be waiting."

A special zone of surveillance had been set up along the Spanish border. One could not enter the *"Zone Interdite"* (Forbidden Zone) without a special pass, which was given only to residents. Moreover, these passes were constantly being changed by the German authorities. Outsiders had to obtain an authorization from the German *Kommandantur,* and it took several days to receive the precious papers, which were issued only after a thorough investigation.

I arrived early and so decided to walk around and reacquaint myself with Avignon, the city where I had once been a student. Climbing up the side of the great rock in the center of town, I found myself at the entrance of the Pope's Palace. The walls rose from the edge of a deep ravine, overlooking the Rhône River. I began to descend through the well-groomed park surrounding the castle.

Tired, I sat down on a bench and waited for my contact. At two-fifteen P.M., Frédéric Rocca came into view. He stood, aimlessly looking around, as if trying to locate someone rather than selecting a place to sit. His eyes drifted in my direction, then paused a moment. I slid along the bench to make room for him. Carefully raising his trouser legs, he sat down next to me. I nodded, waiting for the proper code word.

Apparently he was in no hurry. He watched some children playing, smoked a cigarette, then read a few pages of a local newspaper before nonchalantly turning in my direction. "Are you familiar with the Pope's Palace, mademoiselle?" "Not really. I have just come from the North. Can you tell me about it?"

"I'll be glad to. I have a lot of time."

Passwords exchanged, I now knew he was my contact.

"My name is Anick," I told him with a smile.

"I know. I'm Rocca."

The conversation continued in a pleasant manner, long enough for us to be sure that no one was watching.

A while later, balancing uncomfortably on the bar of his bicycle, I was taken by Monsieur Rocca to his country home, which was located some distance out of town.

Though we'd expected our rendezvous with the Americans to take place the following day, as it turned out, Justin, a liaison agent in Avignon, had postponed it for a day.

At five-fifteen the morning of our meeting, Rocca and I arrived at the entrance to the railway station. An unsmiling young German soldier stared at my identification card, which he placed on his desk. "Anick Durand?" he asked.

"Yes," I answered quickly.

After an alarmingly long wait, he handed me back the paper, pressed a handle, and allowed me through the turnstile.

Rocca looked quite relieved.

There was a group of travelers crowding the lounge. They had been rounded up, and their identification cards were being checked by Gestapo agents. A blond German civilian with a leather coat and fedora was calling them to come in one at a time. Routine checks of rail passengers by the Gestapo were a common occurrence.

Considering my experience in Paris, I couldn't help shuddering at the idea of a roundup. You never knew if you were safe when in the hands of the Gestapo. You might end up going home, to prison, or worse, to your grave.

Justin came through the turnstile and immediately sighted Rocca. Smiling, he extended his hand as he came forward. I noticed two men coming up the ramp close behind him. One wore blue denim overalls and a V-neck pullover frayed at the sleeves. The other had on a rumpled brown suit. When they passed by, Justin nodded slightly. I knew then that these were the pilots I would be bringing to the Spanish guide.

"I'm late," Justin apologized, ignoring the two men. "I was delayed at the entrance."

"So was I," I said, observing the Americans out of the corner of my eye.

Allen was the name of the jovial young man. He had a broken nose, like a boxer, and I noticed the edge of a bandage on his forehead. His quite handsome friend, Stan, had black hair and a tan. Both men looked very tired. I watched them gloomily board the train for Perpignan, a town near the Spanish-French border.

The Americans had been provided with false IDs, for without such cards, a person was totally at the mercy of the Gestapo. Stan and Allen had their instructions from Justin. They knew they had to trust me and depend on my leadership, since they only spoke English. My overnight bag contained sketches, scale drawings, and map overlays. These were to be given to the Americans before they crossed the border.

According to the plan, I was to get in touch with Monsieur Pope in Perpignan, at the church des Augustins. He would provide shelter while I arranged for the guide.

Inside the train, the air was heavy and smelled of perspiration. I eased my way into the corridor and reached the car where the two pilots were sitting. I gave them a quick nod. Holding the brass window rail, I studied the faces around me and felt reassured. Most of the passengers were ordinary French citizens.

Just then a German officer in full uniform made his way in my direction, disturbing the few people sitting on their luggage. He posted himself at the door next to me and started making advances. So gallant and so "correct," he opened a gold case and offered me a cigarette. I readily accepted, knowing that it would be to my advantage to cultivate his interest in me.

I took a cigarette out of the case and pushed my shoulder against his. I exerted no pressure, only made contact. I could almost sense the man's excitement rising. His neck turned red under the tight-fitting collar.

An obliging hand was outstretched with a lighter.

"Do you live in this area?" he asked, trying to look indifferent while puffing casually at his cigarette.

"Yes, I am on my way to visit some relatives."

"I should introduce myself. Captain Kurt Straub," he said, and clicked his heels.

"Anick Durand." I smiled.

He was silent for a while. Then, looking around, he said, "What a crowded train. There is such confusion in this country! It's deplorable," he concluded, lifting an eyebrow in contempt.

I truly wished I could have said, "Go to hell!" but despite how distasteful I found his arrogance, I continued to listen politely.

Leaning against the sliding door of the compartment, I took deep puffs of the cigarette and, through the window, watched the scenery flashing by.

Unexpectedly a sharp whistle rose above the uproar of the wheels on the rails. We were not too far from a station. A train employee moved hurriedly through, announcing, "Be ready. The train will be searched before entering the next station."

The Germans were about to conduct another of their surprise luggage checks. I tensed immediately. Painfully alert, I felt queasy, and perspiration appeared on my forehead. My mind raced ahead, searching for a solution; if they opened my bag, I would be trapped.

The captain, unwittingly, solved the problem.

"I am getting out at the next stop. Are you, Mademoiselle Durand?" His voice expressed his thoughts, but his gaze, I noticed, focused on my breasts.

"Yes," I heard myself answer, not yet knowing what I would do next.

"Good. May we have lunch together, then?" An enticing grin puckered his thin lips.

While resting my hand on his wrist, I nodded, lowering my eyes slightly, changing position so as to relax against his shoulder.

Encouraged, he added, "I know a place in town where we could have a nice tête-à-tête. We might even be able to get a room."

He took a handful of ration coupons from his coat pocket and showed them to me. "I'll have a nice gift for you," he enticed.

I had to look pleased.

The train was jolting heavily as it slowed down. My hands clung to the metal window bar. A group of civilians approached, along with two military men who were opening suitcases and packages at random as they walked along. Those passengers who had been checked already were moving forward to exit.

I shot a glance at the two disconcerted Americans sitting in the compartment, trying to warn them of my next move, but they were too bewildered to understand what was going on.

Turning to the captain, I asked charmingly, "Will you help me with my bag while I get off?"

He bowed. He was thin, with a long, sallow face, and a beaked nose that reminded me of a bird of prey. The triumphant expression in his slate-gray pupils clearly divulged his plans. As he carried my precious bag, we went out together, and the German police saluted at the door.

Realizing that I was getting out, Allen and Stan darted an eloquent and pleading look at me. I could not respond.

Instead, once off the train, I turned flirtatiously toward the SS captain. "I need a little time to freshen up before our lunch date," I told him, taking my suitcase out of his hands. "I won't be long. Wait for me."

He straightened his tunic and threw out his chest. "I'll be waiting at the exit," he said expectantly as he appraised me from head to toe.

I waved back at him and forced my way through the crowd in the direction of the public toilets. Cautioning myself not to run, and thus attract suspicion, I crossed the tracks and returned to my platform.

The train was pulling out. The coaches were gathering speed as I hauled myself aboard, bag and all.

By that time, the inspection team was gone. My strategy had worked perfectly. If my bag had been searched, the incriminating maps would certainly have been discovered.

As I returned to their compartment, a look of incredible relief appeared on the faces of the two airmen. It had been a close shave, but the rest of the trip passed without further incident. The three of us shared the wine and cheese that had been Rocca's gift, and Allen and Stan gradually unwound.

Once in Perpignan, we quickly found Monsieur Pope waiting at the church des Augustins. He was kneeling uncomfortably in one of the church's isolated corners, near a baptismal fountain.

Dipping my fingers in the holy water, I made the sign of the cross and genuflected beside a pew. The two men instantly did the same. Ostensibly, they were still engrossed in their prayers when Monsieur Pope limped by us.

We rose to follow him and were on the steps outside when we stopped in our tracks, alarmed. Coming from all directions toward the church was a crowd sprinkled with a few German uniforms.

We stood there dithering. A short distance away, Monsieur Pope waited for us to make a move.

The situation could have been a disaster. Instead, it became a comedy.

Coming toward us on the main street was a procession, headed by a bicycle with a sidecar strapped alongside it carrying a bride. The young woman looked bewildered as the vehicle rolled down the sloping avenue at full speed. She held on with one hand, and used the other to clutch her veil, which was ballooning like a mosquito net caught in a draft.

The groom followed on a racing bike, handlebars sportingly curved. The cuffs on his trousers were neatly folded, a metal clasp holding them in place so that they would not get caught in the chain. His loose tie fluttered in the wind.

The rest of the company trailed behind him, and they too were on wheels, all merrily pedaling away.

The sight was so unreal that forgetting himself, Allen let out an incredulous guffaw. "Holy cow!"

"*C'est drôle, n'est-ce pas?*"—"It's funny, don't you think?" I cut in, my voice covering his.

It didn't matter to me what he had said, for I couldn't understand, but I knew that to speak English in public was fatal. Luckily, everyone was too engrossed in the parade to have heard his exclamation.

He clammed up after that. It was the last I heard out of him until evening.

The bicycle with the sidecar braked at the steps of the church, and the father of the bride, leaping off his own bike, rushed to rescue his flustered daughter. The bridesmaids left their bicycles at the curb and began to rearrange the girl's tangled attire as she stepped out of the sidecar. Soon the ceremony began.

Following the nuptial benediction, the three of us bravely joined the line of relatives, demonstratively kissing the elated couple before blending in with the departing guests.

Through all of this, Monsieur Pope had sat quietly waiting in one of the back pews. He was totally unruffled.

Later we had dinner and afterward the Americans tried to say something to me, but I could only understand the words "Thank you!"

Pope smiled. "I think they are grateful. They use words I don't know. . . ."

Stan took me to my room. "Boon swear," he said, in attempted French. I gave him a friendly kiss and quietly closed the door.

That evening I slept in Monsieur Pope's bedroom, while the men shared the living room. His bedroom was very small, the furniture evidence of a practical bachelor's taste. A single bed was pushed against the wall, and I sat to undress.

After removing my clothes, I looked at myself in the armoire's mirror. I saw my reflection and approved silently: my waist was trim, my legs and thighs slim and long, and my breasts firm and round. I brooded over the situation that I, a girl of twenty, was in. I found myself among young men most of the time, and yet passion never seemed to work its way into the relationships! Stan, for instance, was very attractive, and he seemed to like me. . . . I shrugged. Why should I care, anyway!

I turned off the light and stretched out on the bed, but I wasn't sleepy. After a while, I could hear the men snoring. My arms folded behind my head, I felt the coolness of the sheets on my naked body. "They'll be gone tomorrow!" I mumbled.

It was a long, discomforting night, a vain jumble of thoughts and desires keeping me from resting. I fidgeted and tugged at the pillow, tossing on the bed in a useless attempt at rest.

I awoke with a start as the Mass bell chimed six o'clock. I had been dreaming and sat up, confused. Remembering where I was, I got out of bed and dressed. After a slice of bread and a cup of acorn brew, I left to contact Paco, the Basque guide who I hoped would take the American pilots to safety.

Paco lived in a small cabin surrounded by a tiny vegetable garden in a northern suburb of Perpignan. The little house was his. He had built it out of stones and mortar stolen from the graveyard nearby.

I rapped at the door.

"Yes?" he asked, inspecting me through the slightly opened door.

"A fine day for a climb," I said decidedly.

"Who said so?"

"Pope, of course. My name is Anick. Are you available?"

"I am the guide you need," came the answer, and the door opened wide.

Paco was a tall, thin man with a dark, olive complexion. He looked more like a bandit than a guide. His occupation was smuggling, and it made no difference to him whether he brought goods or people, as long as he made a good profit. He knew that he could demand a lot from desperate people. He was in an advantageous position, for he knew the trails in the Pyrenees Mountains like the back of his hand.

A strange odor pervaded the room we were in, a combination of stale wine, rancid meat, and tobacco. The chair creaked as I sat near the primitive wooden table.

Under his watchful stare, I recalled Monsieur Pope's words before I had left that morning: "He will not be cheap!"

I did not need the warning, for I could see the greed in his dark eyes as he inquired, "How many are going this time?"

"As of now, two."

"Twenty thousand francs each," he stated flatly.

The price was outrageous. I tried to bargain with him, but he shook his head, saying, "Twenty thousand francs, or they stay!"

"What about clothing?" I asked him. "It must be very cold in the mountains."

"They'll trade their clothes for warmer ones on the way up. It will be arranged."

"With no more charges, I hope!"

Paco gave me a wolfish smile. "I said 'trade.' I keep their belongings."

In desperation, I opened my purse and started counting the money that had been entrusted to me. It was fortunate that Petit-Jean had allowed for emergencies. I gave him half of the price demanded. "The rest will come when they are on the other side."

Exactly five hundred francs (about eleven dollars) remained for my return home.

While Paco counted the money, I threw open the door to let some air into the place.

My mission was almost over. Satisfied with my work, I returned to Pope's place. He was standing near the window when I came in, obviously waiting for me. No sooner had I caught sight of his face than I knew that something was very wrong. He was more upset than he wanted to appear.

"Anick," he rasped, "Rocca has been arrested along with Justin. The Gestapo are hunting for the girl who stayed at his country home. They received information from a German officer. They know you were on the train going to the Pyrenees, and they have your description."

Intense and agitated, he warned, "It's not safe any longer. You had better lie low for quite a while. I can't keep you here."

At that instant, the frustration I felt was stronger than the fear. Everything had *seemed* to go so well! I was tired of running, sickened by the thought of still more danger. I was even willing to pack it all in. But where could I go? This time the Gestapo was close behind me. I didn't want to endanger Monsieur Pope. I expressed my feelings in a flood of words and emotions, then sat, beaten.

Monsieur Pope tried to comfort me. "Anick," he said, "don't give up now." Placing a hand on my shoulder, he continued, "Not every mission can be completely successful. You have to hold back for a while, but look at me, at my age and with my poor health. I'm still fighting!"

I didn't feel convinced.

"The end of the war is near, believe me," he added with an air of conviction. "We're not waging a losing battle."

I wanted to trust him. I passionately believed that I had to follow my destiny, and I had to admit to myself that decisions such as mine never came without pain. Besides, what could I do? At this stage in the war, I just had to stay alive.

Stan and Allen sat there helpless, worried, not knowing what was happening but aware that something had gone wrong.

I sat for a while in a corner of the room, chewing my lower lip absently, uncertainty still trailing in my mind. Finally getting up, I looked at Monsieur Pope and said, "I have to deliver the pilots tonight. Then we'll see."

I brought Stan and Allen to meet Paco at a tiny eating place. We were served a greasy stew made of some indescribable meat. After sucking his fingers, Paco gulped down his last glass of wine, picked his teeth, and motioned that it was time to go. He tilted his Basque beret over his eyes and went to the door.

I signaled to the proprietor, but he was busy behind the

bar serving customers. His wife finally came to our table to give us the bill.

"Can you add three sandwiches?" I asked.

A few minutes later we were all outside and Allen gave me a hug. "*Au revoir,* honey," he said in his bad French. I handed him the travel bag.

Stan took me by the shoulders, bent toward me, and whispered what must have been kind words. His eyes were a little watery, and he gave me a long kiss on the lips while holding me tight against him.

I stood on the edge of the pavement where the narrow street began to curve and watched them leave, until they turned and waved a last good-bye.

The next morning one of Pope's trusted men drove me in one of those incredible wood-burning cars called a *gazogène* to a safe farm in the Pyrenees. I would wait there until the coast was clear again.

CHAPTER TWELVE

Home Again

I spent the next several weeks laying low on a small farm just outside of Axat. Although the fresh air and simple routines of farming life revived my spirits, I still felt uneasy. I couldn't help but wonder what had happened to Rocca and Justin. Were they being tortured by the Gestapo? Had they talked? Were they still alive? Questions raced through my mind. I thought of Didier and wondered if and when I would see him again.

Then, without warning, a note from Petit-Jean arrived one Friday. His message was brief: "Come to Cavaillon. A friend will be waiting for you at the train station on Sunday."

A train ticket was attached to the note.

It was early morning when I arrived in Cavaillon. There were only a few passengers who got off at the small station, and I immediately noticed a young man leaning against a pillar near the exit. He appeared to be searching for someone. His eyes passed over me a couple of times, and after a minute or so, he made a discreet signal in my direction.

I nodded in return, then proceeded to follow him on foot.

The man led me to a mattress maker's shop located in a narrow lane in the old part of the city.

"In there," he said, signaling the entrance of the store with his hand, and continued on his way.

I knocked several times. To my surprise, Hellops opened the door, closing it right behind me.

We kissed each other affectionately and, as I removed my coat, he told me how pleased he was to see me back. Then, fumbling through the cupboard, he retrieved two mugs, which he filled with hot brew.

"You must be tired after a night sitting on the wooden banquette. Let's have something warm to drink."

We sat at the table facing each other. After an offer of bread and cheese, he said, "It's all I have, sorry. This is a temporary shelter."

"Looks good to me," I assured him.

"Petit-Jean is busy along the coast near Toulon. I saw Jackie yesterday. She's on her way to check the German traffic at Istres Airfield. By the way," he added, "she doesn't know that you're back."

He kept talking, giving me time to drink my coffee.

"Monsieur Pope is doing fine. Thought you'd like to know."

I shook my head. "He's old and should retire," I commented.

"One of his men told me you had a narrow escape."

"Yes, but the pilots crossed the border anyway."

It was difficult to keep a warm, friendly conversation going when you had learned that there were limits to what could be said. It had become habit. Our words, no matter how simple, always seemed impersonal, emotionless.

There was no lack of feeling between us. Still, I found it difficult to show my inner emotions.

"I'm glad you had a safe trip," Hellops continued. "We have been quite busy since you left, as you can well imagine. A couple of our agents from Lyons have been arrested."

There was a long silence. Hellops, like myself, found it difficult to talk about our comrades' bad luck.

"Well, Petit-Jean left instructions. You are not to go back to Aix until we are told it is clear. People talk, and it wouldn't be safe for either of us. It's in your best interest," he reiterated.

This was disappointing news. I had been ready to resume my responsibilities as an OSS agent.

"What do you suggest, then?"

He drank the rest of his coffee, hesitating for a few seconds. "I talked to Petit-Jean about you going to your summer house, Saint-Ange. Keep a low profile for a while, and then we'll call you back as soon as possible."

"All right," I said with little enthusiasm.

Hellops got up. "I have to arrange your trip. My advice is not to show yourself outside. This place is safe for the moment."

Before grabbing his cap on the way to the door, he turned toward me. "Welcome back." He grinned, and then shut the door behind him.

Around six A.M. the next morning Hellops took me to the bus station. We held each other without saying a word, not knowing if or when we would see each other again.

Saint-Ange, the family country home in the lower Alps, was a rather large building with a terra-cotta tile roof and a sprawling yard shaded by plane trees.

When I showed up unexpectedly at the beginning of

February, the housekeepers made me feel welcome. But my stay lasted longer than I would have liked. I was able to get in touch with Petit-Jean, and through him I learned that the Milice had made inquiries about me in Aix on two occasions. Fortunately, Mother had no idea where I was.

For the moment, Saint-Ange was safe. I spent my time helping out around the house, reading a lot, and listening to the news on the radio. In June the Germans claimed that the landing in Normandy was "an aborted attempt at invasion." That was all I knew of this historic moment.

When July came, the sundry slopes surrounding the property were like huge mauve carpets when the lavender bloomed, and I enjoyed helping harvest the aromatic plants.

On the sixteenth of August 1944, one of the local boys politely handed me a letter. I sat on a bucket in the yard.

The note was from Jackie. Her round, perfectly formed writing covering the envelope made me smile.

"Hélène, *chérie*," it read, "I am home with *Maman*. Our friends are waiting for you. Hellops says your 'vacation' is over. It is time for you to come back. There is much to be done. I'll be gone for a couple of days to meet Petit-Jean, but come back quickly, quickly!"

I continued to read. Suddenly my joy changed to an immense sorrow. "Didier was killed near Sainte-Mère-Eglise," it said, "on the day of the landing in Normandy. I'll tell you about it when you arrive."

There wasn't much detail, but I could read between the lines. My eyes filled with tears, and I had to wipe them in order to finish reading the letter.

Grief-stricken, I withdrew into painful memories. "Don't worry," he had once told me, when the war was still young.

"At the Liberation, you and I are going to celebrate. We'll go to Paris and see the best places. No more hiding in the cellar for parties!"

No! No more hiding, no more laughing together, no more games with the *Boches*—the Germans—like we used to play. This time the enemy had won the contest.

I felt my throat tightening into a scream of anger, and I furiously kicked at the dirt on the ground.

A flock of black birds rose from the furrows and scattered into the air. I kept an eye on their flight, the intricate patterns they made, hearing their calling to each other, happy, strident cries. They were free and alive.

My wrath erupted as I thought of Jean de Simeon, who was no doubt still in Vichy, killing more people for the insane joy of it.

"Life's a play," I told myself, "a miserable, rotten game where people are simply pawns on a game board.

"Dear God!" I prayed devoutly, "don't let me learn to disbelieve in You!" But there was no answer.

After a feverish night, filled with nightmares, I began to prepare for my long-awaited return home.

The train was nearing Aix. Anxiously, I surveyed the suburbs from my compartment window.

So much had happened since I had left to help the fliers: narrowly evading the Gestapo, escaping to the farm in Axat, then the lazy wait at Saint-Ange. The prospect of seeing Mother and Jackie, of putting my arms around them and kissing and hugging them, filled me with a deep desire and expectation.

"What will I do or say first?" I knew my life would not take its normal path until the war was over.

The locomotive slowed down. I could see the streets. The pace of life here had not changed. And yet, the Germans were lurking nearby, relentless in their manhunt.

It was the seventeenth of August 1944. The Allies had already started their second landing, this time in the South of France.

❖ ❖ ❖

Jackie was waiting for me at the station. I saw her hurrying toward my compartment, taking long strides, her black hair bouncing over her shoulders. She looked just the same, though perhaps a little more slender.

From the minute we were together, I think Jackie sensed that I wasn't the same person she was used to. Oh, it was Hélène, all right, but not the same sister she had known. There was a seriousness about me, a shadow of sadness on my face that she didn't recognize. The smile on my lips was set and empty.

We fell into each other's arms.

"Oh, Hélène, *Maman* and I have missed you so much!" Jackie sobbed.

"I missed you, too, more than you can imagine. For a while I thought I would never come home again!" I wanted to ask so many questions, hear about everything that had happened during my long absence. Was Mother all right? Had she asked about my whereabouts?

Almost as if she had been reading my mind, Jackie exclaimed, "*Maman* is really worried about you."

"I can imagine." I got busy with my bag. "Here, help me."

I handed her a big canvas containing some potatoes, a pound of homemade cheese, a jar of honey, almonds, and a cardboard box with a few eggs from Saint-Ange—enough to improve Mother's meals for a while. Jackie took the bundle from my hands and we began walking home.

"You came back at the right time," she said gleefully. "You should see how the Germans are running, since this new landing on the Mediterranean! The other day," she continued, "they didn't have enough trucks to evacuate Arles. Would you believe they requisitioned all of the carts in the area and harnessed the Mongolians between the shafts, like animals?" She looked at me to catch my reaction. "Isn't that disgusting!"

"Yes," I agreed. "The Germans are not so arrogant any longer."

What's the matter with me? I thought. I should be happy to be home! Why am I suddenly feeling so down?

Sensing my tenseness, Jackie changed the subject. "Petit-Jean will be so glad to see you again. He came back last night. He says there is work to be done immediately."

Deep within myself, the tide of frustration rose and erupted, and I snapped at Jackie, "Give me a little time to settle down, will you?"

Startled, Jackie quickly changed her tone. "Of course, darling. Don't worry, we won't have to meet with him until tomorrow. Actually, this landing has changed many things." Trying to ease the stress, she kept chatting. "I can't wait to hear about your experience in the Pyrenees. Petit-Jean said that you were on special assignment. Is that true?"

"Yes, it is."

"We'll go home first. You must long to see *Maman*. Then

I'll take you to the room I've rented for you in town. Beaugard is still in the hospital—a heart condition, I was told."

I stopped dead in the middle of the sidewalk. "Now, just a minute! Do you mean I can't stay at home?" I thought I would be allowed to spend at least a few days at home. Even while at Saint-Ange, I had to hide from the outside world.

Jackie tried to explain. "I wanted you to stay, of course, but there is a German artillery unit stationed at the house, and they have installed antitank guns in the garden. It wouldn't be wise. As a matter of fact, when we arrive, act very casual."

"Have they bothered *Maman?*"

"No, thank God! Her jewelry is gone, of course, and so is most of the furniture. You'll see."

We arrived at the front gate, back home at last! My heart was pounding. I placed a hand to my chest, trying to slow down the palpitations.

There were the linden trees. The summer flowers were still blooming in the garden, and Mother's roses were wilting in the hot summer sun. I stopped, amazed at what I saw. Deadly Molotov cocktails were stacked up against the outside walls of the villa, jutting like vintage wine bottles in a cellar. Our mattresses and cushions had been brought outside and lay scattered on the gravel pathway. Wool hung from the ripped material, tangled with shrubbery. Most of our furniture had been chopped up for the soldiers' stove, which was now installed by the gate. An enlisted man was working on Father's mahogany desk with an axe. Its four legs were already gone.

In order to enter the yard, we had to step over ammunition, metal containers, leather satchels, and provision bags. Jackie explained that "her cousin" was visiting and the soldiers let us go in without any interference. They knew Jackie, and besides, they were quite happy being where they were.

I found Mother in the study, sitting quietly in her chintz-covered chair, which the soldiers had allowed her to keep. She had changed greatly. Her hair, once shiny and brown, was now streaked with white. She was reading a prayer book, her lips moving silently as she turned the pages.

As I came near, she raised her head slowly. We mutely studied each other.

"Hélène, you've come back!" she gasped in that soft voice of hers.

I sailed into her arms and held her tenderly. I broke down and cried, resting my head in the hollow of her neck. All mothers have this magic, tender, caressing touch, which brings comfort to a child.

"*Maman,*" I sobbed, "forgive me, please. If you only knew!"

"Now, *ma chérie,* don't cry. You have come home at last, and we are going to be happy again." Her old eyes were smiling.

My face paled, all of the life gone from my eyes; I retreated within myself, where no one could reach me. "I'm sorry, *Maman.* I don't think I can stay."

"So soon!" She sighed.

I had to lie once more. I hated to pretend to be carefree and scatterbrained, but I knew that Petit-Jean would be sending me away again. "*Maman,*" I said, deliberately forcing myself to use an easy tone, "I'm afraid I am going to have to disappoint you. I am only passing through on my way to the coast to meet some friends."

She did not answer, but moved away from me, her face

reflecting what her heart feared. She was actually convinced that I had wandered away from home forever.

I wanted to cry out, to explain that my feelings for her had never changed. I looked at Mother's small features, the tightness about her eyes and the lines on her throat, and shook my head. She was so unaware of war and violence.

Doing her best to change the subject, Jackie took Mother affectionately by the arm. "*Maman,* look at what Hélène has brought you."

Like a magician opening her bag, Jackie began to remove the food and display it on the table. Mother stared at me, then at the provisions. She thanked me in a polite, detached tone, then left the room.

Out in the hallway, two artillery soldiers had their guns sprawled next to them on the floor as they rearranged cartridges and ammunition. They were blocking Mother's way. Needless to say, they didn't budge, but the officer in charge of the detachment, a man in his middle thirties, walked over to Mother and, with a certain aristocratic manner, clicked his heels and said, "Madame, do you wish something?"

She looked at him. "Soldiers, guns, killing. Is this all the Germans want?" She hadn't raised her voice.

"We are a warrior nation," he answered in a calm, restrained tone. "For us it is almost a cult. The German nature is to fight." He spoke with a very polite smile on his lips.

Mother shook her head wistfully. "Fanatics! You are all fanatics!"

The soldiers were listening to her.

"*Raus!*" the commanding officer barked.

They jumped to their feet and gathered their equipment on the run.

Mother went by.

Arms folded behind his back, the captain stepped aside.

Jackie and I looked at each other in dismay.

"How did she dare to talk to him like that?" I whispered to my sister.

"She just doesn't realize the danger," Jackie said.

We heard the rattle of a key turning in the lock after Mother shut her door tight. Her books provided a great escape from all of her worries. She had been a scholar of world religions, particularly Buddhism and Hinduism. She sometimes locked herself in her room overlooking the rose garden and read until dawn.

I felt disconcerted and stood near the stairs, unsure of what to do. Finally, I went up to my room. With the door shut behind me, I sat down on my bed and closed my eyes.

⚜ ⚜ ⚜

I didn't know how long I had been napping when Jackie called, "Let's get going. You shouldn't stay here too long, it's not safe."

Reluctantly, I went to the bathroom to wash. A cold shower revived me, and I dressed again. After a last glance, I closed my door quietly, shutting out the tender memories of my youth.

Jackie was waiting in the dining room. The wooden shutters were partially closed to admit just enough air to keep the house cool.

I leaned against the massive oak buffet and viewed the familiar room. I could picture the family sitting around the table: my brother Maurice teasing me, Philippe laughing,

Father scolding us in his stern but affectionate way, and Mother always there to pacify and console.

"Ready?" Jackie was at the door. "We ought to be on our way."

She took me by the hand. "Please don't go see *Maman*. She'll cry if you go now. Besides, the Germans might wonder what's going on."

Seeing me waver, she added, "I don't mean to be unkind or make you angry, you know. I've missed you too much! I'm just trying to protect all of us. Don't think I don't know what you have been going through!"

"You are right," I sighed, "but you must admit that it is hard for me to be denied everything, after being away so long!"

Some of the Germans were in the garden on KP duty and did not take much notice of us when we left. A cook, his waist covered with a dingy, soiled apron, was feeding his field stove with what was left of Father's desk.

✤ ✤ ✤

Early that evening, Jackie and I strolled arm in arm toward the Restaurant Glacier. She was happy to see that I had regained some of my spirit, and she babbled incessantly.

It was still very warm outside, and there was a restrained excitement in the air that seemed to mount as the hours went by. The news of the Allies' landing in the South had brought back long-awaited hopes of freedom. Men in short sleeves, women in cotton dresses, and children in their Sunday attire were challenging the German law that forbade the gathering of more than three citizens in the streets, under the pretext of "conspiracy or rioting."

Some sat on their doorsteps or stood on the sidewalks, busy exchanging the latest information from the BBC, laughing with the typical ebullience of the Provençals.

Jackie and I somehow felt sober, unable to grasp the meaning of the word *liberation,* now that liberation itself was almost within our reach. We preferred to wait, to be certain; we didn't want to experience any more delusions, any more thwarted hopes.

The Restaurant Glacier had tables outside facing the Casino Municipal. We sat down. Soon, an old waiter, white napkin folded over his arm, arrived with a carafe of wine. "Compliments of the owner," he said formally. "We are celebrating."

Petit-Jean had given Jackie a false ration card, so we splurged and ordered steak made of horse meat, garnished with turnips, and a dandelion salad. Glasses in hand, pride shining in our eyes, we solemnly toasted the Allies.

Near the end of dinner, Jackie produced her ration card. She carefully tore two meat tickets out, plus two others for bread, and handed the tickets to the waiter, along with the exact change.

In a lighter mood, we walked to the room I had rented. We had regained our feeling of closeness and were discussing our dreams and secrets. Neither of us found reason to despair now that we were together again.

Jackie sat among the pillows, listening to me tell about my trip to the Pyrenees with the pilots. Pouring my heart out, I found relief, having someone close to listen and understand my loneliness.

Jackie's hand took mine. "How selfish I have been! To

think that all this time, you were hiding out, and I didn't do anything to try and help."

"I didn't want you to come. Petit-Jean told me to stay put. But tell me, what happened to Didier? How did he die?"

Jackie shook her head sadly.

"You are going to cry," she said softly. "He was with his radioman and another agent at the landing in Normandy. They decided to spend the night at a farm near Sainte-Mère-Eglise. The farmer betrayed them. The radioman and the other agent escaped, but Didier was shot in the courtyard. It took him two days to die. The Germans watched him lying there on the ground and never helped him. They ate and drank as they watched his agony."

Tears were running down my cheeks. I couldn't talk or think, and I withdrew into my shell, where no pain could reach me.

I heard Jackie's voice again after a long silence. "Hélène, are you all right?" Her hand touched my face affectionately.

"Yes, I'm all right now." The sadness was still there, but we began talking of other matters.

I smiled kindly. "Tell me about yourself. I have the impression you have something important to tell me. Would it be about Petit-Jean?" I pointed at the aquamarine ring on her finger.

Jackie's eyes suddenly brightened, and she nodded. "Our work together has brought us closer than I expected. I'm in love with him. We're now making plans," she said, looking fondly at her ring.

"I envy you," I told her, a trifle frustrated. I shook my head. Depressed, I continued dryly, "Do you think I will ever find someone? I want to fall in love like you."

Jackie looked at me, those green eyes of hers offering sympathy. "Don't worry, *chérie*. When real love comes, you will know it. It will happen when you least expect it. Take my word."

✤ ✤ ✤

The next day, Jackie and I went to meet Petit-Jean at the Café des Deux Garçons on the Cours Mirabeau. While sidewalk cafés were no longer the scene of merriment that they'd been in the prewar days, one could still meet friends there and cautiously discuss the latest events in low tones.

"What's holding him up?" Jackie said impatiently. He was a good twenty minutes late. I shook my head and glanced around. We both knew the rules: don't wait much longer than the time indicated, and move to the next meeting place before you bring attention to yourself. We were just about to do that when Petit-Jean arrived. I saw him first, heading toward us with a newspaper in hand. He hadn't changed very much. His wavy hair was cut shorter than usual, and his eyes, partially hidden by the rimmed glasses, looked unusually tired. However, his smile, which was sometimes boyishly innocent, was just as warm and friendly as I remembered.

After kissing Jackie, as a lover does, he took a chair and signaled a waiter. "A glass of beer," he ordered. When the drink arrived, Petit-Jean settled back. Then, bending slightly over the table, he quietly started outlining our next assignment.

"You already know that the landing on the Mediterranean coast has started," he said. "We desperately need tactical intelligence about the strength of German troops in the lower Alps, particularly around the towns of Apt and Manosque. A radio operator is already there waiting for you. We have been told by one of our agents that a unit from the Ninth Panzer Division is now making its way in this direction. Our job is to locate them and find out what their unit consists of. I understand they are being escorted by infantrymen. This has to be investigated and reported to our radio operator."

Petit-Jean was flirting with Jackie as he talked, putting his arm around her shoulders.

"You are to leave the village of Pertuis as soon as possible, and I'll meet you in Apt tomorrow morning at eight o'clock. I have to stay behind to meet Bibendum, the ringleader of the parachute drop section. Wait for me at the marketplace. We will then proceed to Apt to pick up our radioman. Keep your eyes open on the road. Any details, no matter how small, should be reported."

He took a cigarette from a pack of Gitanes he removed from his pocket, then left the pack on the table.

"There are a couple of miniature printed booklets rolled inside the pack of Gitanes," he said, "which will identify enemy insignias, matériel, and troop descriptions. Hide them carefully. In the folded newspaper, there is also a map, passes, and letters, all of them with falsified German seals."

Jackie deftly picked up the cigarettes and placed them in her pocket. Petit-Jean bent over and gave her a kiss. They exchanged a look that left no doubt about their being deeply in love. Had a member of the Gestapo been seated nearby, he would have never realized that Petit-Jean was passing orders to agents of the OSS.

He stood up, leaving some change on the table. "I must be off," he said, kissing Jackie good-bye again. "Don't forget our date tomorrow. Take care."

He gave me a peck on the cheek and went his way, turning right on the rue Clemenceau.

I began thinking about our new problem—transportation. No cars were available, since they had all been confiscated. Buses and trains no longer traveled in the direction we were going.

Taking the newspaper with us, we strolled along the tree-lined Cours Mirabeau, trying to plan our next move. Jackie was not much help, for her thoughts were still with Petit-Jean. Finally, she focused on the problem at hand.

"What are we going to do about transportation? Let's stop at Anne-Georges's home."

"No! It's unfortunate that Beaugard is so ill. Frankly, I don't want to ask Anne-Georges. For some reason I don't feel at ease in her company. Petit-Jean should have arranged something for us," I complained.

"He has so much to do. He's counting on both of us," Jackie assured me, taking his side.

I just shrugged, annoyed.

We drifted along the Cours Mirabeau, listening distractedly to the liquid sound of the fountains, all the way to the Rotonde.

Across the street was the German police station. Huge granite caryatids embellished the portal of the occupied sixteenth-century mansion. A rack of requisitioned bicycles had been installed to the side of it. A sentry paced back and forth in front of the building, guarding the vehicles.

We watched, undecided, then Jackie turned to me. "Shall we do it?" she asked, grinning mischievously.

I gave her a smile back. "You suggested it, so you do it. I'll wait here."

The routine was simple; it had worked before. Jackie would engage the guard in conversation, while I "re-requisitioned" one of the bicycles.

She approached the man, flirting outrageously. *"Wie gehts, mein Lieber?"*—"How are you, my love?" she asked him.

The man, captivated by her charm, paused, a stupid smirk on his lips. He then continued on his beat while she accompanied him. Highly pleased with himself, the *Boche* kept on jabbering away in pidgin French to Jackie, who made sure that his back was turned to me.

This was my cue. I jumped on the first bike available and began to pedal. Bemused by Jackie's come-on, the soldier didn't even notice when I passed by. Taking a roundabout route, I made my way home, where I hid my new acquisition behind a large water tank in the garden.

Jackie arrived home shortly after, laughing at the episode. She also had a good giggle about the German, who had made a date with her for after-duty hours.

To obtain a second set of wheels, Jackie telephoned the local police station. She talked, while I watched from the kitchen door to see if anyone was around. After a great deal of arguing and nagging, a Partisan named Louis agreed to let her have his own bicycle.

It would have been unwise to do much packing, so we gathered a few belongings and piled them into Jackie's camping rucksack and brought it down to the dining room.

We were going over the map planning our route to Pertuis when Mother came in from the garden, removing her wide-brimmed straw hat. Guessing that we were preparing to leave, she made a desperate attempt to stop us.

"Oh, please," she said. "Stay home, both of you!" Suddenly, she looked shriveled in her black dress. The bones of her face seemed more prominent, and her eyes were deeply hollowed.

I decided then and there that I had kept my promise to Beaugard long enough; enough covert stories, enough lies. For once, the truth! This time, at last, we had to try to make her understand the gravity of the situation.

I poured out my heart to her.

After hearing the secret I had kept from her for years, Mother had to steady herself at the edge of the table. Jackie helped her to sit down.

She turned her gaze to me. Forgiveness was in her eyes.

"Oh, Hélène," she said helplessly. "Why didn't you tell me?"

"*Maman,* it was for your own safety—no other reason!"

I could see the blue veins marking her temples through the almost transparent skin. Mother wasn't angry, only hurt. She saw me as a different person. Instead of a party girl, I was a young woman consumed with burning determination. Her eyes told me that she was very proud.

Kneeling, I placed my head in her lap, and Mother caressed my forehead lightly. For a brief instant, I was simply her little girl again.

Mother started to talk, but Jackie and I didn't let her continue, afraid of being swayed by her feelings.

"*Maman,*" I said, "we love you so much!"

We were interrupted by a noise at the doorway. A German officer stepped in, followed by four men carrying a wounded soldier.

Jackie opened the buffet drawer and slid the map we had been studying inside.

The captain pushed us aside and helped stretch the soldier onto the dining-room table. The wounded man's face, arms, and legs had been horribly burned, the skin blistered and red. He appeared to be in his sixties; the old and the very young were the only ones left for the German army to call to duty.

"Perhaps *Maman* will understand now what war is about," Jackie whispered.

To our surprise, she reacted calmly to the situation. In a hushed voice, she asked the captain, "What happened to this poor man?"

"His gas tanker was hit on the road. The other man is dead."

Mother shook her head sadly. "There is no mercy any longer. God has abandoned us. Can you do something for him?"

"I'm afraid not. We have been cut off from our medical corps since morning."

She went into the kitchen and brought back a small bowl containing her monthly ration of cooking oil. Delicately, she dabbed the soldier's face with the oil, lubricating the seared flesh. The man was in shock and didn't respond to her touch. She dropped into a chair, sobbing quietly.

The German captain approached her and said in halting French, "Thank you, madame, for your kindness." Then he left the room without another word.

"*Maman,*" I said, bending over, "please forgive us. You know we have to go. We must. The Americans will be coming soon."

She faced us without heroics. "I understand now, and I am proud of both of you. You have my blessings and my love."

I gazed into her soft, brown eyes, giving her a special, warm smile of thanks while kissing her gently on both cheeks. "Dear *Maman,* you *do* understand, don't you?"

"It isn't really understanding," Mother admitted, "so much as it is surrendering."

We went together to the door and kissed good-bye once more.

"Please, be careful," she told us, holding on to the door as she watched us leave.

CHAPTER THIRTEEN

Crossing the Bridge

I t was scorchingly hot outside, for it was August, and the South of France was in the middle of a heat wave, but we did our best to stay cool in our shorts and sleeveless blouses.

We pedaled for about an hour without speaking, still upset about having to leave home.

"I wonder what Henri looks like," muttered Jackie, lost in her thoughts.

I peered at her sideways and laughed. "Who's Henri?"

"You've been away too long. Don't you remember Monsieur Henri? Petit-Jean told us that he is the OSS chief in Algiers. All of our orders come from him."

"Oh yes, I remember now."

"We are supposed to work for him after the landing."

"That's all we need, a fussy old coot!" I commented. "He probably hates women. He'll have us cooped up in an office somewhere filing documents for posterity!"

"That'd be a change!" Jackie chuckled.

We passed a peach orchard on the country road. The fruit was thick; much of it lay rotting in the grass. Obviously, the Germans didn't have time to do the harvesting, and the farmers were gone, having abandoned their crop.

It was too good to resist.

Jackie braked and laid her bike in the irrigation ditch. Holding on to one of the lower branches of a tree, she shook some fruit down. "Come on, join me," she urged. "No one is watching."

Dropping my bicycle, I ran to the first tree. I grabbed the biggest peach I could reach. We giggled at each other while munching the fruit, then helped ourselves to some more. Finally, we got back on our bikes and headed off.

We were beyond the hamlet of Venelles when I called out, "Look there," pointing to a small grove of mulberry trees. In the midst of the foliage I had spotted an enemy ammunition train. A few soldiers were guarding the convoy. Most of them, though, were lolling in the leafy shadows, asleep or playing cards.

We paused near the tracks and leaned busily over our wheels. Jackie forced some air into the tires, and one of the men came over to investigate. Reassured that we posed no threat, he offered his help, while I methodically noted in my mind the number of boxcars and their location—good intelligence information to pass on to our radioman in Apt.

Jackie smiled thinly at the German and thanked him before we headed off.

A single road lay to the east, stretching toward the looming hills. From our position, we could see a narrow line of enemy vehicles on the horizon. Like a procession of ants, trucks, mobile antiaircraft and light machine gun vehicles, and a number of foot soldiers inched toward us.

All of a sudden, a P-47 aircraft roared overhead. Mercilessly, it began raking the convoy with machine-gun fire.

We quickly tossed our bikes into a nearby ditch and raced

for shelter in a sunflower field on the other side of the road. We got down on the ground and lay completely still. The earth was hard and unyielding, and sweat stung our eyes.

The fighter plane made another dive and again began strafing the Germans. Their antiaircraft gun blew up, then several convoy trucks got caught in the fire. The detonations reverberated around us like a cannonade. The Germans must have been carrying fuel, because a long column of black smoke rose into the sky.

The plane leveled off and headed toward the coast. Its wings changed from silver to black as it slowly disappeared into the horizon.

Awestruck, I stole a glimpse at the convoy. Men were scurrying in all directions as flames darted from truck to truck. Within moments, the entire wreck was ablaze.

Taking advantage of the confusion, we crossed the field, stumbling along with our bikes. Soon we reached the main road again.

Next came the crucial test.

Not far ahead was the bridge that would take us across the Durance River. It was supposed to be well guarded by the enemy, but we had been provided with the necessary forged papers, so we were not overly concerned. What really worried us, however, was the fact that the bridge appeared to be deserted. We stopped, observing the guardhouse suspiciously.

"No one's around. A little odd, don't you think?" remarked Jackie.

We moved closer.

"The bridge has been bombed!" I exclaimed. "The guards must be dead."

The nearer we got, the more craters there were in the roadway. The eight-hundred-foot span lay twisted over the river, the cables sagging limply. In the thick mud of the riverbank, we could see the grim outline of one of the large bombs. It had failed to explode. Its gray, angry nose was pointing upward.

We sat dispirited at the edge of the river, cooling our dusty feet. Tiny tadpoles darted away from our toes.

"How do you feel?" asked Jackie as she rubbed her sore feet.

"Worn out!"

"Me too. I don't think I can keep my sandals on," she moaned. "I have blisters all over my heels!"

She got up, barefoot, and I followed her along the rocky stretch. We explored the riverbank, searching for a crossing point, but soon determined that we would have to cross the bridge. The river was too deep and neither of us was a very good swimmer. Still, we had to reach the other side—Petit-Jean and the radioman would be waiting.

"We could cross by holding on to the sagging cable," I proposed, my voice sounding unsure.

Jackie was not the least bit enthusiastic about that idea. "I don't believe we can make it that way!" she said, shaking her head.

"Well, we don't have much of a choice." I looked at the bridge again. "I think we can get a pretty good grip on the loose cable, don't you?"

"If you say so."

Leaving our bicycles on the riverbank, we crept on all fours, soon coming upon the precarious cable. The hot metal seared our hands. The ledge supporting our feet was dangerously narrow. I bit my lip nervously. Uncertain, I looked down, and a wave of panic swept over me. "Jackie!" I screamed, almost losing my balance. "Help me!"

Below, the water spun and churned in ugly, yellow eddies.

Jackie inched her way to me and took a strong hold on my arm. Slowly, at a snail's pace, we edged across the large divide. Halfway across, Jackie yelled out a warning. "The plane is back! Hurry!" The aircraft must have been heading for another target because it kept going, passing us.

We finally reached the last arch in the bridge and lowered ourselves onto the embankment.

As soon as we set foot on the other side, a group of men wearing brown corduroy pants, black berets, and FFI arm-bands circled around us. They were armed with guns and looked hostile.

The Underground had taken over this territory. We had been prepared to meet the Germans, and our forged identification papers were designed to fool them. We hadn't expected to meet our allies.

We were searched, and once they found our papers, they took us prisoner.

Trying to make them understand who we were was useless. Guns were shoved at our backs. There was no emotion written on their faces. They simply ordered, "Let's go, girls!"

We were marched to Pertuis, then interrogated at considerable length by a group of Partisans led by a man with a peg leg. His name was Monsieur Martin. He was the village tobacconist, and had been a sergeant in the infantry during World War I. Our explanations fell on deaf ears. They had never heard of the OSS or its American headquarters in

Algiers, or for that matter, Colonel Beaugard and his network.

"Anick, Petit-Jean, Arnaud, the OSS, Beaugard? What kind of nonsense is this?" they demanded, laughing.

The Underground had a reputation for coming to their verdicts quickly. After a short discussion, the farmers finally admitted that there might be a grain of truth to our story. They decided to wait until the next morning, when Petit-Jean was supposed to arrive to meet us and, we hoped, set things straight.

I had told them confidently, "After all, we are in your hands and cannot escape."

On that note, we were promptly locked up in a pigsty for the night.

Around eight o'clock that evening, one of the FFI men brought us some food on a tin plate, a mixture of eggplant and tomatoes, smothered in a horrid sauce consisting mainly of fat. We were famished after the long, eventful journey but too repulsed to eat. Hellish fleas mercilessly bit our bodies, and lice crawled across our scalps.

A guard stood watch at the door. He was a gangly, acne-pocked fellow, with an old, bolt-action rifle slung over his shoulder. The scratching and twitching of his two prisoners made him laugh inanely, his protruding eyes watering from his laughter.

We were squatting on filthy straw, feeling awful. I had tried hard to control my bladder, but it was aching from the long effort. "I have to go," I said piteously to Jackie.

"Me too. Ask the guard."

I began moving forward, my feet slithering over a film of

greenish slime. The guard's back was half-turned. I pulled him by the sleeve.

"Yeah? What do you want?"

"We must go to the outhouse."

He rubbed a hand on his chin. "I'll have to come along."

He reached for the lamp hooked to the wall. It swung, flickering momentarily.

In that split second, I thought we might be able to jump him, but unfortunately, the rest of the band was camped outside the door.

The guard, apparently reading my mind, looked at me sharply. "No games. You hear? Or I'll shoot!"

He lifted the lamp at arm's length and unlocked the door. A dog yapped as we walked single file along the path in front of the guard. He pointed to a small wooden hut in the nearby field. "In there," he grunted. We would have known anyhow, from the stink.

The shed was about five or six feet by four feet, and as my eyes became accustomed to the gloom inside, I saw a hole in the ground with a plank of wood on each side. I stepped in first and tried to close the door. The nose of the guard's gun stopped it from closing. "Now, now," he nagged.

I couldn't wait any longer and crouched down as he watched. Soon, Jackie replaced me.

"Hurry up," the guard urged. "We can't spend all night out here."

On our way back, several gunshots broke the stillness of the night.

"German snipers!" howled the guard, flattening us to the ground. The rest of the FFIs were now firing from the barn. The skirmish was short-lived. Cautiously, we made our way back on our hands and knees. Our nerves were totally jangled. Nonetheless, exhaustion won out, and back in the pigsty, I closed my eyes for what seemed like only a few minutes.

Around one in the morning the door of the barn flung open and the guard was knocked down with the butt of a rifle. Three men wearing the Communist FTP armbands swaggered in, prodding Jackie and me with the snouts of their guns. They gave orders to follow them to their camp on the outskirts of Pertuis.

We had been prepared to cope with the Germans but had not expected to be held captive by our own countrymen First seized by the FFIs, now we were the pawns of the FTPs!

Perhaps these FTPs thought we were important hostages, and they wanted to receive credit for our capture. And if we were as we claimed, real American intelligence agents, they would use us as barter for the future, especially when the Allied landing in the South had been completed.

Less than an hour after our abduction, Peg Leg, the FFI chief, presented himself to the rival camp with a dozen men in tow, demanding to speak to the Communist leader. Peg Leg's men were armed to the hilt and looked furious.

They launched a barrage of vile obscenities, dire threats, and vulgar, tight-fisted gestures. The Communist leader made the mistake of pointing his weapon at Martin, whose bodyguards disarmed him and kicked him savagely to his knees.

Following a long pause, the FTP man gave us back to the FFIs. "We'll meet again," he hissed angrily. "I'm not finished with you bitches," he warned.

Morning arrived all too soon. Too tired to move, I watched
my sister get up with great effort. She had just awakened and
had a drugged look on her face as she stretched her arms and
legs in an attempt to ease the stiffness that had set in. The
smell of our bodies was revolting.

A woman from the village brought some soup in a large
pan—a watery brew with a few greasy potato slices floating
at the top. We ate what we could, and after allowing us to
bathe our faces and hands in the watering trough, two FFIs
unceremoniously marched us to the center of town, where
the meeting with Petit-Jean was to take place.

In the village square, a fountain splashed gaily, and women
performing their morning chores filled their buckets. As we
passed, they pointed and laughed. Jackie and I were now the
subject of local gossip.

Eight o'clock . . . nine o'clock . . . ten o'clock came and
went. Growing fear paralyzed us. As the empty hours passed,
we silently reviewed our recent experiences and thought of
Petit-Jean's fate. Had he been captured? Had he been in an
accident? Would he ever show up?

"Where in God's name is he?" Jackie murmured.

I shrugged helplessly and gave another look at the street
corner. It was empty.

Our dilemma was grave indeed. We knew the Underground was quick to try and sentence any individual believed
to be a traitor. At this point, they were convinced that we
had lied to them. None too gently, the guards led us to the
city hall.

I had been in the field long enough to realize that by now
our chances for survival were slim.

A final trial was conducted. There were no preliminaries,

no formalities. I studied the jurors' stoic faces and saw no mercy.

When it was over, we listened to the head juror read the charges: "These women are collaborators against France. The proof is undeniable. The papers they were carrying have German seals. There is no truth in their bizarre story of being with the American network."

"I agree," Monsieur Martin said harshly, standing up behind the table. "Girls, you are guilty of treason. The penalty is death."

All of the men nodded in accord and started to leave, one by one, leaving Jackie and me with the guards. Their words were still reverberating in my ears as we were hustled back to the barn.

Around midday, the guards returned and ordered us to move. Perspiring profusely, I shuddered, feeling the coolness of a gun barrel poking into the side of my ribs. Jackie's mouth twisted grimly.

"Come, take my hand," I told her. The flat tone of my voice implied resignation to the inevitable.

She stood up, her body swaying.

At moments of extreme peril, the most obscure, even odd, ideas come to mind. I had a weird thought: What would be said about our disappearance after the war? Missing in action? Executed by mistake? Of course not! No one would ever admit that a mistake had been made. Nothing would be mentioned. We were just a couple of girls lost in this great, big, ugly war, and would be forgotten as if we had never existed. It was so much easier that way, simply scraped off into oblivion with no explanations, no complications!

I was suddenly overwhelmed with self-pity. How sad it was

to have fought so diligently, to have given my life for a cause, without ever knowing the outcome. I lowered my head and laughed bitterly at the irony of it all.

The stillness and the heat in the air were almost palpable, making it difficult to breathe. We were paraded through the village past hundreds of hostile faces. The hum of the crowd rose in waves like the buzz of a swarm of bees around a beehive. A sort of frenzy seemed to possess them, from the everyday housewives to the merchants, these self-appointed patriots who had never lifted a finger during the Occupation. These same people were now coming out in the street demanding justice, spitting at us as we walked by.

When we reached the café in the marketplace, a man motioned to us to sit on a bench inside and wait. His expression was neutral. Turning his back to us, he searched his pocket for a cigarette. He dug out a rumpled one, hesitated, then slid it between his lips.

Large beads of sweat formed on my forehead. I couldn't utter a word. What can you say when fear grips you and death awaits? I wanted to cry, but it was too late for that. I heard a vague whisper. Jackie was praying, "Dear God, please, don't let us die!" And I thought bitterly, Who can choose when to die?

We were rudely jarred from our ghastly, nightmarish thoughts by hoarse orders. Convinced our time had come, we huddled closer together. With the slow, clogged movement of a bad dream, the beaded curtain shielding the entrance parted and in swaggered Bibendum, the ringleader of the parachute drop section.

I recognized him immediately, even though he was rough and unshaven as he stood there in his khaki uniform. I have never been happier to see someone. It was like a visitation from heaven. My feet felt as heavy as lead. I stood mute, unable to move.

It took him a few minutes to adjust his eyes to the lack of light in the room. The moment he recognized me, he came forward and made a broad gesture of relief with his arms.

"I came in time!" he exclaimed. "Some of the FFIs on the road were boasting about capturing two girls. Anick, you were lucky. These men were getting ready for an execution."

"I know!" I managed to say, my voice raspy. "We had no hope left."

Bibendum shook his head, making his massive neck flex. "Come on, girls," he chided, "it's all over now."

He slapped us amicably on the backs and then paused to wipe his forehead. Following his orders, his own men had cleared the tribunal table installed in the middle of the café and had covered it with a red-and-white-checkered cloth.

We all sat, while Martin brought a bottle of red wine in one hand and glasses in the other.

"No hard feelings," he joshed with a broad smile, as if an insignificant misunderstanding had just been settled.

The sweat on my back was cooling as I stonily watched the pesky flies circle aimlessly near the ceiling.

"Is she your sister?" Bibendum asked, looking at Jackie, who sat next to him, pale and dejected.

"Yes," I answered automatically. My hands were shaking so violently that I could scarcely hold the glass that was being handed to me. I spilled the drink down my chin and a purplish stain splotched the front of my blouse.

Bibendum tilted his glass and took a large draft, then

smacked his lips in noisy appreciation. "Not bad! This home-made wine gets to you, though!" He laughed, turning toward me. "I was with Petit-Jean early this morning," he said, putting his glass down. He took the jug in front of him and refilled his glass. "Just one drop more."

His tongue made a sucking noise of enjoyment. He continued, "German snipers got Petit-Jean on the road. Couldn't do a thing for him. The bullet went straight through his heart! We've been hunting for you ever since."

Jackie jolted, then recoiled with shock. She did not utter a word. Her face colored and then went pale. She covered her mouth with the back of her hand as if to hush a cry. After standing up slowly, she went to the edge of the room, where the shadows were deepest.

Bibendum did not understand why she was hunched over in the corner. He wiped his forehead again. With each movement, his muscles rolled under his khaki shirt. His head looked hard under his close-cropped crew cut. He belched, the sound of a man whose stomach is pleased.

"The Allied landing is going fine," he told us. "Petit-Jean and I met last night, but there is no use continuing the mission without him. You are to join the SSS G2 outfit"— Security Service Section, a U.S. Military Intelligence division—"attached to the Seventh American Army in Saint-Tropez."

After taking another sip out of his glass, he continued. "We have no transportation available at the present. You will have to cross this side of the Lubéron on foot. It's not too bad. The main road is still blocked by the *Boches*. Contact Robert in the town of Apt. He was Petit-Jean's radio operator. He's staying at the Hôtel Bremondy on the main street.

Take him with you to the coast. I'll provide you with new passes."

I did not want to look at my sister. I sagged in my chair, cowardly. Feeling desperate for her, I tried to form comforting words in my mind. It was all so very hard to express.

One of the men, thinking Jackie was ill, had given her a stool near the open window. She sat, chalk-faced, absently playing with her ring. The tears falling on her hands must have been very bitter.

Coming forward, I took her in my arms. What can one say to a loved one to make them know that you care?

The heat seemed unbearable when we started for the mountain. The sacred hour of the siesta had come. Animals and their herders rested behind thick walls, while the sun probed mercilessly on our backs.

The road swung away from Pertuis. The heat was sucking us dry, and a mile farther on, we stripped to the waist. There was no one to see us on the lonely trail.

We passed a cairn, probably built by shepherds, a few stones set on top of each other.

It felt as if there was only us and the mountain ahead.

We did not have a bad climb, but it seemed to grow more massive and rocky as we moved up. For about another hour we pushed on without once seeing any sign of life or any movement other than a lone raven strutting among the bushes and some tiny lizards playing among the rocks and dry moss. The little creatures, with their jet-black eyes and panting throats, stopped to stare at us.

Our reddened shoulders and breasts began to burn. Midway up, feeling thirsty and hot, we sat down on a boulder and rested for a short while. Pertuis was already well behind us, hidden around the bend. We knew that the village would reappear as we moved farther on.

At last we reached the summit. It seemed like an oasis after the steep climb. A breeze drifted over the mount and dried the perspiration on our bodies. The earth was pitted with tiny crevices in which small, scraggly mauve-colored flowers grew. Except for the droppings of animals, probably goats, there was still no sign of life.

Jackie was leaning against a tree, her eyes glazed over. All of her dreams had been shattered. Tired and emotionally drained, I lay silent on a thick bed of pine needles. The fragrance of sage, growing wild on the slope, gave a spicy tinge to the air. I distractedly watched a hawk passing through the light blue sky, effortlessly riding the wind.

Both of us let our minds drift. Jackie's, no doubt, followed the road of sorrow. I wondered apprehensively what life would bring me. Would I be spared the loss and sadness that Jackie was experiencing? Would I be as courageous?

Abruptly, she stood up, saying in a taut voice, "We should be on our way, or we'll miss Robert."

"Will you be all right?" I asked.

"Sure."

I brushed the pine needles from my shorts. Since the descent would be easier, we put our blouses back on. The touch of the cotton cloth made my skin smart, as if it were on fire.

⚜   ⚜   ⚜

Upon entering the town of Apt, we passed by the communal washhouse, located near a cold stream that flowed from the mountain. Women were busy slapping and kneading clothes on the flat stone slabs at the water's edge. Sheets and underwear lay out on boulders to dry.

We proceeded to the hotel we had been told to go to and asked about Robert. The inn was run by a Partisan named Pascal, a garrulous old man we found sitting on the front porch, whittling a shapeless piece of wood with a razor-sharp pocketknife. He raised his head quickly when we mentioned Robert.

"You have come too late," he told us. "He left as soon as he heard of the death of his chief. As a matter of fact, he thought that you had been killed, too!"

Jackie rubbed her tired eyes. "Let's stay here until morning," she suggested.

We took the room vacated by the radio operator and ordered cheese and bread. Pascal brought the food upstairs.

Through the window I could see the locals out in force, in a fever of excitement. American tanks were coming up from the coast, and somehow the townspeople knew they were coming in their direction. Throngs gathered in the streets, placards posted everywhere: *"Vive l'Amérique . . . Libération . . . France est libre!"* Housewives were busily decorating their windows and doors with green foliage, in honor of the advancing liberators.

Incapable of joining in these joyful preparations, we lay on our beds, listening to the rumble of activity in town. We were too exhausted to sleep, and our backs and shoulders ached with a murderous sunburn.

At one point while we were resting, Jackie suddenly sat up. Her eyes were wide open, and tears trickled down her cheeks, gathering at her chin. "He's dead! He's dead!" she kept repeating.

I gathered her in an embrace, but there were no words to be said. Childlike, she pressed her cheek against my shoulder. I brushed her face, wet with tears.

A while later, a violent blast sounded. Jackie was now sprawled out on the bed, her head propped up on her elbow. In a tired voice, she said, "They're celebrating."

Alert, I sprang to the window, unprepared for what I saw: German tanks from the Ninth Division were making their way into town. The streets of Apt, which only a short time before had resounded with cheerful calls, now echoed with anguished cries. "The *Boches* are here!"

A head surfaced from one of the armored vehicles. The man's face looked fanatical under the SS beret and goggles. He wore the black uniform of the Waffen SS Obersturmführer. His Zeiss field glasses hung heavily around his neck.

"Get up!" I snapped, grabbing Jackie by the arm. "German tanks are here!"

She scrambled out of bed and snatched her shorts from the chair. Pulling on my shirt, I ran across the room and flung the door open. We both rushed downstairs, barefoot.

Pascal was in the main hall, holding his shotgun. In the confusion that ensued, he almost tripped over Jackie as he pushed his wife and their young maid into the cellar.

I opened the front door. People were scattering in all directions, and we ran with them.

A tank rumbled past and men followed, shooting at will. After bolting over a garden gate, we lay flat in the depths of a tomato patch. Then, keeping to the narrow lanes where no vehicles could pass, we struck out in the direction of the main road.

CHAPTER FOURTEEN

The Longest Night

After jogging for about the first mile on Route 100, we gradually slowed down, our feet tender from running barefoot on the fine gravel.

We passed a shrine that appeared to be perched on a small mound jutting up off the road. A bunch of once-colorful wildflowers, now withered in a rusty tin can, had been placed under a crudely carved crucifix. All around us the scenery was desolate—dry hills, a small parched creek lined with arid, white stones. Fluttering ahead, striped butterflies zig-zagged up and down, like feathers.

As we walked, we began to hear the sound of rolling pebbles. A young woman was coming down a dirt path, which led to a farm. She hadn't seen us yet.

At almost the same moment that we sighted her, five German soldiers emerged from behind a hill. Nearby was a decayed stone wall that at one time had been part of a hovel. It offered some shelter, and skittering and tumbling, Jackie and I jumped behind it, landing in a large bush of blooming gorse. The stunted branches whipped and scratched our faces and legs, leaving long, red streaks.

We lay as if turned to stone. Bees buzzed around our eyes and noses, gathering pollen out of the delicate yellow flowers.

The woman kept on coming down the path, slowly, her head down, searching for ways to avoid the rough spots in the road. With both hands she pulled her cotton top down over her obviously swollen abdomen. At last, she looked up, noticing the soldiers. Her pace slackened immediately, and it was clear that she wanted to turn and go back the way she had come.

The men were close now, and she evidently decided to try and walk by them. Pulling her shirt even tighter around her figure, she advanced. They met in front of our hideout.

The woman attempted to pass on the left, but a short, stocky NCO, in charge of the German patrol, grabbed her by the arm as she tried to go by and threw her into the hands of the man next to him. The two of them pushed her around, almost as if they were playing ball with her, and she stumbled on the slippery pebbles. She said nothing but was quivering all over. Her black hair, unfolding from her untidy chignon, gleamed in the sunlight.

The instigator of this game caught her once more. This time he held her by the collar, then ripped the shirt open, exposing her breasts, which were enlarged with pregnancy. The woman mumbled something, a sort of inarticulate plea.

One of the soldiers said a few words in his guttural language, and they all laughed. Then he dragged her by the hair across the rough path into the bushes.

I saw Jackie close her eyes tightly, and felt her faint against me. I covered my mouth with my hand so that I would not cry out. We could hear the woman weeping and begging. After a short while, one of the men came out of the underbrush with his fly open, holding her panties. Then there was another, and another. . . .

Suddenly a dreadful, heartrending scream shattered our ears. "Aaah!"

The German soldiers continued on their way by the stone wall, the crunch of their boots treading the dry soil, fading as they went down the hill.

The silence had a different quality now. A blue jay flew up from the parched bracken, rattling twigs with its wings, and in the distance the pine trees stirred, rustling their branches. We waited a good fifteen minutes, then crossed the trail.

As soon as we reached the spot where she lay, my head snapped away in a reflex action. The woman's body had been discarded behind a rock. She had been ripped open with a short-blade bayonet. Stark horror was frozen in her eyes.

I shut my eyes, hoping never to have to open them again. I tried to believe that this was only a horrible nightmare, that the vision would go away. I blinked. . . . Dear God! The woman was still there, her mouth open in a final plea for mercy.

The survival instinct I had learned through my work shook me out of my paralysis. It gave me the strength to drag Jackie along past some bushes to the shade of a tree. Breathless and drenched in perspiration, I knelt down next to her. Jackie was inert, and I tried slapping her face. Her cheeks turned as red as a beet, and she began to regain consciousness.

She looked around, bewildered, as if she had lost track of things. Finally she straightened up lamely. "Are they gone?" she asked, trembling.

"The patrol was heading for Apt."

We remained there a while longer, then, without looking back, continued in the opposite direction.

We finally met a band of local Maquis posted on the edge of the road, and after showing the passes given to us by Bibendum, we informed them of the critical situation in Apt.

"There is a woman who needs to be buried almost a mile down the road," I told the men. "She's on the dirt road near a farm." I could say no more.

After living through Petit-Jean's death that morning, and then the ordeal on the road, Jackie began acting strangely. She had lost her normal vitality. Her face had changed in the space of a day. She looked worn, and the skin beneath her eyes was the color of chalk.

I, too, felt like an empty shell.

Around six P.M. a man who had been able to escape from Apt reported that the town was under siege and the enemy was searching all the homes for Partisans.

From our vantage point, we could hear the shooting. Through the leader's field glasses, we caught glimpses of German soldiers who, like a blight of locust, had begun to go through every house, smashing furniture and doors, ripping clothing and bedding, looting, and killing.

Antoine, the Maquis leader, took us to a truck hidden under some trees branches. It was loaded with weapons, some parachuted to them by the Allies, others stolen from the Germans. He handed each of us a Sten submachine gun, then some grenades. "We might be attacked during the night," he said dryly.

A recent order given by General Alfred Jodl, assistant to General Wilhelm Keitel, Supreme German Commander of

the Occupation Forces, had been placed on the streets walls
in every town as a warning:

> It has come to our attention that our troops do
> not act with sufficient harshness. Severe reprisal
> measures against the population of any dwelling
> showing insubordination must be carried out, to
> include the burning of villages, if necessary. Do
> not hesitate to shoot, hang, and set fire. Our
> headquarters will follow through, to ensure that
> our command has been performed with sufficient
> force.
> To summarize, there is to be *no exception*. For
> instance, when crossing territory infested by the
> French Underground, place French women in
> front of German convoys for protection.

Antoine, the head of this local Maquis, was a gaunt,
nervous man with narrow shoulders and shrewd, little
brown eyes. As fate would have it, the man accompanying
him was the FTP Communist who had threatened us in
Pertuis.

"So we meet again," the FTP spat.

Antoine wiped his hair away from his face, and told us to
go to the Americans and urge them to send a rescue party. As
he spoke, tension contracted his face to the point of ugliness.
The grenades hooked around his cartridge belt looked like
evil fruits dangling from the branch of a tree.

"I'll give you a driver and the small Simca parked near the
path. You must find the Americans. They'll listen to you,
since you are working for them," he said sharply. "If you

cross the German lines tonight, you can reach the town of Forcalquier by dawn. You should be able to make it, if you take the road to Reillanne."

The Communist from Pertuis had been listening to Antoine's words attentively. He slung his gun over his shoulder, and straddling his bicycle, left the camp.

Jackie had not said anything since the awful incident earlier in the afternoon. She pulled me by the arm, her hands shaking. She had a strange expression on her face when she whispered, "Let's wait until morning. Please, let's not go now!"

She had always been willing to go anywhere, anytime. Now her voice was troubled and her eyes were expressionless. For a moment, I weighed the alternative of staying here and letting someone else go instead. But we had to find the Americans. At least some good would come from all this death.

"The trip at night should be fairly easy," I said, not altogether certain.

Jackie finally agreed to go. Turning to me, she said soberly, "Take it, darling." She handed me the engagement ring Petit-Jean had given her. "I may not make it."

Her spirit was so low that a few pessimistic words would have been enough to sap all of her remaining strength. Placing my arm around her shoulders, I asked gently, "Jackie, can you go on?"

"Yes." She smiled a smile that appeared to light up her entire face. "I'll be all right. Don't worry." Then the light vanished and she turned away.

An improvised field kitchen had been installed at the foot of the hill, and one of the Partisans offered us a generous portion of thick, stringy vegetable soup in a can, with a slice of black bread.

Jackie pushed the food aside, then went to stretch out on the ground, where she rested her head on her folded arms.

Respecting her need for solitude, I strolled with the Maquisard to the edge of the temporary camp. We settled down with our backs against the trunk of a tree, where my companion tore up the bread with his fingers and hungrily sucked his soup from the can like a starving animal.

A short distance down the rutted trail, a man was sitting alone on a boulder, his hunting gun between his knees. He looked totally distraught.

"What's the matter with him?" I asked. "Is he wounded?"

"No, that was his wife whom you saw die on the road. He joined us only yesterday, when he heard the Allies had landed." He shook his head, distressed. "Life is shit," he said, then continued eating.

Antoine approached. "Are you ready?" he asked me.

I looked at him indifferently.

Frustrated, Antoine shook me angrily by the arm. "Do you hear me? Be on your way within half an hour. The car is ready," he ordered.

"Very well," I finally answered.

Night had yet to fall. A ray of light still outlined the ridge of the hills. The tiny black Simca was parked a few feet away. I lingered awhile longer with the Partisans.

The driver waved impatiently from across the road. "Come on," he urged. "Let's be off."

There was no more time for rest. I called out, "Jackie, they're waiting for us."

Silently, she got up and joined me.

After getting into the back of the small car, I tucked my legs into the cramped space. Jackie sat in front next to the driver.

Progress was slow as darkness set in. For cover, we drove without our lights on. A brilliant moon was rising over the horizon, but the road was tortuous and narrow. Ahead, a hare hopped out of the bush. Hearing our car approach, its ears quivering, it turned and ran back into the shrubs.

Surrounded by an almost unnatural silence, we drove at a slow pace through the night to our unknown destination. The Simca snaked over the moonlit route, its canvas roof flapping and rattling too much for our liking. Jules, the driver, stuck his head outside the car every so often to keep the car on the road.

My conscience was nagging me, urging me to turn back. I couldn't stop thinking of Jackie's premonition. Still, we had to reach the Americans before dawn. I chose to go on, thinking that her foreboding had been triggered by the horrors of the day.

After a while, Jackie suggested I switch seats with her. "It's your turn to relax," she said.

"No, not yet."

But she wasn't listening. She had already stood up, her legs straddling the front seat. Without thinking, I followed suit.

Just as we settled down in our new positions, shots rang out from the side of the road. It was the crackling, shattering noise of submachine-gun fire.

Jules frantically pressed the accelerator to the floor in an attempt to get away. Hunched over the wheel, he shouted, "The sons of bitches have spotted us! Get down!"

I clawed madly at the seat, instinctively bending over. My chin was between my knees as the car lurched crazily under the sudden speed. It swerved onto the shoulder of the road, and my head slammed against the dashboard.

Looking up, I could hear voices bellowing and cursing in German as shadows ran along the side of the road. The sounds faded as we drove on, stunned.

A short while later, from the opposite side of the road, a second fusillade hit the car. This time it was from a single automatic weapon. There were flashes in the dark. Jules kept on ducking and bobbing his head, while watching the road as best he could.

In the back, Jackie tried hard to stay shielded. Instinctively, I covered my face with both hands as splinters from the shattered windshield flew in all directions. I peeked through my fingers and saw blood on my hands. Glass, like powdered sugar, was all over my lap, the front seat, and the floorboards.

I howled at Jules, "Don't stop! Don't stop! They'll kill us." He raced blindly ahead.

"We'll reach the village of Reillanne soon," he yelled. It was then that I heard Jackie cry out, "I'm hit!"

At first, I didn't understand the appeal in my sister's voice, for she hadn't screamed or shouted. Her muffled cry was one of distress, not despair. A lump traveled up and down my throat.

Amidst the gunfire and confusion, it was impossible for me to tell how badly Jackie had been wounded. The air began to escape from her lips in short, gurgling gasps. Helplessly, I reached into the semidarkness behind the seat and patted her gently on the head, talking to her as one might soothe a child.

The shooting stopped as quickly as it had begun. Silence returned. The uncanny quiet was suffocating.

Jackie was still. We were almost at a safe intersection near the foot of the hills where the village of Reillanne was located.

"Jackie, *chérie*," I said, touching her hand. "You are safe now. We can take care of you."

The car stalled, coming to a stop. I turned back in my seat. "Don't worry, we—" I stopped talking.

The moonlight was on Jackie's face, and I realized her expression had not changed. Her inert body lay piteously crumpled in the back of the car, her lips parted.

I took several long breaths, unable to regain control of myself. "She's dead!" I whispered, my hand holding my side, as if I had received the mortal wound myself.

That moment will prey on my mind every day for the rest of my life.

Unable to start the car again, Jules ran to the first house on the roadside, and I followed him several paces behind.

He banged at the door with his fist, but no one answered. I called out loudly, "We are French!"

There was movement in the house. A light shone on the second floor and heavy footsteps came down the stairs. "Coming, coming," said a drowsy voice.

A man poked his face out from the door, raising a smoky oil lamp in our direction. He was in a long nightgown and was rubbing the corners of his eyes. He stared blankly at us.

"What's going on?" he asked us. "The Germans are not far away, and this is no time to attract their attention!" he protested.

We told him of the ambush and what had happened to Jackie.

The man's wife joined him at the foot of the stairs. She had the strong, defined cheekbones of a peasant, her mouth full and wide. The light from the lamp gave her an earthy sensuality.

The man backed away into the shadowy house and beckoned to his wife. "What do they want? Send them away!" she pleaded.

"Hush, Honorine!" the husband admonished. "Go and wake up the mayor. Someone has been killed. By the Germans probably," he quickly added.

His wife let out an anguished cry and started trembling. She did not move.

"Go on. Hurry up," he insisted. "Go, while I get dressed." He backed away and started up the stairs. Oddly enough, he was fully dressed under his nightgown.

Resentfully, the woman threw a black shawl over her head and disappeared into the night.

Jules and I returned to the car to wait.

The road was deserted. Together, we removed Jackie's limp body from the Simca and set it down on the macadam. Against all security rules, Jules focused the headlights on her.

She was so pale! Perspiration, in tiny beads, moistened the locks of her dark hair. Already her green eyes had that faraway gaze that death bestows on the endless traveler.

Kneeling, I placed her head in my lap. I stroked her face and closed her eyes, tears welling up inside of me. "Oh, Jackie, Jackie," I sobbed uncontrollably, cradling her body in my arms, rocking back and forth. "What have they done to you!"

The most dreadful part of my sorrow was the utter helplessness I felt, the knowledge that I couldn't share my grief with anyone else, just my own heart. Fate had irrevocably closed the circle, and I was alone again.

"No, no, no!" I moaned, trying to deny or negate the sorrow that was drowning me.

"There was nothing I could do," pleaded Jules. He lit a cigarette with shaky hands.

I could see his pale, emaciated face fleetingly through my eyes, swollen with tears. Then the match went out.

I opened Jackie's blouse. The bullet had come through her back and pierced her left breast, leaving behind a grayish circle framed in blood. The bullet had gone through her heart—just like Petit-Jean.

Numb with shock, I stared at the wound with somber fascination. I was totally drained, my mind overcome with grief.

Fingers touched my arm. It was the farmer's wife, who had returned from the village. She was holding a folded white sheet. "It's all I can give you to wrap her in," she said apologetically. The woman appeared to want to tell me something else.

I took the linen from her hands and said, "I'll do it myself."

Her husband called from the porch, "Honorine!" He was buttoning his jacket. The armband of the FTP Communists was pinned to his sleeve.

Blindly, I wrapped my sister in the sheet. In life she had never been a heavy girl. Dead, she felt twice her weight. The sheet slid easily over the gravel on the ground.

I withdrew my hand, sticky with blood.

"Jackie!"

I let out a sob, loud and choking, so filled with anguish that I felt as though my heart had stopped beating. Turning away from the body, I ran toward a fountain a few yards away and rubbed my fingers in the water, as if to erase the indelible crimson stains.

When I returned, people were coming out of their homes, descending the hill, slipping out of the shadows, soundless and furtive like night predators. They came one at a time, or in groups of two and three. They appeared to be gliding more than walking toward Jackie's body, which lay on the ground in stark relief under the bright rays of the moon.

The Communist FTP from Pertuis was there among them, with the farmer and Jules.

They stared at the corpse as a hole was dug. Someone brought a French flag, and I wrapped Jackie in it.

There was no coffin. Jules and I placed her body in the crude grave, gently, carefully.

The village FFI leader was a doctor named Maurice Brun, code-named Pierre L'Hermite. He removed his beret and gave a brief eulogy: "Jacqueline, young girl of France, you gave us your courage, your belief, your life. In the name of France, in the name of my men, in the name of the Maquis, thank you and farewell."

I have no coherent recollection of what followed. It was as if life had slid away from me, as though my emotions were suspended. Bright pictures of our life together unraveled before me. I covered my face with my hands and remembered one of the last visions I had of Jackie alive, when she handed me her ring: "Take it, darling," she had said sadly, "I may not make it."

A sudden tremor shook my body.

✤ ✤ ✤

I remained at Jackie's grave for hours. The sun was rising, giving way to a clear, warm day. Lost in my sorrow, I did not feel the tap on my shoulder.

"Mademoiselle Anick, do you want to go now? The car needs repairs, but I have a motorcycle, and I can take you," a man from Reillanne was saying.

I nodded silently and got up, bleary eyed. I had no more tears. I felt barren.

My legs were still stiff from having knelt for so long, and I held on to the man's arm and spoke in a hoarse whisper. "I want to see a priest before going."

The man seemed annoyed. "You shouldn't waste time," he said. He was trying to get rid of me. I could feel it! I stared vacantly at him without moving.

"Oh, all right!" he said angrily, beckoning me to follow, then leading the way along the winding lane of the hill.

Darkness prevailed as I entered under the Gothic archway of the local church. My steps echoed along the cold marble floor. I dipped my fingers in the water stoop, and after genuflecting in the center aisle, moved directly toward the Virgin Mary's chapel to light a candle. I had to express the infinite emptiness of my heart to comfort my soul.

After dropping a coin in the wooden box nailed to the wall, I ignited the wick of one candle from another that had already burned to a gutted stump. It lit quickly, and I placed it in its holder.

I closed my eyes, humbly asking, in a hushed prayer, for relief from my grief. I felt faint and leaned against a pew, the fragrance of burnt incense intoxicating me.

Furtively, a priest passed by on his way to the sacristy. Discreetly, I signaled to him. "Father, please. May I speak to you?"

"What can I do for you, my child?"

Fixing my gaze on the priest, I tightened my lips. "Father, my sister was killed during the night."

"Yes, I've heard," he responded.

"You did?" I asked, my face hardening. I thought back to the burial. He should have been the first one to come, but now I recalled that he hadn't been there at all.

"I thought you would have been on your way by now," he told me.

There was that feeling again. Everyone here wanted me to go. *No, I must be wrong. He's scared, that's all! But then, what does he have to fear here?* I thought with contempt, looking around the house of God. *He certainly won't get killed in his own church!*

I opened my wallet and handed the priest all that remained of Petit-Jean's money. I was brusque and sullen when I asked, "Please, see that a cross is placed where she is buried, so I can find her grave when the war is over. And please, pray for her."

I left abruptly, in the middle of his blessing. Brushing it aside, I met my driver at the door.

The priest never looked up to watch me go. Something was very wrong.

I was leaving behind two unanswered questions:

First, the last burst of fire had come when we were close to the village. Why didn't the Germans, if it was them, follow us to Reillanne to arrest me and my driver?

And second, the villagers, including the priest, seemed nervous and wanted me to go. Why?

Perhaps one day after this wicked war ended I would find the answers.

✤

The Americans

T he road was clear, and we went speeding down the highway to meet up with the Americans.

At the entrance of the town of Forcalquier, we were stopped by our first U.S. military policeman. He scrutinized the motorcycle riders sharply, his helmet jauntily tilted to the side on his head.

I had to admit that we were an odd sight, the driver in civilian clothes, with a Sten gun slung over his shoulder, and his companion, a barefoot girl in torn shorts.

"ID cards, please," the policeman asked in English.

"What does that mean?" the driver from Reillanne asked me.

I shrugged. "I don't know."

The sentry summoned a man, who addressed us in French with the inimitable rolling *R*'s of a Canadian. "He wants your identification papers," he explained. We complied immediately. I gave him my pass from the FFI in Pertuis.

"I am with the OSS," I told the Canadian. "I have to report to SSS G2 Headquarters in Saint-Tropez."

He led me into a tent, where we met one of the officers in charge of the Task Force Butler Armored Division, a man who wore an eagle on his collar. The Canadian explained that the officer was a colonel.

I identified myself and the driver and gave an approximate location of the German Panzers, as well as a brief account of the ammunition train in Venelles, the enemy soldiers roaming the countryside, and the situation in Apt.

As I was talking, a courier walked into the tent and placed a large envelope on the folding table in front of the officer. Forgetting all about the two civilians for a moment, the colonel glanced at the contents, then spread out a scale map of the lower Alps. He immediately started to work, tracing red circles with a pencil and giving orders to his staff.

"What's the name of the town you were talking about?" he asked me through the Canadian.

"Apt."

He searched for a minute or so on the map, and upon finding the location, rested his finger on it. "I will do my best to send out a rescue unit. Unfortunately, I cannot give a precise date. Good luck," he told me, and left the tent.

Satisfied that action would soon be taken, the driver turned toward me. "I have to go back now to give the good news, if you don't need me anymore."

"Go ahead. I'll find transportation of some sort to reach the coast," I told him.

"I'm on my way, then."

We both stepped outside, and he got on his motorcycle and started the engine. With a broad smile directed at the soldiers milling around us, he commented, "Isn't it great to see the Allies!" And with that, he was gone.

Bewildered, I stood in the middle of the camp. The

foreigners moved busily around me, speaking a language I could not understand. No one paid any attention to me.

In an olive grove on the side of the road, a few men sunned themselves. Sitting under a dwarf tree, a group of GIs were warming up some food in tin cans. I couldn't help but be attracted by the aroma coming from there. I had had no food since the night before, and I began moving in their direction. As I approached, some soldiers looked up at me, surprised to see a woman among them. Others passed by, indifferent.

One man moved out of a semicircle, smiled, and pulled me into their group. Thinking I was begging for food, he handed me a mess tin filled with Spam and beans. I nodded in thanks since I knew no English. *"Merci."* I started to dig into my food.

"Hey, Anick!"

It was a familiar voice, and with a feeling of relief, I spun around abruptly, spilling the food off my plate.

It was Hellops. His handsome, bony face had that disarming roguish grin I knew so well. He was sitting on an empty oil drum, his legs dangling like a puppet's legs on a string. His soft brown eyes, almost sunken in their sockets, were watching me.

"What are you doing here?" It was all I could say to him, I was just so surprised to see him.

He jumped off of his perch. "What else? I'm on my way to the coast. How come you are alone? Isn't Petit-Jean with you?"

"He's dead. And so is Jackie!"

Hellops was silent for a long time. "When?"

I began to tremble all over. "Yesterday."

He seized me by the shoulders and shook me hard. "Stop

it!" he said firmly. "I know how much you must hurt, but you have to get ahold of yourself. I'm here with you."

The trembling subsided, and he held my shoulder gently as we walked around the camp. I tried matching his gait along the path.

"Come along with me," he suggested. "I'm going to Saint-Tropez." Tightening his grip, he continued, "We'll start all over again from there. We'll do it for Jackie and Petit-Jean."

I agreed with a weak smile, a wave of affection spreading inside me.

We took a path that led to the POL—the petroleum, oil, and lubricant post. At one point, Hellops, who was leading the way, stopped and turned to me. "Look, I even have transportation," he bragged, pointing to a black Citroën parked in the shade. "I filched it from the *Boches*. Now wait for me. I have some business to discuss."

Like any con artist at work, he used his talents so convincingly on the fat NCO in charge of the POL that in no time he was able to get an extra jerrican of gas.

Back at the car with me, he said triumphantly, "We can make our way to the landing now."

Shortly after, we took our leave of the Americans and headed toward the Mediterranean coast.

PART III

1944–1945

CHAPTER SIXTEEN

Pete

August 20, 1944

The Allies originally planned a simultaneous invasion of northern and southern France for May of 1944. The famous D day landing in Normandy was only half of what was meant to be a two-pronged attack. However, because the Allies were held up in Italy by German resistance, they were not able to attack the South of France until later that summer. By the end of August, the southern invasion, code-named Dragon, was in full swing.

In peacetime, Saint-Tropez was just another quiet little harbor bathed in sunlight. In the middle of war, it was unrecognizable.

Hellops and I could hardly believe our eyes that afternoon when, weary with travel, we drove into town. We were amazed by our first glimpse of the mass of mechanized military power moving up the beach.

The place was a hub of excitement. LSTs (liberty boats), liberty ships, and DUKWs (cargo amphibious trucks) filled the harbor. The seawater gleamed with rainbows of oil. Jeeps darted crazily in all directions, their drivers beeping urgent horns; trucks, men, and cars were everywhere. The sky was dotted with barrage balloons protecting the landing against any air attacks; only a few JU-88 German planes risked an appearance. And above this cacophony of mechanical noise, we could hear the deep thud of mines exploding along the beaches.

Hellops stopped the Citroën. A group of GIs were standing near a truck.

"Where is G2 Headquarters?" he asked them.

"Follow the harbor until you get to the main street," one of the soldiers answered. "It's the last hotel on the left, just outside of town."

When we arrived at the G2 Section, we were separated immediately and taken to different rooms for debriefing.

My debriefer was a French-speaking CIC (Counter Intelligence Corps) officer, about forty years old, rather short and slim. "I'm Captain Goyrand," he told me.

He got up from his desk, looking at me curiously. I must have appeared strange with my red puffy face and matted hair. The smell of the pigsty in Pertuis still trailed behind me. His nose wrinkled.

"Identify yourself," he stated in an impersonal tone.

I handed him the pass given to me by Bibendum, adding decidedly, "My code name is Anick, and I am designated H-1 in Colonel Beaugard's Underground network. I have been working with the OSS under the command of Petit-Jean, network Jacques I, of the Penny Farthing Chain."

I added, "Petit-Jean, as well as my coagent, Jackie, are dead. They were killed on our way to the coast."

"Oh." He showed no emotion. I didn't, either. What was the use? They meant nothing to him.

For about two hours, he plied me with questions. I discussed my last mission, Gestapo and Milice agents, recent sightings, as well as those political personalities who had been under investigation since the landing.

At one point the phone rang. Listening attentively, Captain Goyrand took notes.

After a few minutes he hung up and searched for his cigarettes. Finding them, he offered me a Camel.

"You're cleared," he said from behind his desk.

We conversed for a while longer in a more relaxed manner. After a vigorous handshake, the captain led me to the main room, where Hellops was waiting.

"Is everything all right?" he asked me.

"Yes. It will be fine, I'm sure."

An enlisted man handed each of us an armband with the American flag printed on it, which he pinned on our left sleeves. A U.S. insignia was added to our collars.

Shortly after, Hellops received further orders, then got ready to leave.

"Cheer up! It's our turn to win," he said. He gave me a kiss on the cheek. "Let's make a deal. When we receive the pay due to us since we started, and tickets to go to the States, let's go together."

This made me smile. "You forgot to add if all goes well!"

Like Hellops, I too had a destination: the SSS G2 Headquarters. I had been assigned to the original SSS staff of twenty-three, which had just landed.

A jeep took me there. I was delighted with the ride in that funny, bumpy, crazy little car. The wind blew through my hair and restored the color to my face.

The SSS G2 Headquarters was entirely separated from any other military installation. It was located in a villa that had once belonged to René Clair, the famous French movie producer. Its roof had been ripped away by a shell from one of the American Navy guns during the Landing.

I had been told to report to a Lieutenant Peterson.

"He's not here at the moment," said Girard, one of the agents stationed at the villa, in French. "I'll give you a room, though," he added. He led the way and I followed him across a long patio.

"Here it is," he said, gesturing for me to step through a large French window that was almost crumbling.

All that was left of the former bedroom were the four walls, a mattress on the tile floor, a cracked mirror, and one chair. The whole atmosphere was quite depressing. Still, the Americans gave me food, clothing, and—most important— a place to sleep. I desperately needed the rest.

Shortly after supper on the second evening, I stepped out of my room. The sun had set, and a blue haze danced along the tops of the olive trees. I watched a flock of swallows flying overhead. For what seemed a long time, I sat alone, listening to the sea, watching the waves playing along the shore. How much I missed Jackie! Such a tragic death, and when victory was within reach!

It was a moment of total depression. I felt completely alone in the wake of my sister's death. A void filled my heart, an emptiness that could never go away.

The four years I had spent with the Underground and the OSS had taken everything from me. I felt as though I did not exist. During my time with the Resistance, my own country and traditions had become foreign to me. Having lived in a permanent state of fear for such a long time, I felt like a hollow shell.

I thought of my early life. I had had a childhood filled with

love and tenderness, something I'd known so little of during
the war. All that happened seemed to belong to some book I
must have read a long time ago. I had known sleepless nights,
experienced desperation, wanted to run away, looked constantly over my shoulder, and could never relax ... and
Jackie, always Jackie! She had gone so quickly out of my life,
like someone who simply closes a door and vanishes, leaving
me alone, with the burden of living.

Looking back, I realized I had undergone such conflicting
emotions during those years. My body and mind could no
longer respond spontaneously to everyday life. I felt old and
used. Suddenly, my thoughts were interrupted by somebody
calling my name. "Anick, are you there?"

Surprised, I turned and looked straight into the face of a
tall, phlegmatic American in a paratrooper's uniform. "I'm
Lieutenant Peterson," he said, his slightly foreign accent
making his French pleasant to my ears.

We looked at each other without a word. His profile was
prominent against the now-colorless sky, etched like a sculp-
ture in stone. I noted the straight nose outlined with its
strong bridge, the tanned flesh, taut on high cheekbones, his
lips full and sensual.

I felt instantly aware of him, and a deep, unfamiliar thrill
ran through me.

Later, I remembered that he wore a scarf around his neck
made of a piece of parachute silk.

After a long talk, which extended into the early hours of
the morning, we walked, hand in hand, along the water's
edge, where a cool breeze carried the scent of the sea. During
the days that followed, I was overwhelmed with new feelings,
elated at any moment we could share together.

Jackie had been right. She had always said that war and

violence brought primal emotions to the surface that no one could control or prevent. Love had come when it was least expected. Pete's vitality fed my life and dispelled the sadness that weighed so heavily on my heart.

At first, I had little time to explore these feelings. I was to report to the OSS chief of the French desk, who was now at the Allied Forces Headquarters, in the Mediterranean Theater. He had arrived earlier, but had been treated at the nearest army hospital for a nasty bout of hepatitis.

His name was familiar to me. Jackie and I had talked about him only a few days before, trying to guess what he would look like. We had imagined a portly, middle-aged man, with a receding hairline and glasses. But Henry Hyde turned out to be tall, handsome, and young, with a charismatic appearance and green, restless eyes. He was always on the move, snobbish at times, and conscious of his own importance.

One minute he would utter a cutting statement, then the next replace it with a joke. His staff was staunchly loyal to him, though the one thing that distinguished him from them was his eloquence. A man of great intelligence, he spoke impeccable French and possessed an abundance of charm, which he used effortlessly. Until he arrived in France, French agents had known "Monsieur Henry" only through the many secret messages that had come from him and had been decoded under dangerous conditions. Now, he was a person, not merely a name.

One evening, I was about to doze off when Henry strode in with his usual swagger, sat on the edge of my mattress, and began talking. My head hurt, and I wished I could have slept, but he commanded attention.

Propped against a pillow, I talked about my missions and

life in France during the Occupation, while Henry discussed
the arrival of new agents and future missions. Soon I began
to yawn. Looking out across the patio, and beyond to the
inky dark water reflecting a full moon, I asked, "What time is
it? It's getting late."

He glanced at his watch. "Almost one A.M."

"Pete and I have a date tonight," I said, hoping he would
get the message. "I had better get some sleep."

Henry removed the cigarette from his lips and held it
carefully between his forefinger and thumb. "Sorry, not tonight," he replied irritably as he stood up to leave.

I looked at him and frowned with disappointment. The
consternation clearly written on my face seemed to annoy
him. He shrugged and said, "I doubt that he'll be back in
time. Pete is leaving on a mission at dawn. Good night."

Unable to sleep, I tossed and turned for hours, my anxiety
building.

At the breakfast table, Pete wolfed down powdered
scrambled eggs and bacon, followed by a cup of steaming,
black coffee. Burning himself in the process, he cursed.

I noticed his hands as he held the coffee cup. They were
long and lean like the rest of him. He stood up and looked at
me. I knew he was reading my thoughts. He cracked a broad
smile and said reassuringly, "I'll be here tonight. Don't
worry."

I nodded doubtfully as I watched him walk away. Tall and
lanky, he took long strides in his paratrooper's boots, an
obstinate expression on his face.

I submitted to fate. I didn't want to, but I had now accepted the sad fact that there was no hope, no future, and no
tomorrow. Survival depended on the luck of staying alive

from one day to the next. I had learned my lesson all too well, and I suddenly felt powerless against the overwhelming odds that dictated my destiny.

Around noon Henry Hyde drove up in a jeep with Girard and a Texan named Bill. "Let's go swimming. You need to get out," he said.

Welcoming the opportunity for a diversion, I agreed and we took off on the coastal route. Henry drove cautiously in the center of the road to avoid the mines buried in the soft ground.

The sea was warm and inviting, and even though the beach was off limits due to uncleared mines, we greatly enjoyed the swim.

Henry was unusually silent on the way back, and I suspected that something was up. After a while he declared, "Tomorrow, we head for Marseilles. Bill, you will team up with Parsons. Girard will take the two Frenchmen who came last night. Anick, you will go with Pete."

Back at the villa, the rest of the day dragged for me. I couldn't contain my restlessness thinking of Pete and his mission. It grew darker, and finally it was dinnertime. I had no appetite and went out on the patio in an effort to ease my mind.

A full moon loomed heavily over the sea. It was one of those incomparable Mediterranean nights.

Suddenly, I felt Pete's presence. At the same time, by some indefinable instinct, I sensed that something was wrong. Turning abruptly, I found my body against his, and my arms linked around his neck. He winced, a faint moan escaping him, and stepped back unexpectedly, almost losing his balance. He reached out and held on to the balustrade.

"Pete, what happened?"

"Get a jeep. We're going to the hospital," he said hurriedly. This was not the time for questions. I ran inside immediately to get help. A short while later, we were speeding on our way, with Bill behind the wheel. Pete was holding his leg, and along the torn trousers a dark, ugly stain was beginning to spread from the knee down.

Bill nudged my elbow. "Look under the seat. There's a bottle of scotch. Give it to him." Fumbling in the dark, I found the flask and handed it to Pete. He brought the neck of the bottle to his lips and gulped down several mouthfuls.

Before long we arrived in the courtyard of the dispensary, which was installed in one of the hotels near the water's edge. Bill helped Pete to the stairs, where a nurse took over. Large beads of sweat were running down his face. He looked pale. I followed the nurse, insisting on staying with him, but she brushed by me with evident irritation.

"Wait here," she ordered curtly, looking stiff and antiseptic in her white, starched uniform.

An ambulance was backing up to the door. An orderly came toward me. "What's the matter? Are you sick?" Seeing the blank expression on my face, he repeated in French, *"Vous êtes malade?"*

"No, I'm waiting for someone."

Nodding, he hurried past me.

"Watch it, lady!" someone said behind me. I looked over my shoulder. It was a patient, wrapped in a blue robe. His feet shuffled to and fro in oversized slippers. I pulled myself up and, moving aside, watched the man wobble down the stairs. Time inched by.

At last, the front door reopened, and I turned anxiously.

Bill came out smiling, and my face brightened. "What is happening? Is it bad?" I asked him.

"Okay, he's okay," Bill said reassuringly, "but they had to sew him up a bit!"

A moment later Pete was coming down the steps behind him, limping, but he was looking more like his old self. I stretched out a hand, and he placed his arm around my neck. We moved slowly toward the jeep, which was parked nearby. Bill and I helped him in, and as we lifted him by the arms, he winced painfully.

"Be careful. Stretch your leg," I said, concerned.

He laughed. I watched his face. It was good to hear him laugh, but I did not take things so lightly. "What happened?" I questioned, still troubled by the sight of his blood.

"I met a German patrol on my way back and got a knife wound before I could get away. I was lucky at that!"

Although he was making light of the episode, I could picture what he must have gone through. I drew closer and rested my head on his shoulder.

Hugging this moment to myself, I felt happy and light-headed.

Love was what I desperately wanted—not hate, not revenge, just complete surrender. I wanted to live through each hour, each minute, as though it would be my last. There was no other moment but now! I knew that nothing else would satisfy me.

Upon arriving back at the villa, Bill parked the jeep in front and went inside. "See you later," he said, and left us alone.

The sky was a deep, dark blue, studded with millions of shiny stars. This must be the way a love affair should start, I thought: unexpected, exciting, and promising. Pete had swept me off my feet.

The understanding in my eyes compelled him to wrap his arms around me. My lips met his, trembling, and we had a warm, soft, intoxicating kiss. Pete had to have felt the passion emanating from my body.

We spoke in whispers, while he stroked my hair, mussed by the sea breeze. "I'm falling in love with you," he said earnestly.

I realized that I had come to a turning point in my young life. Before the night would end, I would make love for the first time.

Together, we went inside. My room was dark, and the musty smell of mildew caught at my throat. I went to the window and opened the wide panel and shutters. At the edge of the terrace, the sea rippled in a restless sigh. That certain special magic of Riviera nights seemed to have spread its languid rapture just for us.

Pete turned his head, looking long and hard at me. Reaching out, he brushed my lips with his fingertips. "Anick," he whispered, the excitement mounting within him, making his voice slightly hoarse. He took me roughly in his arms, his mouth searching mine, and our passion grew.

We made love, again and again, wildly, desperation bringing ultimate fulfillment to our senses, for we knew that this glorious moment might never come again.

Dawn came, and I lay with Pete's arms around my waist, reliving the previous night.

The sky, with its touch of blue, rapidly unfurled traces of red into the clouds. A distant reef stood out from the sea through the light mist. My gaze went back to the beach, where sandpipers greedily pecked at the sand and the waves scalloped their frothy fringe of lace.

As the sun rose, we dressed without a word.

The night had been ours, alone. Today we were back in the battlefield.

01370

Number
Numéro

CIRCULATION PASS
Permis de Circuler

Name: (Surname / Christian Name)
Nom: DESCHAMPS HELENE

Address
Adresse 120 ROUTE DE NICE

AIX EN PROVENCE

Identity Card Number
Numéro de carte d'identité

Permission to
Autorisation de CIRCULATE IN

THE ZONE OF THE

7th ARMY

For the purpose of
Pour OFFICIAL BUSINESS

FOR G-2, SSS

THIS PASS IS VALID UNTIL OCT 24, 1944
VALABLE JUSQU'A

The holder may/may not be out of doors
during the hours of curfew.

Le possesseur peut/ne peut pas circuler
pendant les heures de couvrefeu.

Issued at 7H ARMY H.Q.
Délivré à

Date
Date Aug 24, 1944

8. (Name, rank; printed or typed)
Par ICHB Yo

Signature
Signé J. Bennett

Official Title
Titre Officiel MAJ GSC

THIS PASS IS TO BE CHECKED AGAINST
IDENTITY CARD FOR NUMBER UPON
PRESENTATION, AND THE DESCRIP-
TION OF THE PERSON VERIFIED ALSO
WITH THE IDENTITY CARD.
CE PERMIS SERA CONFRONTE AVEC LA
CARTE D'IDENTITE POUR VERIFICA-
TION DU NUMERO DE CETTE CARTE ET
DU SIGNALEMENT DU PORTEUR.

INTERFERENCE WITH MILITARY TRAF-
FIC WILL CAUSE THIS PASS TO BE
REVOKED. MISUSE OF THIS PASS
WILL CAUSE YOUR VEHICLE TO BE
CONFISCATED.

TOUTE PERTURBATION CAUSEE AU
TRAFIC MILITAIRE SERA SANCTIONNEE
PAR LE RETRAIT DE CE PERMIS. TOUT
ABUS DANS L'UTILISATION DE CE PER-
MIS DE CIRCULATION ENTRAINERA LA
CONFISCATION DU VEHICULE.

DATE

CIVIL AFFAIRS

Official OSS pass issued to Hélène by Henry Hyde, August 1944.
Courtesy of author.

Allied troops land in southern France, August 1944. Photo courtesy of AP/Wide World Photos

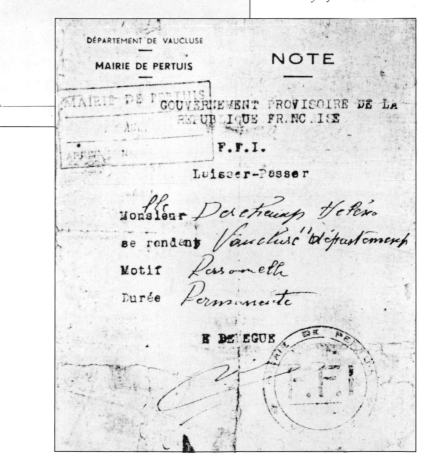

2677 HQ. CO.
INCOMING MESSAGE FORM

Date Auguat 22, 1944

To AIG IERS From SIMPSON

Action HHH Information EG TSR AJM FILES

27.

LES TROUPES ALLIEES VIENNENT ENTRER DANS APT A ONZE HEURES
QUARANTE GHT X ATTENDS VOS ORDRES XQ

LEFT: Decoded message announcing the liberation of Apt by the Allies. *Courtesy of National Archives and Records Administration.*

BELOW: FFI Pass given to Hélène in Pertuis. *Courtesy of author.*

DÉPARTEMENT DE VAUCLUSE

MAIRIE DE PERTUIS

NOTE

MAIRIE DE PERTUIS

GOUVERNEMENT PROVISOIRE DE LA
REPUBLIQUE FRANCAISE

F.F.I.

Luisser-Passer

Monsieur Dereheux Hélène

se rendent Vaucluse département

Motif Personnelle

Durée Permanente

E DELEGUE

F.F.I.

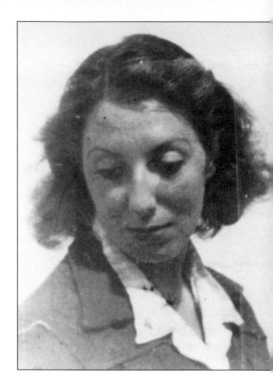

Hélène just
after Jackie's death.
Photo courtesy of author.

Jackie's grave.
The inscription on
the wooden plaque
reads: "To our much
loved friend Jackie,
who died for France."
Photo courtesy of author.

Jackie: Underground martyr.
Photo courtesy of author.

This memorial just outside
Reillanne was erected by
the French government on
the spot where Jackie died.
The inscription reads:
"Here fell on August 20,
1944 Jacqueline Bouquier,
24-year-old heroine, a
victim of her patriotism."
Courtesy of author.

Hélène on route to the Château Gleisol. *Photo courtesy of author.*

Frank Schoonmaker,
chief of the OSS station
at 3, rue Gabrielle,
Marseilles.
Photo courtesy of author.

Once a city was liberated, FFIs could round up German sympathizers. This is FFI headquarters in Toulon. *Photo RG 208-MFI-1C-4. Courtesy of National Archives and Records Administration.*

Hélène was a featured presenter at the 1976 Bicentennial celebration in Washington, D.C. Here, she recalls her experiences as an OSS agent. *Photo courtesy of author.*

Hélène and Henry Hyde, 1992. *Photo courtesy of author.*

CHAPTER SEVENTEEN

Marseilles

Henry seemed irritable the next morning at breakfast. He distributed his directives from across the dining-room table in a very detached tone. "Girard, you'll drive toward Brignoles. I'll see you in a few days in Marseilles."

He took a quick sip of his hot coffee. "Bill and Parsons, you'll go toward Cassis. The First Armored Division is coming up. Watch the road; it's mined. You'll enter Marseilles with the troops. Pete and Anick, you are to reach Marseilles from the northeast. The Underground has cleared the area, but the city is still occupied by the enemy, so watch it. Establish contact with the FFIs. Get information on the German garrison defending the town and their troop movements. You'll get a radio operator there."

"Do we contact anyone in particular in Marseilles?" I asked.

"Yes, a guy by the name of . . . just a minute." Henry fumbled with his papers. "Ah, yes, Mimile is his name. He has a room somewhere above a café near the avenue de la Canebière. Here is the number to call."

"Oh, him!" I laughed, recalling that I had heard about the man from Beaugard. "He's quite unusual. . . ." I was going to continue, but impatient as always, Henry cut me short.

"Well, you had better be on your way," he said. Then, gathering his papers, he got up.

Cars had been requisitioned in town for each team. Henry gave some final directives and then went off alone in a jeep.

♣ ♣ ♣

The Germans in Marseilles were still holding their position, but isolated groups of soldiers, cut off from their command units, were roaming the countryside. They continued to plague the population by burning and shooting at anything in sight.

Pete was still limping, and before departing, he had his bandages changed. As we were getting ready to leave, Pete asked me, "By the way, do you have a gun?"

I shook my head.

"You should," he insisted, and handed me a small Beretta, which fit easily into my handbag. He himself carried a heavy Colt, which hung from a leather strap across his chest.

We both were tense. For the time being, thoughts of love were put aside. We took the inland route, driving for about an hour or so without speaking.

In an open area near the villages of LeLuc and LeMuy, we sighted several wrecked gliders. Judging from the appearance of some of the aircraft, with their cockpits and wings completely ripped apart, their landing must have been extremely rough.

At a bend in the road, a temporary POW camp came into view, consisting of a few tents encircled by jagged, high barbed-wire fences. The prisoners looked at us with empty eyes, standing motionless or sitting listlessly on the ground. Some wore bloody bandages. There were infantrymen of all shapes and sizes, mostly very young and very old; grim, expressionless men who resembled caged animals, with their greatcoats, dusty and torn, hanging loosely about their ankles.

Here and there a few men squatted, answering nature's call. Some others had slipped off their tunics and were delousing themselves. One loner was leaning against a wooden post. He had extracted from his inside pocket a small object and was holding it preciously between his fingers, stroking it and smiling. He slowly raised his eyes; they were the vacant eyes of a madman! I felt an overwhelming distress for the whole human race.

"Keep your pity for those who understand pity," Pete counseled dispassionately.

And I remembered Jackie. I thought bitterly, He's right. Why should I feel sorry? In war, you live or you die. It was them or us.

The Underground helped us enter Marseilles during the night. The air was warm and smelled of the sea. We found the town in turmoil. Half the town was liberated, but the 224th German Infantry Division was still fighting desperately. Pete and I found our way to a small family hotel some distance up the avenue de la Canebière, near the church des Réformés. Centrally located and yet very discreet, it became our temporary home.

I had chosen the hotel because it was safe. Madame Brunet, the owner, was the sister of our housekeeper at Saint-Ange. She ran the place while her husband, an FFI, was off fighting to free the city.

Mimile (short for Emile), our contact in Marseilles, was a pusher and a pimp who had proven to be useful to the Underground on special raids against the occupiers. In addition to being an expert with a knife, Mimile had connections throughout Marseilles that made him a number-one informer.

His "business office" was located on the third floor of a bar near the place Gambetta. The landlord had rented him a back room, a narrow cubicle with no window. It was there that he held court.

His men, as he pompously called them, were a pack of ill-dressed mobsters who carried miscellaneous weapons ranging from small pistols to World War I bolt-action Lebel rifles to knives of every size. They brought back to him up-to-the-minute information on all German movements in town.

Pete and I called Mimile from Madame Brunet's phone, and one of his trusties came to fetch us in an old Renault. The rusty jalopy took us directly to the *patron,* the boss.

CHAPTER EIGHTEEN

Separation

We entered Mimile's room with little ceremony and found him straddling a chair, waiting. He received us somewhat as Napoleon would have met one of his inferior officers.

"Who's the girl?" he asked scornfully.

"She works with me," Pete told him.

A wolfish grin stretched across Mimile's face. "That's what I call a clever man!" He laughed admiringly and turned his back to me.

"Let's talk business," Pete said coldly.

The pimp shrugged. "You start."

He accepted our gift of American cigarettes and placed one behind his left ear. When Pete promised him a few gallons of gasoline, which were stored in the trunk of our Peugeot, he became more malleable.

Soon, Pete and I had become his best friends.

For two days we waited at our hotel as a French battalion, backed up by the First Armored Division, entered the north side of Marseilles. General de Monsabert, commandant of the Third Algerian Division, had set up headquarters at the Hôtel du Quinzième and begun negotiating with General Schaeffer, commandant of the German garrison, but so far they had failed to come to an agreement.

The 224th German Infantry intended to fight for the city. They were holding the sector near Notre Dame de la Garde, just south of the harbor, as well as several forts along the water's edge.

The church of Notre Dame de la Garde stood high on a hill, like an eagle's nest, and was an ideal observation post. The Germans had dug bunkers, corsetted the rocks with tons of concrete, and requisitioned a number of rooms in the church in which they stored their ammunition. They had also installed telephone lines that went clear to Berlin.

Two battalions of Allied infantry, supported by tanks and a detachment of Algerian *goums,* were attacking from several directions. Finally, on August 22, the area between the church and the entrance to the port was mopped up. Fort Saint-Nicholas surrendered. We fed all of this information to Henry through the radio operator supplied by Mimile.

Back at the hotel, Pete and I kept to our room and waited to be contacted by other OSS agents. We ate our C rations, which we had brought with us from the villa in Saint-Tropez, and Madame Brunet provided us with fresh fruit and bread, in exchange for powdered coffee and sugar.

One afternoon, Pete and I stretched out on our bed, engrossed in our own personal thoughts. The hotel was quiet in the heat of the August afternoon.

"Pete," I asked, putting my arms around my pillow, "do you think this war will ever end?"

"I don't know. Perhaps it won't be too long now," he answered, propping himself up on one elbow.

"I hate the war!" I closed my eyes. "Wouldn't it be great if it would end tomorrow?"

"It's just a matter of time before the German army crumbles."

I leaned toward him, smiling into his face. "Will you show me America someday?"

"Sure! You'll like it in California. There are beautiful beaches there. You can also go skiing in the winter, just like here, with the Alps so nearby. And there are places where the redwood trees are so huge you can hardly see the sky."

"I thought California was hot, with palm trees and sandy deserts," I exclaimed naively, remembering a book I had read before the war.

"Not where I live. You'll see."

We were completely lost in the illusion that some future together would be possible. There had to be something for us. We wanted to believe, and for a short while we were able to dismiss the fear and uncertainty. We behaved as if we might have a future under freer, happier circumstances.

Two days later, Bill and Parsons arrived. That evening we decided to go out and have a good time.

"Are you coming?" they asked me.

"Sure, why not?"

Off the avenue de la Canebière, on the rue de l'Arbre, was a shadowy place that had been hastily renamed the Blue Bird in honor of the Americans—everyone in France, it seemed, like to use Anglicized words.

The music hit us as we entered. We took a table near the dance floor and watched the procession of faces, trying to adjust our eyes to the haze of cigarette smoke. A pair of unescorted girls were sitting and waiting in a corner. They eyed every man who came in, hoping for a prospect.

Relaxed, I rested my gaze on a man sitting a short distance away. His chair was tilted back, and he was observing me narrowly. I knew his brutal face immediately and felt his cold stare penetrate me.

I leaned over to my companions. "Quick! See that man near the pillar, with the brown suit?"

The three pairs of eyes searched but didn't spot him soon enough. Before I knew it, the chair was empty.

"It's too late," I said regretfully. "He was a Milice agent from Vichy."

The band was playing. Promptly forgetting the incident, Pete asked me to dance.

"What about your leg?" I asked him.

"I'll manage!" he answered jokingly.

Pete was not the best dancer in the world—he had absolutely no sense of rhythm. Moreover, his injured leg was still bothering him, no matter what he pretended, and he soon gave up. We went back to our table and left the floor to a couple of GIs who were teaching their dates to jitterbug.

Everybody was having a grand time celebrating the liberation of the city.

Around midnight, Bill complained that he was tired. The few cheap drinks had made him drowsy.

"I'm tired, too," I admitted.

Pete and Parsons downed their drinks and the sandwiches they had ordered. I led the way out of the club as Parsons held the door open. Pete followed.

Suddenly the sharp snap of a revolver filled the air, and a bullet whistled past my ear, splintering the club's wooden door.

"Get down!" Pete shouted, grabbing me by the neck. I rolled behind a parked jeep, bashing my chin on the pavement. Parsons and Bill ran across the street, followed by Pete. I could hear them as I lay breathing heavily in the gutter. I had a glimpse of my assailant. It was the *Milicien* in the brown suit.

Some minutes later, the three men came back. Pete was furious.

The man had vanished into the darkness by turning down the rue Longue des Capucins. A crowd had formed outside the club, and the MPs were expected any minute.

"Let's get out of here," Pete grunted.

It took me a long time that night to unwind. I was scared and could feel my stomach doubled up like a fist. I shuddered at the thought of how narrowly I had escaped being killed.

In bed, my hand reached out to Pete, as though I was afraid of not finding him there. "Are you awake?" I asked in a hushed tone.

"Yes."

Sensing my restlessness, he moved closer to me and brushed my ear with his lips. He talked softly while warming me with his body. He folded his arm around my waist, and I buried my face in the hollow of his shoulder.

Gradually, the tension lessened and I abandoned myself to him. Avidly we found each other and escaped into a world of rapture. The rage of love transcends everything.

Afterward, his hand cupped my breast, and I curled up in his arms, my back against his body. We were quiet for a while.

I asked, over my shoulder, "Do you think about me when you are away, or does it begin when we are together? Is the memory of me erased when you are away on a mission?"

"We should be happy for the moments we have together. There may not be a tomorrow," he answered.

I woke up early the following morning, conscious of nothing at first beyond a vague, uneasy feeling of loneliness. Pete was already gone. I watched a flood of sunshine brighten the room, streaking across the bed, then got up and sat on the edge of a chair, slipping my clothes on.

Madame Brunet knocked at the door. "Lieutenant Peterson asked me to wake you," she told me. "He'll be back by noon."

She entered the room, carrying a tray of clattering crockery. "Come and eat," she urged, displaying a plate of bread and butter and some fresh fruit. She placed the tray on the night table.

She looked at me fondly, her fat arms crossed over her stomach. "Eat well, dear, you are as thin as a thread!"

Toward noon, when I was getting ready to go out, Pete arrived back at the room. He gave me a quick smile that softened the severity of his face for a second. Without speaking, he drew a sheet of paper out of the drawer, sat down, and began writing. As he continued to write, I realized that the hour of parting had come. Inevitably, I was to lose him.

Incapable of controlling myself, I bent over his shoulder and read:

Frank Schoonmaker, HQ 7th Army SSS G2
3, rue Gabrielle, Marseilles

Dear Frank,

I have been called to Grenoble suddenly and have no idea if I'll be back. As you know, Anick

and I have been a team since Saint-Tropez. She will
explain what happened last night, but she must not
be left unescorted. She is in danger in Marseilles.
There are still too many Gestapo and Milice agents
at large who fear her denunciation. She has been
working for us for a year. Try to take her with you
until the situation clears up.

I have located several vehicles this morning. Major Crosby says it is best to ask the FFIs to requisi-
tion them for us in their name and hold them until
the 7th Army gets their vehicle situation straightened out.

I am sorry I can't explain the affair personally,
but I know everything will work out satisfactorily.

Sincerely,
Pete

Pete stood up and handed me the letter. "Give this to
Schoonmaker. He'll take care of you." Schoonmaker was in
charge of the Marseilles OSS station, during Henry Hyde's
absence.

I nodded. "I wish to God I'd never fallen in love with
you!" I said angrily. "You are going away. Just like that!
Leaving me nothing!" My voice was bitter, and I choked a
little.

Peter encircled me with his arms. "It has to be. You knew
that," he said soothingly. He let me go and started picking up
his belongings from the bed and chair.

Yes, I knew. But it was hard just the same! "Don't forget
this," I told him, holding the scarf made of parachute silk.

Pete lifted his head, and I read in his face all those things that could not be expressed in words.

He left without turning back.

A man has his strength. He goes, he acts, he thinks clearly, looks ahead and finds consolation. A woman remains with her sadness, and nothing distracts her from it. She falls to the bottom of it, and cannot forget her pain.

I stood for a long time where he had left me, unable to move or think. For a man like Pete, love was secondary to the adventures and dangers of war.

Moving about the room, I mechanically collected my clothes, then sat at the dressing table brushing my hair, a familiar gesture. The mirror reflected the rumpled bed, where the imprint of his head remained on the pillow.

Unable to endure being alone, I went to the hall to call Schoonmaker and explain the situation. After a brief conversation, I walked back to the room to get my bag and went to wait with Madame Brunet for the car that was coming to pick me up to take me to Schoonmaker.

Across the street, a soldier was kissing a girl. They were standing against each other, and his arms were around her waist. They were acting as if no one else was around. They didn't care. I was envious of their happiness and turned my head away.

The jeep drove up the street and stopped in front of the hotel. The prospect of something to do restored a little liveliness in me. Work offered some hope, some distraction.

Upon arriving at the rue Gabrielle, I went directly up the long flight of marble stairs to the second floor and turned the doorknob resolutely. Schoonmaker looked at me from across his desk. He was a tall man with short black hair. Leaning

back in his chair, he ran his eyes rapidly over the letter I
handed him. I had already explained briefly, by phone, what
had happened at the nightclub.

The clouds that had been gathering during the morning
finally burst. Outside, the noisy downpour quickly became
monotonous.

Leaning against the wall, I asked, "What do you want me
to do?"

He hesitated. Resting his elbow on the desk, he looked
straight at me and cleared his throat with a sort of rattling
sound. "You'll travel to Lyons with us. Jérôme, one of our
agents, just joined us this morning. He was in Montpellier.
He'll take care of you."

Picking up the phone, he gave a quick order, then placed
the receiver back in its cradle and with obvious pleasure lit a
cigar. His glance at the Baby Ben clock on his desk indicated
that he was eager for me to be off.

"Major," I said, "will you do me a personal favor?"

Without waiting for his answer, I continued. "My mother
lives near here in Aix. Please call her for me and make sure
she is all right. I couldn't contact her while Marseilles was
still occupied. Besides," I added, turning away, "I am a
coward. I have to find peace within myself before I can
explain my sister's death."

"Don't worry. Your mother is well taken care of. Henry
has set up a temporary base at your home for a few
days."

"I feel better," I told him gratefully. "I'll go now."

Jérôme was waiting for me under the archway, hunched in
his oilskin poncho. He cranked the jeep's engine to life,
shifted the gears, and pulled out.

Even though Jérôme had never met me before, he could sense my restlessness and remained silent. Besides, he had other things to think about without worrying about me.

We stopped at the POL to fill the car with gas and get another jerrican for the trip before getting started for Lyons. I had yet to utter a word.

Rain fell heavily. Midway to our destination at La Coucourde we were forced to make an abrupt stop. We stared in disbelief at the scene of carnage stretching ahead of us on Highway 7.

The German Nineteenth Army disintegrated under the combined blows of the American Seventh Army and the most intense air attack on ground troops in history. German losses were prodigious. Long convoys were destroyed, and the entire area was covered with a mass of burned trucks, trains, and equipment. Eleven thousand German soldiers lay dead, decaying on the road. Fifteen hundred horses perished. The Germans had lost a total of 2,100 vehicles and six 380-mm railroad guns, the mighty long-range guns they were so proud of.

Jérôme inched his way along. The road seemed cluttered with helmets, skeletons of cars of all sizes, lost gas masks, hand grenades, and guns. Hundreds of bloated bodies of German soldiers were strewn along the roadside, still smoldering in the aftermath of battle.

The men had died in bizarre positions, some cowering in heaps, others crawling, sprinting, shooting, yelling, or even imploring heaven with a final plea. Rain was falling into their open mouths, running slowly over their gray, dead lips. Here and there, an outstretched hand had beckoned for help.

Jérôme and I drove silently through the carnage, the stink of rotting flesh impregnating the air we breathed.

As if in a strange trance, I kept on staring at the horrifying sight.

"Sweet Jesus! What is the world coming to?" Jérôme exclaimed bitterly.

"Please, let's get out of here," I begged, gagging.

He tried to speed away from the macabre scene, avoiding as best he could the shell craters, yawning open on the highway. Then there was a thump, and the jeep stopped moving. It was stuck in a mortar hole, and the front wheels were sliding in the mud.

A house nearby was still standing, and from the road I could see the interior, with its floors neatly sliced open like a layer cake ... the colorful pink, blue, and yellow wallpaper, the paintings on the walls, a mirror reflecting the leaden sky. The dismantled walls were still standing, gray and wet, dripping black rivulets. Dirty water ran down the gutter. In the back of the building were the remains of a small vegetable garden, a few dry cabbages and bean stalks seeding to the ground.

"Damn it!" Jérôme swore under his breath. He got out. "Stop feeling sorry for yourself and help me, will you!" he shouted impatiently.

"I can't drive," I moaned, feeling a wave of nausea rising.

"Try anything, damn it. We'll rock the car back and forth. It's not that heavy. Take the right side."

As I got out of the vehicle, he collected some loose bricks scattered around and lined the edge of the muddy crater. "Now, push! I'll take the other side."

We tried again and again, and this time the wheels rolled over the edge. There were several minutes of wheel-spinning before the jeep started to move, waddling off the road, splashing slush in all directions.

Jérôme looked around, a grim expression on his face. "Jesus! What a stink. Let's get the hell out of here!"

It was the middle of the night when Jérôme and I arrived at SSS G2 Headquarters, located in Château Gleisol, outside of Lyons.

I was assigned to a room by a man on duty at the billeting desk. It was elegant, but damp and cold. As the days went by, I noticed that people were gone one day and back the next. New faces cropped up and disappeared periodically. No one ever asked questions. Everybody was friendly enough; drank straight scotch, vodka, or whiskey; and remained aloof with an I-don't-give-a-damn attitude.

I was still occupied with Jackie's death, and with trying not to think about Pete.

Weeks went by. I missed the thrill and stimulation of a mission, and the wait became intolerable. Living on the edge had become a habit, and I fervently hoped that my inactivity would not last much longer.

Early one morning I was summoned to meet with Henry Hyde. The narrow hall at the end of the stairs dead-ended at what was called the map room. I knocked and entered in a single motion. Henry was reading a report, and I knew the instant I saw him that my layover had come to an end.

It was a pleasant room, with beautiful Oriental rugs and a rich oil painting over the marble mantel. There was a round central table covered with deep green felt. The leather-bound books lining the hand-crafted bookshelves lent a worldly, lived-in ambiance to the room.

Henry was not very talkative, nor was he relaxed. He looked very weary, no doubt from the weight of fatigue and heavy responsibility. His personal secretary, Ann, had not arrived yet, for OSS female personnel showed up only after it was determined that an area was "safe."

I had not seen him since my departure from Saint-Tropez, and yet he gave his orders without any friendly preamble. He was all business.

I tried to second-guess my assignment. I had heard that American troops were moving fast to the east.

"You are looking fit," he remarked from behind his desk.

"I'm fine."

"Good." He reached for a pack of cigarettes in his shirt pocket and drew one out.

"You will leave by noon with Bernard, the radio operator, and go to the Jura Plateau." He paused, and I could see that he was sizing me up.

He struck a match and spoke between puffs of his cigarette. "We need a report on German strength and movements, anything that might be important to the military, such as bridges and road conditions, artillery posts, river crossings, approximate numbers of enemy troops, and so on. You know what we need. It will be difficult terrain. The Germans are all over. We are expecting a big move. You can do anything you think is necessary to obtain this information. It's your option, as long as we get what we need. An agent will contact you in Arbois when your mission is completed."

"Very well," I replied. I paused, then asked, "Is Pete coming back?"

Henry held his cigarette motionless and stared at me.

Then, frowning, he looked down at his papers. "Not yet," he answered impatiently.

There had been no verbal rebuke, but the curtness in his tone made me self-conscious.

"Bernard will give you some funds. You will need money to pay off any informers. I am sorry you have to go," he added, giving me one of his famous smiles.

There was no question of our shaking hands.

I walked out and closed the door behind me. Back in my room, I prepared a small bag. Then, ready to leave, I went downstairs and left the rest of my belongings in the storeroom.

"I'll be back in a few days," I told the enlisted man in charge of storage.

CHAPTER NINETEEN

The Jura Plateau

September 1944

The German opposition to the American advance had stiffened, particularly in the Jura and Vosges sectors. The uncertain front line was now perilous to cross, and the Seventh Army G2 was obliged to depend more and more on the OSS SI (Secret Intelligence) agents to obtain information from behind enemy lines.

Bernard and I arrived by jeep in the small town of Arbois. Strong, biting winds and a granite sky set the scene. The ground was cloaked in a thick fog. Upon stopping at a small grove on high ground, we got out of the jeep and surveyed the lush pastures surrounding us. Bernard carried his well-traveled suitcase with the radio and a map.

Crows flapped above us, only to settle with a loud cawing in some trees a short distance away. A church bell tolled in the distance, and a small herd of cows walked unhurriedly, single file, out to pasture. The atmosphere was peaceful.

Squatting over the army blanket I had spread on the ground, Bernard unfolded his map and began the briefing. "We're on the border of enemy territory," he told me. "The lines are tightening, and nonresident civilians who cross them are shot on the spot."

"What a start!" I mumbled. I moved closer, trying not to look too apprehensive.

His finger ran over the map. "As far as we know, at least up until yesterday, the *Boches* are all around there—those hills over there, behind you."

I turned around and surveyed the outline of several looming hills. Even from afar, the terrain already looked hostile and treacherous.

Bernard continued, his breath smoky in the damp, icy air. "You'll be crossing a stream. It's shallow. Keep on going to your right and try to make yourself scarce. Head toward the safety of the forest."

I nodded, listening intently.

"You'll find some farms if you follow that path. The people are on our side. They'll give you information about what's going on. Here's some cash for emergencies, and here is your route. Good luck."

He handed me the map. I kept my eyes focused on the red pencil marks, studying the route to follow. Then I gave it back to him.

"By the way," he added, "your password is 'Such bad weather,' and the response will be 'For the past week.' "

He thought hard for a minute, then, looking at me, suggested, "I think it would be good to have a story ready, in case you are caught. How about this? You are searching for members of your family who ran away from Arbois at the approach of battle. You are lost. Ask them to help you find your way back." He hesitated. "I think it will work."

"It sounds logical," I agreed. Then, after a moment, I

stood up. "Well, I should probably start getting on with my assignment."

Bernard looked up at me, an uncertain, quizzical expression on his face. "Are you scared?" he asked.

By this point, I had seen and experienced more than a lifetime of hardships and challenges. I laughed inwardly, thinking of the proper young lady I had been taught to be. My way of thinking and speaking were different now and had become more "liberated" than what might be expected from a well-mannered young lady.

I bit my lip and said, "You're damn right I'm scared. Those Germans aren't just out sightseeing!"

"Christ!" he said. "Don't get mad at me!"

I shrugged. The tension was getting to me. "Oh, forget it. I'm nervous, and yes, I'm scared. I'll be back tomorrow at about the same time—I hope—if everything goes okay."

I attempted to appear casual about the upcoming mission. "See you."

I turned and walked away in the direction of the distant hills that rose above the icy, cold haze. A cloudburst bathed the countryside and turned the trees into faint shadows in the morning light.

I had been walking for about an hour through the hills, avoiding the country road and choosing instead to follow the dense edge of the forest so I could hide in case of an emergency, when the sudden sound of vehicles coming up the hill filled the air.

My heart pounding painfully, I took cover behind a large

thicket, waiting for the intruders to arrive. Unseen, I watched a German troop carrier approach. Then, a few minutes later, a Skoda staff car appeared with a couple of high-ranking officers sprawled in the backseat.

After the vehicles rumbled past, I was about to come out of my hiding place when a motorcycle with a sidecar approached, carrying a German soldier and his companion. I remained hidden until the sound of the motor had disappeared.

Alone again, I surveyed my surroundings, noticing a small farm up ahead. It was badly kept, the stone walls crumbling in places. I could see a barn on the side. The hinges of its door were broken, the stalls were empty, and there were no animals except for one cow who started to bridle nervously at my approach.

A short, stocky, middle-aged man with an unkempt black beard passed by the corner of the main building, then turned his head instinctively in my direction as if he knew someone was there. After a minute of indecision, he opened the front door and went in.

I followed him and knocked at the entrance. A minute later the door opened slowly, and the double barrel of a hunting gun greeted me.

"What do you want?" the man asked, holding the weapon.

I peeked through the open door. "I am from Arbois. I'm searching for my family, who left at the approach of battle. I'm lost. Can you help?"

The farmer observed me through narrow eyes. "What's your name?"

"Hélène Massière," I lied, purposely adopting the name of a woman I knew of in Arbois.

"I don't know what you want, but I know you are not from around here."

As a last resort, I said, "I am lost, and it's such bad weather."

The man's face relaxed. "Yes, such bad weather for the past week."

He had completed the password. I extended my hand in recognition. He turned his head toward the back of the room.

"You can come out, Lucie. Did you hear? She's one of us."

His wife came out from the other room with the trace of a smile on her face. "Sit down and rest," she invited, and a moment later placed a bowl of fresh milk in front of me. She sat on a chair, rested her hands on her lap, and studied me. I sensed that she did not approve of my work or my appearance. Frankly, I must have looked strange to her— disheveled and dirty, mud clinging to my shoes.

The man was fretting nervously. "You need information, don't you? A German convoy was here last night. I only understand a little German. They were talking about reaching Vesoul and trying to make a stand. They also mentioned blowing up one of the bridges on the Doubs River. That's all I can tell you." He paced back and forth while I drank my milk. "Listen, I have one contact for you. Tournaire is his name. He's a poacher. I'm sure he will help you." He gave me directions. "Be careful," he added in parting. "The Germans are roaming around. They are everywhere."

The woman seemed eager to see me go, and I did not blame her, for it was not possible to harbor strangers without becoming suspect in the eyes of the enemy. Wasting no time, I started on my way.

Soon, I approached a wooden fence surrounding a small cottage. I was about to cross the yard when a figure appeared at the far end of the trail, cycling along the dirt path. He was a man in his forties with a smooth, pink face.

"Hello," the man greeted, coming near. A dead hare was limply bobbing from the handlebars of his bike. "You wanted to see me?"

"I lost my way, and it's such bad weather."

The poacher looked at me, mumbling a few unintelligible words while dismounting his rusty bicycle. He finally answered, "Yes, for the past week. Come," he said, opening the door to the cottage.

The room we entered was dark, lit only by the fire in the hearth. He added a log, then dropped the hare in the sink near the window.

"Are you hungry?" he asked without looking up.

"Something warm would be good. I have been on the go since early morning."

He brought out a bottle of plum liquor and filled two little glasses.

"This will keep you warm. It's one hundred proof. I make it myself." He drank his own glass in one long gulp, then placed some *pâté de campagne* and bread in front of me.

"So," he started, sitting down across the table from me, "what can I do for you? You've got the right password. Who do you work for?"

I quickly swallowed my food. "I need information on German moves and installations in this area. I work for the Americans."

He expertly rolled a cigarette, placing the tobacco in the

thin paper, then licking the edge before inserting it between his lips.

"I didn't know the Americans used women agents," he said, and shook his head disapprovingly. "To each his own!"

Quickly changing the subject, I asked, "Is there anything important you can give me?"

"Sure, I hear the Germans are moving a lot of troops toward Besançon and Luxeuil-les-Bains. I think they are trying to regroup behind their own border. Also, they have installed heavy artillery along the Doubs River. I was also told that one of their fuel depots outside of Besançon contains more than seven hundred thousand liters of gasoline."

"Any news on the defense of Besançon?"

"I don't know anything about that, but I can take you to my Resistance friends. They have connections."

He got up. "Finish eating and then we'll go."

I watched him rinse off his knife and wash his hands. At the same time, I noticed the rifle resting against the kitchen chair, and I suddenly shivered at the thought that I didn't know this man at all. He could just as well have been a collaborator. Passwords offered so little security. I had to trust my life to people I had never met and had no way of judging.

To chase the thought from my mind, I studied my surroundings. The cottage was neat and clean, but the few utensils indicated that there was probably no woman living here.

"Ready to go?" Tournaire inquired, adjusting his beret.

"Sure." I removed my cold feet from the warmth of the hearth, and we left on foot, following the thickly wooded, twisting road into the Jura hills.

It was a long, brisk walk, and finally we reached a tiny hamlet of five or six houses scattered at the edge of a rather large, babbling creek. It was silent all around, and the commune appeared deserted. One of the houses was burning.

"Germans' work," the poacher said, pointing at the flames. The bad weather had not lifted. Rain clouds were drifting low over our heads. I was cold, and the humidity penetrated my clothes. A stray dog came sniffing at our feet, shyly wagging his tail. On the side of the road, up the creek, was what was left of the German motorcycle and sidecar I had seen earlier that morning. The bodies of the two soldiers lay in the mud next to their machine.

Even though there were no sounds or movements, I felt we were not alone. Soon I began hearing the switching of branches, the breaking of twigs, but my companion did not appear concerned. Four Resistance men suddenly appeared out of nowhere. They wore the FFI armband and carried automatic weapons.

They must be the ones who killed the two Germans, I thought.

One of them called out, "Hey, Tournaire, you brought your girlfriend along?" They laughed.

When they were close enough, the poacher took them aside, and I could vaguely hear him confide, "She's with the Americans. She needs information about the *Boches*."

"We'll be glad to help," they declared, turning in my direction with broad, friendly smiles. And they did help.

After hearing what the Resistance men had to offer me, I continued on my way. I spent many exhausting hours on the march or in hiding. At times, I stopped at a friendly home long enough to gather intelligence or drink a glass of milk or munch on a piece of cheese. It was incredible how fast news traveled from farmers to herdsmen and villagers, even across great distances.

Before long it was already late afternoon. I was walking along when I spotted a single-story house perhaps a hundred yards inside the woods. A gully cut across my path, and I crossed it, jumping from rock to rock. I could now see better. The house, I realized now, was more like a large hovel with a gray slate roof.

I stood listening to the whisper of the wind through the tall trees and to the faraway call of the birds. I entered the forest, making a wide detour around the house. The ground was covered with ferns, muffling the crunch of dry acorns under my feet.

Just then, a woman stepped out from the front door and began sweeping the porch, humming a soft, indistinct melody to herself. With a wave of her arm, she chased away the mongrel that had stretched out along the top step. She continued to sweep the dirt aside. From the hovel, the wail of a baby brought the woman running back indoors.

I weighed the situation. It certainly appeared normal enough. I stepped forward, and the dog let out a weak growl as I went by. When I approached the front door, the woman, who could see me from inside, restrained a cry of surprise.

"You needn't worry," I hurriedly reassured her. "I won't hurt you. We are on the same side."

Seeing that I was unarmed, the woman relaxed a bit. I asked her where the men were. She pointed a finger in the direction of the woods.

"Over there," she said.

"Can I come in and wait for them?"

She nodded while wiping the infant's nose. "Yes."

She did not appear unfriendly, so I went in and sat on a stool near a wooden table. The woman brought me a piece of country bread, and I dunked it in the bowl of soup placed in front of me. We didn't talk.

A good half hour passed before I heard voices and heavy steps approaching the front porch. The door opened and two men entered. The older one carried an axe on his shoulder; the other brought logs into the bare room. They appeared startled upon seeing a stranger.

"My name is Sorbier," said the younger one, placing a log on the fire. "What can I do for you?"

"Perhaps help me," I responded, holding his unblinking stare. "It's such bad weather," I recited, waiting for a reply.

The man nodded. "I see what you mean. Bad weather for the past week," he answered. He quickly came forward, and we shook hands.

"This is my father, and my wife and son."

"Do you have any news for me?"

Sorbier shook his head. "Our home has been raided many times in the past few days, and we do not have visitors from the outside. But Tournaire, the poacher near the creek, went exploring yesterday and—"

"Yes, I know. I have been there already."

"All I can tell you is that the German troops are scattered everywhere. You had better be on your guard."

As he spoke, the dog began barking furiously. The old man stood motionless for a few seconds, then turned his head toward the door, clearly wondering what to do next. Sorbier quickly positioned himself in front of the dirty plate and placed the soup spoon between his fingers.

The wife was a faster thinker. "In there," she urged, and she pushed me into a cupboard in the wall that was used to store fruit. I lay on a pile of apples, afraid to move and have the fruit roll out from under me. A sour, fermented odor filled my nostrils, and I pinched my nose so as not to sneeze.

Between the thin planks of wood hiding me, I saw the front door thrust open with a kick of a boot, and three German soldiers stomp in. I caught a glimpse of Sorbier's emaciated face as he nervously rolled a thin cigarette paper between his fingers and inserted the homemade cigarette between his parted lips. I held my breath and caught an apple as it began rolling off the heap.

The German in charge was swaying and nearly incoherent from drinking. He moved forward clumsily, a machine pistol under his arm.

"Eat, eat," he repeated over and over again, gesturing with his finger to his mouth.

"Give them some food," Sorbier ordered his wife. "Give it all!"

The woman shakily handed them a loaf of bread and a potful of soup. They greedily filled their mess cans. Then the drunken sergeant jabbered an order, and they immediately started looting the shelves, throwing potatoes and dry cheese into their knapsacks. Passing by the potbellied stove in the center of the room, they kicked it, fortunately not hard enough to topple it over.

"*Auf Wiedersehen.*" They left with their spoils as abruptly as they had arrived.

Nobody in the hut spoke a word.

The peasant wife knocked softly at the cupboard door, and I crawled out and stretched my stiff limbs.

"I'll be on my way now," I said, straightening my crumpled clothes. "I don't want to bring you any trouble. Thanks for the food."

They still could not speak, stunned that their last rations had been taken away. I left some small change on the table and then left, closing the door quietly behind me.

My mission had not been futile. I had collected important information during the day. I was now on my way back, and after some hiking, the dying day's twilight spread among the autumn trees.

I continued walking, crossing pastures and apple orchards, and eventually came upon a rutted dirt road and farmstead, where I noticed a great stir of activity. A gust of wind whirled a cloud of leaves into the air, momentarily obscuring my view of the barn. When the leaves settled, I saw that the yard and path leading to the village were full of men milling about and bellowing orders. Suddenly I realized I was looking at the familiar field-gray uniforms of the Wehrmacht.

The metallic clanging of tanks jarred the air, and I hurriedly jumped into a muddy ditch, slush spattering my face. I peeked up over the embankment. Ahead, two Mark IV tanks were maneuvering heavily along the path, their big single guns erect as sinister sentinels.

To avoid detection, I remained in the ditch until I could crawl in the darkness to a bed of leaves behind a dense patch of undergrowth. A well-trod path ran narrowly between two hedges, and I carefully studied my position before settling in.

It had rained during most of the day, and I was drenched

and cold. Clumps of mud clung to my shoes and coat. My feet ached and blisters were swelling my heels. I grew progressively colder, and hunger poked at my ribs. Taking a piece of vitamin chocolate from my pocket, I munched on it slowly.

Exhausted, I let my head bow with fatigue, and ended up nodding off. I awoke suddenly and glanced around. It was now pitch dark, and I immediately felt reassured. Rain fell steadily, whipping my face. Around me, the countryside was a gloomy carpet of mud and water. Ill-shaped trees bent over and twisted their branches, submitting to the first autumn assault.

Shells were exploding in the direction of the town of Dôle. The explosions came without interruption, and brilliant flares arced into the sky, glided, and vanished into the night. Parachute flares danced in the air, illuminating the ground.

My legs had cramped, and I stretched them carefully before getting up to start down the hill. After sitting so long on the rain-soaked ground, my clothing was saturated all the way down to my undergarments and felt uncomfortably heavy.

My progress down the hill was painstakingly slow. As I reached a steeper path, I stopped dead in my tracks. My neck tensed. My sense of hearing had become keen in the dark, and I heard an unmistakable scuffling of stones in the distance. The sound stopped for an endless minute. All I could hear was the absence of footsteps . . . complete silence.

Not daring to move, I continued to listen and heard fresh noises ahead. The icy wind blew my hair and rippled my coat. It was bitterly cold, and somewhere out there was a German patrol. Crouching down, I remained motionless and held my breath at intervals as I waited for the crack of a gun. In the orchard, apples fell from the trees and plopped onto the wet earth. The silence lengthened.

It became intolerable, squatting in total gloom like a cornered animal. I wiped the rain from my face as I rose and started down the hill once again, making my way through the orchard. I carefully avoided breaking twigs as I advanced along the uneven terrain. Then a *snap*. A sprig crushed under my weight. The answering crack of a submachine gun broke the silence.

Tac, tac, tac. A flash lit the darkness. Collecting all of my energy, I vaulted over a low stone wall and landed within a short distance of a soldier. In that split second, I distinguished the outline of a German helmet.

My pulse was pounding. I realized it was useless to crouch now, for he knew just about where I was. I felt afraid of death, lost and alone, and I broke into a zigzag run. My breath came in short, hard gasps through parched lips.

A second burst echoed from the hill, but I was already a good distance away, sheltered by the dark trees of the orchard. Branches slashed my legs as I raced in the direction of Arbois, with my skirt tucked up tightly in my hands.

Suddenly I tripped and fell over a rock. I whimpered in pain, feeling the skin of my knee peel, then rolling back on my feet again, I continued to run. Nearby, a rooster disoriented by the shelling and the flares lighting the sky started crowing long before dawn.

The orchard thinned, and I came out into the open. The shelling had stopped, but the rain kept on falling. The dismal, muddy streets of Arbois were alive with men from the American 143rd Division leaving for combat. Some of the soldiers looked straight ahead with their jaws set, thumbs under the slings of their rifles, faces void of expression; others were laughing and whistling halfheartedly.

I stood limply with my back against an iron fence, feeling dirty and drained. As I watched the soldiers go forward to the same front line I had just passed, one of the men called, "Hi, honey!" He threw me his combat jacket. "Looks like you need it more than I will up there!"

Little did he know that the young girl to whom he donated his jacket was bringing back information that would perhaps save his life and those of his comrades. The rest of the unit went down the street. I listened to the thud of their footsteps and the clanging of their equipment. I felt sick, and I sat on the ground, totally exhausted.

The shops still had their iron shutters rolled down. It was very early. The few inhabitants in the street glared at me as they passed. Some stopped to stare, and others pointed at me. When the troops were completely out of sight, I stood up and walked to the far edge of Arbois, guided by the tall spire of a church in the distance.

I found Bernard sitting quietly on the ground in the same place I'd left him twenty-four hours before. He had built a small fire, but it was not burning well. A thick, opaque smoke rose from the wet branches.

"Welcome back," he muttered, disengaging his headset. He poked at the sputtering fire and pushed the wood that was burning onto a damp clump not yet ignited. "How was it?" he asked.

"Muddy all the way!"

"Want a drink? You look like you could use one."

I nodded. He extracted a small flask from his pocket and

handed it to me. I took a generous swig of cognac. The strength of the alcohol made me cough and shiver all over. The burning liquid felt good running down my throat.

I dropped down heavily beside him and drew a Lucky Strike from the pack he had placed in front of me. I watched the pale flames of the fire for a while, pleased with the warmth on my hands and face.

"We'll go back to our rooms as soon as I get through. You must be beat!" Bernard grinned as he removed some twigs embedded in my hair. "Do you have much for me?"

I nodded and took another sip. "Yes. The people in this area were quite talkative."

As I gave him the information, he began coding the message. Luckily, the air was clear enough, with little interference. Plugging in the earphones, he listened to the static and muttered, "I'm getting it," and he got busy.

He received a reply and started the message. It went through: *Many obstacles on the road leading to Mouchard. Bridges blown around Dôle, and main road sown with explosives. Important enemy field depot located by FFIs some twenty kilometers east of Besançon. Heavy enemy artillery installed along the Doubs River. Besançon occupied by an estimated three thousand German troops. Luxeuil-Remiremont road heavily defended by enemy. Road from Luxeuil to Plombière still open.*

Orders sputtered back immediately through the clattering static: "Wait. Contact man on his way. Out."

The fire faded to ashes, the branches collapsing inward with faint sparks. Bertrand packed his gear, rolled the blanket up, and we drove back to Arbois.

Madame Massière, our landlady, was a kind, thoughtful

woman in her late seventies, who was still bewildered by the war. When Bernard and I came in, we found her sitting in the old-fashioned parlor, mending a threadbare knitted vest. Seeing us, she bit off the thread and set the garment down. She took a look at me and was startled at how disheveled and drenched to the bone I was.

"Come in at once," she said. "You'll catch your death! Take that coat off this instant."

Madame Massière rushed off to the kitchen as fast as her old legs permitted and returned a few minutes later with a bowl of steaming soup. It was marvelously hot. I cradled the warm bowl in both of my hands and drank from it slowly. The woman fussed over me, meanwhile fluffing pillows and rearranging the cream-colored doily that covered the chair in which I sat next to the fireplace.

The flames blazed brightly and surged as if determined to clear the room of humidity and shadows. Bernard had removed his combat boots and socks and stretched out his feet near the fire. A small tabby cat that had curled up near my chair opened an eye and yawned indolently. My clothes smelled damp and musty, and the hem of my skirt started to steam with the heat.

After a while I took inventory of my bruises. My left knee had been badly cut during my flight through the orchard.

"Let me see," the old woman said, putting on her spectacles. I stretched out my leg. Dirt and mud were all over the open wound and cuts. The knee was very sore.

Madame Massière pulled open the drawer of a small cabinet, then extracted dry leaves from a tin box and yellow powder from a bottle. Adding pharmaceutical oil of some sort, she ground the mixture in an enamel bowl with the back of a spoon and mixed it all together. I winced with pain when she applied the healing concoction to my skin. After she was finished, she bandaged the knee with a piece of cloth.

I was aching all over, and I sneezed several times while rubbing my drippy nose. "I don't suppose running in the rain did me much good," I said, trying to make a joke. The landlady looked up at me with feigned disapproval. She asked no questions.

After swallowing two aspirin, I took a hot-water bottle from the kitchen and climbed the creaking staircase to my room. Poking his head through the banister, Bernard shouted, "A contact will arrive tonight."

Feeling snug and warm in the carved wooden bed, I could have almost believed that the war had never happened, that I had never been through all the anguish.

Sadly, I tried to contemplate what was ahead of me. It seemed like a long, long road of utter loneliness. I considered what it would be like to go for a stroll in the streets without fearing injury or attack. I wondered what it would be like, to be at peace with the entire world, and with myself.

I had tried to be a good agent; I had gone behind German lines many times, escaping their patrols and bringing back lifesaving information. But what of my life? What was left for me? I had lost Jackie and perhaps even Pete. I had no answers but to rest and face the next day.

When I awoke it was five A.M. It was with much effort that I got up, took the water pitcher, and washed. The icy coldness shook me awake. Heavy shelling was still rumbling, this time closer, in the direction of Besançon.

Downstairs, Madame Massière was busy at the woodstove. Bernard was sitting nearby, his feet propped up on the brass bar of the stove.

"Your cold better?" he inquired matter-of-factly. I didn't answer.

"We have to leave right away," he added. "We're going back to Château Gleisol. Henry will give you your next assignment. The new contact will stay here."

I swallowed my cup of hot milk and stepped out. Bending my head out of the jeep, I waved good-bye and blew a kiss to the tiny old woman who stood on the porch.

The great offensive to drive the Germans west of the Rhine River had started. Since I spoke very little German, I was of no use to the OSS in the upcoming German campaign.

Henry Hyde assigned me to the OSS station at Château Gaillard in Annemasse on the Swiss border. During this time, I saw very little of Pete. I was later moved to Thonon, on Lake Leman, where I became involved in a new project: interrogating people who had escaped from both concentration and forced-labor camps, as well as German POWs. We collected as much information as we could, then sent it to Seventh Army G2 Section. We also trained Polish officer escapees, many of whom were later dropped behind German lines to organize espionage and sabotage networks.

CHAPTER TWENTY

Alone Again

Thonon, January 1945

When the jeep came to a halt in the courtyard, it was about eight o'clock in the morning. The Thonon unit had gathered in the dining room for breakfast as usual.

I raised my head to see Pete and Bill enter.

I knew immediately that Pete had seen me as he came in, but his eyes avoided mine and traveled across the room instead.

"Hello," greeted our group chief, Major Thompson, with an inviting gesture to join us.

"We are just passing through," Pete announced as he sat in one of the empty chairs. "I brought some papers for you from Lyons." His voice was croaky, as if he had a cold.

Bill was already helping himself to scrambled eggs and sausages.

My first impulse had been to run to him as he entered, but a distance seemed to have come between us. I sat dumbly waiting for Pete to speak. Instead, he turned abruptly to his left and engaged one of the men in a discussion.

I felt myself go cold. Why show up now, when I was just

starting to forget him? We had hardly seen each other since our quick good-bye in Marseilles.

Swallowing quickly to loosen my throat, I addressed him directly. "Hello, Pete," I said, my voice faltering.

"Hi."

We gazed at each other mutely. There was such a passionate expression on his face that I lowered my head to try not to betray the rush of feelings his look had awakened.

Leaning over my cup of coffee, I struggled to sip and swallow the hot drink.

The conversation had started again. Even though Thompson was aware of what was going on, he kept on talking evenly as if nothing had happened.

Damn Pete! How foolish I had been to hold on to my dreams, to foster them, while all along deep down I knew they would never materialize? *Go on, go to your room before you start crying and lose your pride.* I got up abruptly from the table, but Pete caught my arm.

"I have to see you before I leave," he said. "Can we talk?"

I remained where I was, conscious of his hand on my arm. I studied his face. It was so tense that it gave him a hungry look.

I turned to go toward the stairs, and he came after me. We went up without exchanging a word. A dull pain throbbed in my temples. I opened the door to my room and let him in, then went to sit near the bedside table.

There followed a moment of utter silence. It was the silence of full awareness. My whole body stiffened in a reflex action of self-defense.

Pete lit a cigarette and stubbed it out after only one or two drags. "Anick," he began huskily, "Headquarters has not looked kindly on our relationship. You know that. Lovers and spies do not mix. They think we cannot function to our fullest capabilities, being involved as we are. I have been assigned to Germany."

I flinched but didn't protest as the words washed over me. There was a sad inevitability about what he was saying, but my feelings were so intense that I only wanted to retort with something bitter and cruel.

The words, though, only swam meaninglessly in my head. I couldn't even control my lips enough to speak. My face had settled into a mask. I sat very straight, with my feet tightly pressed together and my hands clasped on my lap, like a schoolgirl listening to a reprimand.

Finally, I turned to gaze at him and out of despair gave him a sad smile of infinite tenderness. There was so little time left for us together. I was amazed at how well I remembered even the slightest detail about him.

I sighed. It wasn't so long ago, the wonderful love we shared, but it was haunted by the awareness that it could end anytime. There is no hope really in daydreams, but what would be left without them?

I looked at the tall, lanky figure in the paratrooper's uniform and the stubborn eyes in his lean, tanned face. I wanted to fill my memory with his image, for I was consumed with the devastating knowledge that I would never see him again.

As strange as it was, even with our closeness, he had never known my real name! The realization that we had to part thrust like a dagger.

"You are the first man I have loved, Pete. The first one who has made love to me!"

He brought me against him with an almost brutal strength, and with my body against his for the last time, I felt the sensuous warmth I had discovered that first night in Saint-Tropez.

"I'll never forget, darling," he was saying. A gaunt smile flitted across his face without really touching it. He was searching for words. "Things will be all right. You'll see."

Then he stepped back away from me and turned to go. A second later he was gone.

I felt the prick of tears. All of my emotions escaped out of me, but I made no gesture to stop him, knowing that he had already walked out of my life.

The sound of a jeep's engine brought me to the window. Heavy frost had drawn weblike designs on the window glass. Using the sleeve of my sweater, I rubbed off the grime, vaguely aware that I was shaking violently.

A pale ray of sun pierced through the cottony snow clouds, warming the place where I pressed my forehead.

Pete gave a last glance from the car, looking up and catching the gesture of my hand.

I watched the funny, bumpy little vehicle bounce along the graveled driveway.

I realized then that it was time for me to quit. I couldn't go on anymore, and moving away from the window, I shut myself in from the outside world. In the turbulent life of an agent, I was learning there was no gentle good-bye.

I'll remember, Pete. I'll remember! I kept repeating inwardly, as if afraid to pronounce the words aloud.

March 1945

I was passing through Annemasse, on my way home at last. I had planned to stop in Paris, where they were starting to officially confirm and recognize the people who "really" had fought in the Underground and, in my case, in the Resistance and the American OSS. I wanted to receive my papers. Also, I was considering going to French Indochina, where, I had recently learned, my older brother, Maurice, had died.

From Château Gaillard's main hall, I watched Bernard coming up the front steps. He had just arrived from Sélestat in the Rhine lowland; his muddy car was still parked in the driveway. He threw down the pouch he'd been carrying over his shoulder and noticed me standing there.

"Hey!" he called from the door, waving in my direction. "I hear you are going home. Good luck!"

Just then he turned around, waiting for me to catch up with him. "I almost forgot. Did you hear about Peterson?" he asked. "You worked with him during the French campaign, if I recall."

I nodded. "What about him?" I asked, thinking he was going to say that he had seen him in Germany.

"I got the news this morning. He was killed crossing the German lines. I was asked to let you know."

Everything came to a standstill. I was aware that Bernard was speaking to me, but I could not hear the words he was saying.

I automatically said good-bye to him, never noticing when he left. I only stared at the heavy snowflakes falling outside.

I was numb with an ineffable sense of loss and withdrew into my only escape: memories. I took refuge in them and drowned myself in them, as if they were my last moments.

Almost five years . . . Five years of my life I had given. Where were the people I had worked with, or tried to help? Dead or still decaying in concentration camps. Jackie was gone, having tried to follow in my footsteps, believing in my patriotic ideas. Would I ever forgive and free myself from her loss?

Didier, too, was dead. Petit-Jean, and now Pete. Everyone I had loved or cared for was gone! The pressure was so violent within me that it stifled for a few moments any other emotions. It reached the point where my soul, parting for an abstract instant from its earthly cocoon, was able to look from the outside and say, "I'm sorry, so sorry for you!" I leaned back against the wall.

My thoughts continued to wander. . . . I wish I had been with Pete when he died. I would have whispered simple, tender words to him, which would have carried him gently on to his endless voyage. My God! I am losing my mind!

I looked around with dry, burning eyes. Desolate, I stared once more out at the peaceful, gentle snow. It seemed to appease my stirring feelings and emotions.

Who knows, I reasoned, perhaps, yes, perhaps there will be another spring for me, too. And another, and another.

Epilogue

October 1, 1983

A few days after my return from New York, where I had attended one of the annual events organized by the Veterans of the OSS, I was sitting on the edge of my bed, glancing at the headlines of the *Palm Beach Daily News.* There it was, a story that made the Veterans of the OSS appear to be a glamorous group of ex-spies:

OSS Veterans Honor Man Called "INTREPID"

At the top of the New York party list last week was the William Donovan Award dinner aboard the aircraft carrier the Intrepid, *which now is a museum.*

The "party" could have been labeled "The Ship of Spies." More than seven hundred turned out for the gala black-tie event, and most were members of the Veterans of the OSS, forerunner of the CIA. William Donovan was the founder and chief of the OSS. Recipient of the illustrious award was Sir William Stephenson, who flew in from Bermuda.

Known as Britain's "Master Spy" during World War II, Sir William Stephenson, code name

"Intrepid," was charged by Winston Churchill with directing all intelligence activities in the Western Hemisphere. His past exploits are legendary.

Past recipients of the Donovan Award include President Dwight D. Eisenhower, the Earl Mountbatten of Burma, Allen Dulles, a long-time director of the CIA, and the British Prime Minister, Margaret Thatcher. Edwin Meese, counselor to President Reagan, was guest speaker. Among the dignitaries was William J. Casey, present director of the CIA.

Seen among the crowd was the ever fashionable Evangeline Bruce, talking with the handsome Canadian Consul Kenneth Taylor. Taylor had spoken at a luncheon earlier that day at the Union Club. He made headlines a few years ago when he helped smuggle Americans out of Teheran during the hostage crisis.

At one table was Henry Hyde, the well-known international lawyer. Hyde was chief of the French desk of the OSS, attached to the Allied Forces Headquarters, and was interviewed that morning on CBS. Fashion designer John Weitz, former OSS member, and his wife, Susan, were chatting with Lorna de Wagen and the Peter Sichels (his wineries in France provided the evening's fine wine). . . .

Tossing the newspaper aside, I smiled to myself. How times had changed! The band of daredevil, do-or-die spies now shared equal billing with the swells of New York society.

"Was it all for one . . . or one for all?" I asked myself,

remembering the loyalty and unspoken camaraderie of by-
gone years. That was then, this is now.

I had flown to the city the night before the event and checked
into the Carlyle Hotel. I always looked forward to these
reunions. With an unwavering sense of loyalty, I still saw my
former comrades-at-arms as if it was yesterday. In my mind,
time had stood still, and the image of my wartime colleagues
remained unspoiled.

For me, they were still Henry, John, Bill, Joe . . . never
mind the white hair, the telltale limp, or the way the years had
etched deep lines across their familiar faces. Of course, I too
had aged, but there had always been a difference of ten to
fifteen years between me and most of them.

As much as I enjoyed attending these reunions, though, at
times I couldn't help but feel the sting of disappointment. I
was surprised to observe how status-conscious some of my
devil-may-care friends had become, in their everyday routines and lifestyles. A caste system appeared to have been
established, and it seemed odd, even foreign to me. I
couldn't help noticing how quickly my longtime friends had
forgotten the equality that had been shared by the fighting
men and women in the intelligence field.

During the war men and women accomplished the same
missions and endured the same hardships. Now, I thought,
biting back a touch of cynicism, it was a man's world.

It was almost noon when I arrived at the Union Club, where
cocktails and lunch were being served to the OSS Veterans.

Through an open door, I spotted Bill Casey, dressed in a charcoal, pin-striped suit. He was in deep conversation with former deputy director of the CIA Ray Cline. Casey's head turned as I walked into the room, and he greeted me with a friendly sweep of his hand.

"Hélène, here you are. I appreciate your thoughtfulness in sending me those letters you dug out recently."

"I thought you would like to have them," I told him.

I moved over to Geoffrey Jones, president of the OSS Veterans, who wore the jovial air of a man who expected everyone to have a good time. He was discussing the special invitation extended to him by the French government to attend the fortieth anniversary of the Landing, slated for 1984.

Soon it was time for lunch. I was seated next to Kenneth Taylor, the Canadian consul. The man to my left introduced himself, but the room was now noisy, and I was only able to catch his first name. Ben was a fleshy-faced, facetious-looking man of medium height, with a corpulent frame. Horn-rimmed glasses, posed on a bulbous nose, gave him an inquisitive air, which I must say I didn't find very appealing.

The legendary French colonel Pierre Fourcault, a former right hand to de Gaulle, presided at the next table. Wheezing and moving his hands with dramatic, impressive gestures, he recollected one of his famous war yarns with Gallic verve. A captive audience listened with deference.

Several toasts were made, and a speech was given by Consul Taylor. Ben, the former agent seated to my left, was notably curious about my wartime experiences. He inquired as to which OSS team I had belonged to.

"I was one of Henry Hyde's people. I worked in the field," I replied.

"Well, then, I probably knew a few of your comrades," he continued. "Perhaps you knew Poniatowski? I teamed with him during the French campaign."

"Of course. And perhaps you knew Peterson?"

I sighed. Suddenly the room grew smaller and the boisterous noise around me seemed muffled. I felt as if I had been catapulted back in time, and I had to catch my breath.

"It was sad how Peterson was killed after reaching the German lines," I said, my voice trailing off.

Ben broke off the ash of his cigar. "Pete isn't dead. He lives in California," he replied matter-of-factly.

I had been lifting my wineglass to my lips. Stopping, I stared at him incredulously. All I could hear was a distant voice addressing me.

"Geoffrey Jones tells me you lived in Iran," said Consul Taylor.

I fought to regain my composure. I believed that as long as I remained within the realm of logic, emotions could be controlled, but suddenly it was difficult to do so.

"Yes," I heard myself reply abstractedly, my lips moving seemingly in slow motion. "I lived in Teheran for five years." My voice sounded stilted and strange, as if someone else was speaking for me.

Ben was now talking to another guest. I had the uneasy sense that the conversation was about me, judging from the fleeting glance he shot in my direction. He appeared amused by what his friend was saying, and I found myself disliking the man intensely.

"Where did you live in Teheran?" Taylor inquired.

"I had an apartment near the Royal Teheran Hilton on Pahlavi Avenue."

"You must have known many Iranians, then."

"Yes, yes . . . Americans were liked at the time. I knew the Shah's family. Two of his sisters were friends of mine, Princess Fatemeh and Princess Shams," I responded absent-mindedly.

I was grateful when he let the conversation drop, obviously sensing my preoccupation.

Bittersweet memories of the war reeled through my mind. Wanting to escape from the noise encompassing me, I retreated to the quiet of the powder room.

The fluorescent light over the vanity table made me look sickly pale. I studied my face in the mirror, noticing the gray streaks in the reddish blond hair. Involuntarily I traced with my finger the furrows at the corners of my eyes.

"What would it be like to see Pete again?" I asked myself, and for a passing instant, I caught, in the glass, the vision of my younger self.

I shrugged lightly. What would be the use? It was so long ago. "You're too old, girl!" I told the face in the mirror. Yet suspended memories of the past remained.

I was thinking of the winter in 1944, when I was twenty-one, when I saw Pete for the last time. I could picture the Joe House (safe house) in Thonon, at the edge of Lake Leman, snow covering the ground, and the trees with their wintery, naked branches . . . the room where we last met. Pete was saying, "Headquarters has not looked kindly on our relationship. . . . They think we cannot function to our fullest capabilities, being involved as we are." The voice faded.

I gazed again into my eyes in the mirror and remained that way for a few long minutes. After all these years, I could not visualize Pete's face any longer. He had disappeared out of my life a long time ago.

Pensive, I sat on the ottoman. I kept still, as if it was the only way to stop time from running away. I felt a quick chill course through my body. Guarding myself against sadness, I tried to find good memories.

In the days following the Landing, I recalled, the Americans couldn't understand how much one young French girl, working for them, had gone through. How could they comprehend, coming from their brave new world, what a hell it had been living under the cruel fist of the German Occupation?

The undercover work I had carried out for some five years had been extremely hard on me, and when Jackie died next to me, I thought I had reached the end of my strength. Nothing seemed to matter. There was no room in my mind for anything but grief, and I had felt that I would never overcome it.

Then one day Pete had entered my life, making me realize that wounds could heal, even after the most harrowing circumstances. Life was worth living after all. He had brought back warmth to my heart, and, in return, I had loved him uncompromisingly.

But in the secret world I lived in, love between agents was as chancy as the trade we worked in. Passions, illusions, and hopes were torn apart and promises were broken. Deception, lies, betrayal—all of this had been a part of my life.

I closed my eyes. Memories tumbled over one another. There was the morning when the radio operator, Bernard, had come in from the front lines. His cheeks had been chaffed and ruddy from the freezing gale sweeping through the crystallized trees. Snow had been falling heavily, covering the landscape with an immaculate white carpet. . . . Bernard, the one who had so bluntly told me that Pete had been killed.

I blinked, trying to remember how he had phrased it. "I was asked to let you know. . . . He was killed crossing the German lines." Someone had told him to let me know! Why had they bothered?

I had mourned Pete's death for a long time.

The click of the door opening brought me back to reality.

I knew it was time to find out the truth once and for all, to leave the past behind.

Back at the table, I uneasily lit a cigarette before turning to ask the question I was afraid to ask.

"Did I hear you say Pete is alive?" I finally asked Ben, my voice slightly hoarse, faltering with the words.

He raised his eyebrows in a semblance of surprise. "I never said that. You misunderstood me," he replied coolly, his gaze unwavering.

I watched him for a sign but saw only a blank face. I saw nothing, not a look of interest or understanding, not even a stir.

Forty years was not long enough for me to forget the artifices of my profession. His offhand manner reminded me of the old days, and the impersonal way they used to run an operative.

"My mistake!" I let out the words slowly, while rising from my seat.

"Come, come now," Ben's smug voice continued, "it's such a nice reunion. Let's enjoy it."

Ignoring him, I turned away and strode across the room with some of the departing guests and, upon reaching the entrance, took a deep breath of the cold, crisp air. I left the club and began walking at a brisk pace. Soon I was lost in the midafternoon rush on Park Avenue.

That evening, upon boarding the *Intrepid,* the guests were greeted by a Marine honor guard and a brass band.

Following the bizarre revelation earlier that day, another surprise awaited me. I was seated at Henry Hyde's table, and there next to me was a man who, at first, appeared vaguely familiar.

"Aren't you going to kiss your old friend?" he inquired, standing up.

Squinting, I stared at him, incredulous.

"My God!" I exclaimed at last. "Hellops! Is it possible?"

It was my oldest and dearest friend, Robert Viret, with whom I had teamed in France. I hadn't seen him since we separated at the Landing in August 1944.

We fell into each other's arms, overwhelmed with emotion. After recovering from the initial shock, I finally was able to speak.

"You don't know how often I have thought of you all these years," I told him. I was still holding him in my arms. "I had heard a few rumors about your fate from headquarters, but with our lifestyle then, one never knew if the information was accurate."

Hellops shook his head. "I was taken prisoner by the Wehrmacht the first days of October 1944, near the town of Baccarat, in the East, while trying to cross the German lines."

"That's what I heard. I got word when I was pulled off the field for a while. Did you escape?"

He sat down next to me. "No, they kept me for a week in a cellar at Badonvillier."

I listened, fascinated, murmuring to myself, "I can't believe you are here next to me!"

Hellops smiled, then continued. "When the Germans started retreating, they took me across the Rhine River. I was transferred to the camp of Shirmeck, then interned at Hasbach, Baden. In April 1945, during a transfer, I escaped near Singmaringen and was liberated by the French army on the first of May. After spending some time in a field hospital, I finally went home to Lyons, where my mother had a restaurant, if you remember."

"Of course I do. I stopped there as we were going to the East. But tell me, is this your first visit to the States?"

"No, I came to the U.S. several times, but had no idea you were still alive. I flew in yesterday. Henry had sent me an invitation for the affair. He said in his letter that he had a big surprise for me—and here you are."

Hellops brought his chair closer to mine. "Tell me a little about your life."

I collected myself for a moment. "There is so much to cover. I'll give you a brief idea of what happened after we parted in Saint-Tropez. If you remember, they sent you with the 45th Division, Seventh Army, as a G2 agent. I was attached to Henry's OSS SI Section. I went through the French campaign with him, up to the German border. Since I didn't speak German, I was assigned to the OSS station on the Swiss border. I left the OSS in April 1945." I added laughingly, "I hope you are here for a few days, so we can continue our journal."

"Who did you team with during the French campaign?" Hellops asked.

I reflected. "Isn't it strange how things sometimes connect? It's like a merry-go-round. Only this morning, I was convinced that I had left the past behind." I felt my old friend was studying me. Finally, I replied, "I teamed with a Jedburgh [special OSS parachute agent] named Peterson."

Hellops shrugged. "Don't think I knew him. I left Saint-Tropez before you did."

I was Anick again, and the passage of time seemed curiously warped. Past and present were now one and the same. I became silent.

Hellops rested his hand on mine and then squeezed it gently. "Why the sudden sadness?"

I looked at my friend with woeful eyes. "I was remembering the ones you and I knew. The ones who are now gone."

"Anick, don't think for a minute that I have forgotten them. Did you ever find out who killed Jackie?"

I slowly removed my hand from his, taking my time before I spoke. When finally I did so, my voice was neutral, my emotions contained, kept at a distance.

"Yes," I acknowledged. "In the summer of 1976, I received a long letter from Mireille, a friend of mine who owns some land near Reillanne. In the letter, she said she had learned from her aunt that the person who shot Jackie was a kid of fifteen at the time, and that he had never used a gun before. The village FTPs posted him on the road with an automatic weapon with orders to shoot at a black car approaching Reillanne. He followed those orders, and Jackie was killed.

"The poor kid was so distressed that he tried to kill himself by stepping in front of a bus. He was badly hurt, but only recovered physically, not mentally. I was told he found a job in Marseilles several years after the war, and a month later, one evening, he went to a bar, ordered a jug of rum, and blew his brains out in front of everyone."

"How terribly sad," Hellops said, shaking his head.

"Mireille's letter also mentioned that no one in Reillanne ever talked about that night and Jackie's death, even though the townspeople knew the FTPs were responsible. Now I know the truth."

I lit a cigarette nervously, took a deep drag, then put the cigarette out. There was a cold, remote feeling in me as I asked myself, *Were all those patriotic ideas, all the fighting for freedom, the missions behind the lines, the loneliness and frustrations, all worth it?*

My mouth tasted bitter. I looked with my mind's eye at Jackie's pert little face, the dimples on her cheeks, and her sunny smile. Then I saw her face again, this time etched in the awful mask of death, her green eyes forever lifeless. I felt tears well up and desperately tried to contain the feelings welling up within me.

Was it really worth it? I wondered again.

I wanted to believe it had been but could not help feeling cynical about how history repeats itself. There still were the same political intrigues, the hate groups that thrive on terror and human misery, and I knew that there were enough egos and self-indulging crusaders to fuel another war, and another. . . .

The huge deck of the *Intrepid*, which had resounded with the bustle of conversation earlier, now fell to a hush. Sir William Stephenson took the podium.

Looking at the crowd gathered around, I silently wondered, *How many of these people present were really engaged in actual fighting, like we had been?*

A quote from John le Carré jumped to my mind: "There's fieldmen, and there's deskmen, and it's up to you and me to see the distinction is preserved."

Voiceless, I responded, *It shouldn't be difficult to differentiate between the two. Field people were the pawns in the game of chess. Desk people played out their fate.*

I let out a sad little chuckle. "We were the expendable ones. That should make the distinction!" I muttered.

"What was that?" Hellops asked.

I shook my head. "Oh, nothing. I've been talking to myself. This comes with age, I guess."

Sir William Stephenson's voice was growing progressively weaker. He was a man who had reached a venerable old age, and all of the hoopla of the evening was apparently weighing heavily on him.

The party was quickly winding down. I turned to Hellops and affectionately wrapped my arms around his shoulders. I smiled this time without restraint.

"We have to celebrate our own reunion!" I declared.

My friend gave me a devilish grin. It was the same smile filled with the carefree audacity I had loved in the old days.

"I know just the place. We'll go to the Oak Room at the Plaza, and drink the champagne we had planned to have at the end of the war," he announced happily.

We had our night of reminiscing—so many people, so many stories we had forgotten until now. It was a wonderful night. Yet as we held each other to say good-bye, I had a fateful premonition.

I hung on to my presentiment with fear, as if I knew, deep in my heart, that the parting for us had come. The last I

remember of my friend was that roguish smile of his. It
lingered in my mind for a long time afterward.

Hellops died, suddenly, on May 6, 1986. We were supposed to have met that month and never did. His final
gesture, I was told, before being taken to the hospital, was to
place a small piece of notepaper in his wallet. It was the
paper on which I had scribbled my address when we bid
farewell for the last time.

Today, on the hilly road to Reillanne, a monument erected by
the townspeople of Apt and Reillanne commemorates the
place where Jackie was killed.

I, Hélène, live alone. It was my destiny after all. I never
really adjusted to a routine life, with regular hours and
chores. My free spirit has never accepted the transition. I
rebel when I feel forced into a situation. Even though I am
not so terribly old, I feel that I have lived longer than most
people.

Someone will ask, "With all the ruthlessness, frustrations,
and anger of war, do you recall love?"

"I think I do," I answer. "I recall that I once loved."

Within, I cannot help smiling as I remember that young
girl, the recollection of missions, people, and places, and
amid all the violence and cruelty, remembrances of warmth
and tenderness.

It seems so long ago! Yet this life of ours escapes so fast, so
very fast.

For sorrow, one must have time to cry!

The Opposing Forces

After Germany defeated France in June 1940, the country was divided in two halves. The Nazis governed one part directly. The other was nominally still French, but the Vichy government actively collaborated with the Germans. Soon, Resistance groups grew up throughout France to combat both the Vichy government and the German Occupation. Yet these groups, which had competing political views, were often as divided against one another as they were devoted to defeating their common enemy. These definitions should help explain this many-sided conflict.

Anti-Nazi Forces

Forces Françaises de l'Intérieur (FFI):
In English, "French Forces of the Interior." A Resistance movement inspired by Charles de Gaulle.

Francs-Tireurs et Partisans Français (FTP):
A Communist-controlled French Resistance group.

Maquis:
Literally, "the scrubby underbrush." The first Maquis were young men who fled to the hills and woods of southern France to escape the Milice. Supplied with arms parachuted in from England, the Maquis quickly became a formidable fighting force. By the time the Allies landed in southern France in 1944, the Maquis had secured many important locations.

Office of Strategic Services (OSS):
Forerunner to the CIA, the OSS was established in 1942 by Franklin D. Roosevelt. Beginning in late 1943, OSS agents were sent into France to organize and equip local Resistance groups for the upcoming Allied invasion of Europe. On October 1, 1945, the OSS was disbanded.

Pro-Nazi Forces

Milice:
Established in 1942 by Pierre Laval and headed by Joseph Darnand, the Milice was created to enforce Nazi law and order, to suppress Resistance efforts, and to round up all opponents of the Third Reich. A volunteer force, the Milice quickly gained a reputation for cruelty and violence.

Vichy:
Shortly after the German takeover of France, the French government moved first to Bordeaux, then to Vichy, a city in the heart of France (see map, page 2). The Vichy government remained under the strict surveillance of German officials.

Index